HINDU PLACES OF
PILGRIMAGE IN INDIA

This volume is sponsored by the
Center for South and Southeast Asia Studies,
University of California, Berkeley

HINDU PLACES OF PILGRIMAGE IN INDIA

(A STUDY IN CULTURAL GEOGRAPHY)

By
SURINDER MOHAN BHARDWAJ

UNIVERSITY OF CALIFORNIA PRESS
BERKELEY, LOS ANGELES, LONDON

University of California Press
Berkeley and Los Angeles, California

University of California Press, Ltd.
London, England

First Paperback Printing 1983
ISBN 0-520-04951-9

Library of Congress Catalog Card Number : 73-174454

Photosetting by
Thomson Press (India) Limited, Faridabad, India,
and printed in the United States of America

To the countless dedicated pilgrims
whose footprints have given meaning
to India as a cultural entity

A NOTE ON TRANSLITERATION

Throughout the text, the transliteration of Indic terms usually conforms to the scheme used by the Center for South and Southeast Asia Studies, University of California, Berkeley. Diacritics have not been used for modern Indian place names. When place names are taken from a translated work, the spellings conform to the specific source for easy comparison.

PREFACE AND ACKNOWLEDGEMENTS

It was in the Winter Quarter of 1964, during the course of a seminar in cultural geography, that Professor J. O. M. Broek aroused my interest in the study of sacred places of pilgrimage of India. In the seminar paper "Places of Pilgrimage in India—The Significance of Their Study from the Viewpoint of Cultural Geography" I tried to evaluate the available literature on this subject and suggested the need for field investigation. Geographers, particularly Indian, had paid only scant attention to this important mechanism of religious circulation. However, in 1966 Robert Stoddard completed his Ph.D. dissertation, *Hindu Holy Sites in India.* He attempted to account for the distribution of Hindu sacred places essentially as points optimally located with respect to the Hindu population, using modern census data and other published works. Rigorous testing of this hypothesis by him proved the existence of no such relationship. This was only to be expected, because the pattern of important sacred places had been developed over two thousand years ago—long before the present pattern of population distribution. Stoddard's work was a further inducement to understand Hindu pilgrimage in historical-cultural context and by conducting firsthand field investigation. There appeared, however, no immediate source of financial support to go to India.

The Graduate School Doctoral Fellowship from the University of Minnesota for the year 1966–67 allowed me to carry on library research in the historical aspects of pilgrimage in India. Later, on the kind recommendations of Professors J. O. M. Broek, Joseph E. Schwartzberg, and Burton Stein, a Junior fellowship for field research in India was made available by the American Institute of Indian Studies, for the year 1967–68. I am deeply indebted both to my teachers and to the American Institute of Indian Studies for their support, without which this work would not have seen the light of the day.

In the organization of my field work in India I got generous and much needed help and encouragement from Dr. Gurdev Singh

Gosal, my former professor and Chairman, Department of Geography, Panjab University. Professor B. N. Goswamy, Chairman, Department of Art History, Panjab University, introduced me to many *purohits* (priests) at several sacred places. Without his personal interest it might have been difficult for me to study the pilgrim records kept by the priests.

I am grateful to the many *purohits* from whom I have been able to learn part of the complexity of the sacred places. I am especially thankful to Pandit Raj Kumar Sharma, Sardar Ram Kumar (both of Hardwar), and Pandit Chandra Mani of Kangra. For carrying out interviews with pilgrims I thankfully acknowledge the help of Sardar Joginder Singh, Sardar Darbara Singh (both M.A. Geography of the Panjab University), Shri Naresh Bandhu Roy (M.A., LL.B.), Shri Pradyuman Singh, Shri Chu-ing Lama (of Rewalsar), Sri Vineet K. Sharma (B.A., LL.B.), and Professor S. D. Varma, Chairman, Department of Geography, Government College, Dharmsala.

My teachers at the University of Minnesota have been and will remain a source of inspiration for my life. I also wish to express my sincere thanks to Professors Robert F. Spencer and Luther P. Gerlach of the Department of Anthropology, who directed my interest in cultural anthropology. The numerous and valuable suggestions, and critical comments I have received from Professors J. O. M. Broek, Joseph E. Schwartzberg, and Fred E. Lukermann have made it possible for me to achieve some clarity in my research. I wish to record my profound gratitude to Professor Schwartzberg for his painstaking help in the better organization of this work, and for having given me the opportunity to develop my interest in the ancient geography of India while I worked under his immediate guidance in the South Asia Historical Atlas Project for two summers.

Ever since, and even before, the inception of this study Professor J. O. M. Broek has been an unfailing source of inspiration and guidance. Because of my numerous deficiencies, linguistic and methodological, I have made much demand on his valuable time. But, in the tradition of a true scholar and teacher, he has always given me good counsel in abundant measure. In one of the faltering moments during my field work in India he wrote a letter (Berkeley, November 26, 1967) with advice which I treasure: "And take time to reflect on problems. ... Good dissertations grow from the quality of the spirit, not from the quantity of data." I am painfully aware of the fact that my work falls far short of what he may have expected, and yet if it has any value, much of the credit must go to his keen insight and his abiding interest in my work.

For the calculations of my field data I am thankful to the University of Minnesota for providing computer time and to the ever friendly Les Maki, who personally helped to make and run the programs and supplied information even while I was not at Minneapolis. The arduous task of drafting the maps was cheerfully done by Roxana Rohrich, Staff Cartographer of the Department of Geography, Kent State University. I am grateful to her for the much needed help. I sincerely appreciate the kindness, encouragement, and support of Dr. Jordan A. Hodgkins, Chairman, Department of Geography. The Graduate School at Kent State University has been financially generous despite the current squeeze. I wish to thank Dean J. W. McGrath and Associate Dean A. H. Coogan of the Graduate School for their consideration. I am grateful to the Center for South and Southeast Asia Studies for the sponsorship of this work.

Vinay, my wife, has gone far beyond the call of duty in helping me to complete this book. Without her constant encouragement and relentless perseverance in the many difficult moments at home and in the field this task would have been impossible. I owe her a most special debt of gratitude.

S.M.B.

Contents

LIST OF MAPS AND GRAPHS

LIST OF TABLES

HINDU PLACES OF
PILGRIMAGE IN INDIA

Introduction

The institution of pilgrimage to holy places *(tīrtha-yātrā)* is an ancient and continuing religious tradition of the Hindus. Numerous sacred places distributed in various parts of India attract millions of pilgrims; some places draw pilgrims from all over the country, others largely from the neighboring villages. Thus, religion assumes an important role in generating a circulation mechanism in which all the social strata of Hinduism participate. The liberal distribution of sacred places throughout India has created an essentially continuous religious space in which the otherwise great regional cultural diversity becomes less significant for the movement of pilgrims over long distances. Religion provides the basis of pilgrimage by offering the reward of purification of the soul and the attainment of objectives related to the problems of mundane existence. The study of this circulatory mechanism of Hinduism, with its roots in religion, forms the subject matter of our inquiry.

HINDU PILGRIMAGE, ITS NATURE, DEVELOPMENT, AND MOTIVE

Every religion has its sacred foci to which men of faith periodically converge. From the most ancient civilizations to the present times sacred centers have exerted a powerful pull on the believers. The Sumerians of antiquity, who reverently ascended the steps of the Ziggurat to reach the gate of heaven, have their modern counterpart in the devout Jews and Christians who visit the Holy Land, and in the multitudes of Muslims from diverse parts of the world who undertake the hajj to Mecca. Millions of Hindus, since time immemorial, have similarly been attracted to their numerous holy sites in India. Pilgrimage is thus a panhuman phenomenon albeit its importance is reduced in the industrial-commercial nations of the Western world. The concept of pilgrimage exists in all major religions, although, not unexpectedly, its meaning varies widely within the canonical structure of each religion.

Hindu Pilgrimage

The nature of Hindu pilgrimage is capsuled in the Indian expression *tīrtha-yātrā,* which literally means "undertaking journey to river fords." In common parlance, visitation to sacred places is considered *tīrtha-yātrā.* There is, however, much more implied in the term *tīrtha-yātrā*, and it is essential to understand those implications in order to avoid confusion, which is bound to arise if the English expression "pilgrimage" is equated with the strictly Indian terminology. Agehananda Bharati has rightly pointed out that Indian terms for pilgrimage are often to be understood metaphorically.[1] A *yogī*, for example, may physically stay put and yet, through a specific type of meditation, may "perform a pilgrimage" to the seven "shrines." Here both the "pilgrimage" and "shrine" are to be understood in their generalized meaning. Pilgrimage here means to "partake of" and the "shrine" implies a certain quality such as "truth." We may further clarify this metonymy by referring to a verse from *Skandapurāṇa* (a religious treatise): "Truth, forgiveness, control of senses, kindness to all living beings and simplicity are *tīrthas*."[2] Thus, *tīrtha-yātrā* not only means the physical act of visiting the holy places but implies mental and moral discipline. In fact, without the latter, pilgrimage in the physical sense has little significance in the Hindu tradition.

The practice of pilgrimage in Hinduism follows from some of the basic underpinnings of its philosophy. Four dominant ideas have persisted in Hindu thought concerning attitudes to life. These are *dharma, artha, kāma,* and *mokṣa*.[3] *Dharma* is characterized by "considerations of righteousness, duty and virtue."[4] *Artha* entails material gain, worldly advantage, and success. *Kāma* signifies love and pleasure. The fourth, *mokṣa*, is the spiritual realization and self-emancipation which has been equated by some scholars with salvation or freedom from transmigration.[5] The first

[1]Agehananda Bharati, "Pilgrimage Sites and Indian Civilization," p. 85.

[2]Free translation of a verse from *Skandapurāṇa* as quoted in *Kalyāṇa, Tīrthāṅka,* p. 30.

[3]For detailed discussion on this topic see S. Radhakrishnan, *The Hindu View of Life.*

[4]V. Raghavan, "The Four Ends of Man," in Theodore de Bary et al., *Sources of Indian Tradition* (New York: Columbia University Press, 1958), p. 211.

[5]See Franklin Edgerton, "Dominant Ideas in the Formation of Indian Culture," *Journal of the American Oriental Society,* Vol. 62 (1942), pp. 151–156. Cf. Radhakrishnan, *Hindu View of Life.*

three aspects of life converge toward the final goal, spiritual bliss. Within this philosophical concept of life those activities, observances, rituals, and rites become meaningful which help in the attainment of liberation of the self from the bondage of repeated birth and rebirth. Hinduism provides a wide variety of courses that individuals may take toward religious fulfillment. For example, there is the path of knowledge, *jñāna-yoga*; the way of action, *karma-yoga*; and the path of unmixed devotion, *bhakti-yoga*. Pilgrimage, though not one of the major recognized paths of achieving *mokṣa*, is nevertheless accepted as a desirable practice to earn religious merit within a life lived according to *dharma*. It is *one* of the many ways toward self-realization and bliss.

Pilgrimage to sacred places is of no avail if a person does not lead a moral life. There are repeated references in Hindu religious literature that suggest moral life as a precondition for deriving any merit *(phala)* from sojourn to holy sanctuaries and bathing in sacred rivers.[6] Journey to sacred places provides opportunity for the householder to detach himself for some time from the cares and worries of daily life and to devote that time to prayer, contemplation, and listening to the spiritual discourses of holy men.

Development of Hindu Pilgrimage

Several scholars have expressed their views on the origins and development of the practice of *tīrtha-yātrā*, and it is not my purpose in this introduction to examine these views in detail. I shall merely attempt to point out the salient features of the development of Hindu pilgrimage.

Perhaps the earliest allusion to the practice of pilgrimage in Indian literature is to be found in the *Āitareya Brāhmaṇa* of the *Ṛg Veda*:[7]

> Flower-like the heels of the wanderer,
> His body groweth and is fruitful;
> All his sins disappear,
> Slain by the toil of his journeying.[8]

[6]See, for example, *Kalyāṇa, Tīrthāṅka*, p. 31. Several selected verses from the *Purāṇas* convey this idea.

[7]The *Brāhmaṇas* are "expository liturgical texts" attached to the Vedas. The period of composition of the *Ṛg Veda* is usually considered to be between 1500 and 1000 B.C.

[8]*Āitareya Brāhmaṇa*, VII-15, as translated by A. B. Keith, *Rigveda Brahmanas*, p. 320.

In the previous stanza of the above verse it is suggested that "Evil is he who stayeth among men." It is possible that the concept of pilgrimage may have existed in some form at such an early time period. Even today the ideal pilgrim undertakes the journey to sacred places for purification and redemption from sin. I am not suggesting here that pilgrimage of today has the same ritualistic content as that of the Vedic period, but a conceptual similarity seems to be there. If this view is tenable, we need no longer accept the assertion of R. V. Russell (and of those who followed his belief) that "the feeling which prompts the undertaking of the journey is not a very great advance on the primitive reverence for certain places as the abodes of spirits."[9]

The Aryan people of the Vedic times revered the rivers, as is clear from the famous river-hymn *(nadi stuti)* of the *Ṛg Vida.*[10] Perhaps, from the Aryan reverence of the rivers grew the concept of *tīrtha* (ford). Bharati believes that pilgrimage proper is not mentioned in the Vedic literature.[11] I feel, however, that at least two strands of the concept pilgrimage, namely, the merit of travel and reverence for rivers, can be considered to have been continuous from the Vedic times, to which later developments in Hinduism added further content and meaning.

A further reference to the practice of *tīrtha-yātrā* is found in the classic Aryan lawbook *Manusmṛti,* although the relevant verse tends to attach relatively little importance to visiting the Ganges and the Kurukṣetra—both celebrated as sacred in later times:

> If thou art not at variance with that divine...
> Who dwells in Thy heart, Thou needest neither
> Visit the Ganges nor the (land of the) Kurus.[12]

I must emphasize that even today no Hindu scholar claims that

[9]R. V. Russell, in *Census of India,* 1911, Vol. VIII, *Central Provinces, Report,* part I, p. 9.

[10]*Ṛg Veda,* X.75.5, as quoted in *Kalyāṇa, Tīrthāṅka,* p. 620, and Radha Kumud Mookerji, *The Fundamental Unity of India,* p. 27.

[11]Agehananda Bharati, "Pilgrimage in the Indian Tradition," p. 137. See also W. Crooke, who expressed the same idea in "Pilgrimage" (Indian), *Encyclopaedia of Religion and Ethics,* p. 24.

[12]*Manusmṛti,* VIII.92, as quoted in F. Max Müller, ed., *The Laws of Manu,* translated by G. Bühler, p. 270.

bathing in the Gaṅgā (Ganges) is superior to meditation. In fact, within the religious armory of Hinduism the emphasis is always on the control of sense and meditation, for which pilgrimage is no substitute. It is always considered an *additional* redemptive practice, an adjunct to other forms of worship.

Following the Vedic period the practice of pilgrimage seems to have gained considerably increased popularity as shown by the relevant sections of the great epic *Mahābhārata* (ca. 300 B.C.).[13] As Hinduism became more formalized religion the significance of ritualistic elements within it increased greatly, as is clear from the voluminous literature of the *Purāṇas* (to be discussed later). Bharati has observed that "medieval and modern pilgrimage is certainly due to Brahmin revival, and to the ritualization of religion in the Hindu middle ages through its partial absorption into local, non-Brahmanic cults."[14]

Once the ritualistic details got committed to writing and the *Purāṇas* became accepted as the authority in the matter of common religious observance, the practice of pilgrimage, glorified by the *Purāṇas*, achieved a higher status in Hindu beliefs than in the previous times. It must also be pointed out that the offerings made at the sacred places are sources of livelihood for the officiating priests. The latter are therefore more than inclined to extol the merits of visiting sacred places, particularly, of course, where they are the controlling priests. In my visits to numerous holy places I have been struck by this motive of the local body of priests.[15]

The practice of pilgrimage, with its ancient and diverse origins, continues to be popular among the Hindus. In fact, one can maintain, without fear of contradiction, that more people now visit more sacred places than ever before in the history of India. It is not that the Hindus have become more religious; rather it is because modern means of mass transportation have made it possible for larger numbers of individuals to undertake pilgrimages. The number of pilgrims each year visiting the well-known Hindu

[13]In a subsequent chapter I shall discuss in some detail the importance of this epic for a study of Hindu pilgrimage.

[14]Bharati, "Pilgrimage in the Indian Tradition," p. 137. Also see Crooke, "Pilgrimage." The two views are almost identical.

[15]I am inclined to suggest that the evolution of specific sacred places as economic enterprises is a legitimate hypothesis and may shed considerable light on their relative prominence.

tīrthas is to be reckoned in several millions. Specific occasions, such as the *kumbhamelā* at Hardwar and Allahabad, may attract over one million devotees eager to bathe in the sacred rivers.

Motives in Hindu Pilgrimage

The purpose and motives that impel individuals to undertake pilgrimage are diverse and have been fairly thoroughly investigated by Diehl.[16] Two broad categories of motives may be distinguished. First, there are specific motives concerned with mundane existence. They usually involve a commitment or vow to the deity whose blessing is sought for the solution of a problem the pilgrim is afflicted with. They may also be concerned with such rites as the first haircut of a male child or expiation of a ritual impurity that an individual may have acquired. [17] The second category of motives consists of earning religious merit. It is hard to define such motives, but they may include holy bath on a specific climactic occasion, the *darśana* (sight of the deity), or visiting holy men. In the first category of motives the deity is the focus of pilgrimage; in the second, deity per se is less important, the event of pilgrimage more significant. This question of motives will be discussed at some length in another chapter. The exact rituals to be performed in connection with a given pilgrimage depend largely on the motive of the pilgrim himself and the religious occasion on which the sacred place is visited. The rituals for each specific motive and occasion are prescribed in the appropriate religious treatises, but in actual practice they are carried out by the officiating priests of each sacred place.[18]

SYSTEM OF SACRED PLACES AS AN INTEGRATIVE NETWORK

So far I have introduced to the reader pilgrimage only as a religious practice in Hinduism. It has, however, another highly significant dimension. The innumerable sacred places of the Hindus can be conceived as a system of nodes having varying degrees of religious import. Within this system, some places may be the focal

[16]Diehl, Carl G., *Instrument and Purpose*.

[17]For details, see Bharati, "Pilgrimage in the Indian Tradition."

[18]Ritualistic aspect of pilgrimage has been well summarized by Bharati in "Pilgrimage."

points for pilgrims from the entire vast Indian subcontinent with its variegated cultural mosaic. Other, more modest places may serve as centers of congregation of devotees from the immediate vicinity. Between these two extremes there are sacred places of several intermediate levels. Sacred centers of each "level" have their corresponding pilgrim "fields." The holy places thus generate a gigantic network of religious circulation encompassing the entire Hindu population. Pilgrim "flows" are the connecting links between the Hindu population and its numerous sacred centers.

The number of Hindu sanctuaries in India is so large and the practice of pilgrimage so ubiquitous that the whole of India can be regarded as a vast sacred space organized into a system of pilgrimage centers and their fields. Scholars who emphasize the linguistic, regional, and social diversity of India often tend to minimize the integrative role of institutions such as sacred places. More and more social scientists are, however, beginning to be conscious of the indigenous forces of cultural integration. Professor Mandelbaum has rightly pointed out that "there is a traditional basis for the larger national identification. It is the idea, mainly engendered by Hindu religion, but shared by those of other religions as well, that there is an entity of India to which all its inhabitants belong."[19] Speaking specifically about the role of pilgrimages in India, he observes: "Pilgrimages to super centers reinforce religious precepts but also impress the pilgrim with the vastness, the diversity, and—seemingly paradoxically—the oneness of the society."[20]

The system of large and small sacred places in India has not developed as a result of an overt effort by some supreme centralizing authority, because there is no such authority in Hinduism. There is no single, explicit organizational mechanism in Hinduism and hence no neatly structured, hierarchically ordered system of religious authorities, such as is characteristic of Roman Catholicism. The "ranks" or "levels" of sacred places have evolved for over three millennia as a result of absorption of many local cults and reconciliation of numerous traditions. Thus, Hindu sacred places are not to be conceived as a hierarchy of the "pecking order." The informal hierarchy or ranking of Hindu sacred places has resulted from the many, partially overlapping, subsystems of

[19]David G. Mandelbaum, *Society in India,* II, 401.
[20]*Ibid.,* p. 402.

sacred places. These subsystems may have had regional-cultural, caste, or cultic orientations.

OBJECTIVES OF THIS STUDY

The chief aim of this study is to understand the nature of interconnections between the Hindu sacred places of different levels and their pilgrim fields in both the spatial and the social dimensions. However, since these interconnections are rooted in antiquity, it is not possible to fully appreciate the present religious circulation without explicitly demonstrating its intimate ties with the past.

The need for this inquiry arises from the fact that there is no single study known to me which explicitly formulates the various levels of sacred places and relates these levels to the spatial and social aspects of Hinduism. In a survey of the relevant literature (chap. 1) I briefly discuss the geographic and other works which have studied either a single sacred place or several; but none of them is concerned with the significance of levels of these places. Furthermore, there seems to have been no serious attempt made to trace the ancient pattern of religious circulation and link it with the modern one.

This research is conceived in the framework of cultural geography, not religion, although the latter provides the needed data. The study of the spatial order of places, their character, and their manifold interaction with other places and areas lies at the core of geography. My inquiry into the levels of sacred places, their nature, and their relationship with the correspondingly varied pilgrim fields (in the spatial and social dimensions), in the cultural context of India, thus forms a study in cultural geography.

ORGANIZATION

This study is divided into two main parts. The first part begins with a survey of pertinent literature on the Hindu holy places. Following that, I have attempted to establish a direct continuity of the broad spatial pattern of Hindu sacred places from the time of the epic *Mahābhārata* (ca. 300 B.C.) to the modern period. It has been possible to trace the basic pilgrim circulation pattern in ancient India from the sacred place-name lists of the epic. Toponymic information from the *Purāṇas* and other religious and literary sources has been used to map holy places down to the present. The distribution of places of pilgrimage broadly delimits the area of Hindu religious circulation, which leaves a residual area deficient in Hindu holy sites and largely occupied by the tribal population. Thus the sacred places provide a basis for spatial-cultural differentiation.

The second part of this study, beginning with chapter 6, attempts to formulate certain levels of sacred places and suggests the significance of these levels in the spatial and social context of Hinduism. This part is based exclusively on my field data collected at selected sacred places during the period October 1967–September 1968. The formulation of levels of sacred places rests mostly on average distance traveled by the pilgrims to a given place. Levels thus derived are further refined by studying the diversity of the pilgrim field. The diversity of the pilgrim field is determined partly by the standard deviation of the distances traveled by the pilgrims and partly by the linguistic diversity within the pilgrim field.

A combination of the historical-geographic approach and the synchronic study of religious circulation, I hope, sets the institution of pilgrimage into a wider perspective. It allows certain generalizations to be made at different scales and at different levels. It is not necessary here to make a case for the historical-geographic approach, for that has been ably argued by scholars in the field of geography.[21] I shall merely state that an institution through which the ancient tradition of India continuously reiterates and revitalizes itself cannot be comprehended fully without understanding its deep relationship with the past.

The value of the synchronic study lies in the fact that religious as well as historical literature in India neglects the social dimension of this institution. It seems unlikely that this aspect of pilgrimage can be understood properly without field observation. In the caste-ranked society of India it is imperative to study the socially differentiated interaction patterns between the sacred places and the pilgrims. Although the religious literature suggests that some places are of greater sanctity than others by eulogizing them more or less, it gives us no uniform basis for such a ranking. The bases for ranking can only be established by applying objective

[21]See, for example: J. O. M. Broek, *The Santa Clara Valley, California*; Broek, "The Relations between History and Geography"; Carl O. Sauer, "Foreword to Historical Geography."

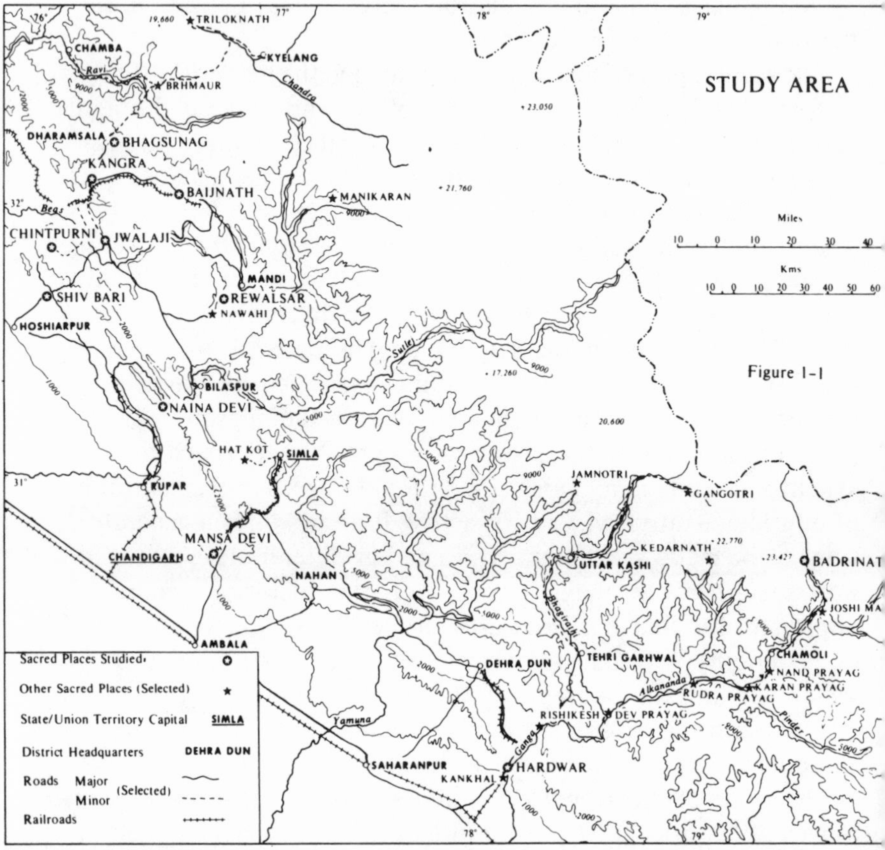

STUDY AREA
Figure 1-1
Miles
Kms
TRILOKNATH
KYELANG
CHAMBA
Ravi
BRHMAUR
Chandra
DHARAMSALA
BHAGSUNAG
KANGRA
BAIJNATH
Beas
MANIKARAN
CHINTPURNI
JWALAJI
MANDI
SHIV BARI
REWALSAR
NAWAHI
HOSHIARPUR
Sutlej
BILASPUR
NAINA DEVI
HAT KOT
SIMLA
RUPAR
JAMNOTRI
GANGOTRI
MANSA DEVI
CHANDIGARH
KEDARNATH
UTTAR KASHI
BADRINAT
NAHAN
JOSHI MA
AMBALA
Bhagirathi
TEHRI GARHWAL
CHAMOLI
DEHRA DUN
NAND PRAYAG
Alkananda
KARAN PRAYAG
RUDRA PRAYAG
RISHIKESH
DEV PRAYAG
Pinder
Yamuna
Ganga
SAHARANPUR
HARDWAR
KANKHAL
Sacred Places Studied
Other Sacred Places (Selected)
State/Union Territory Capital
District Headquarters
Roads Major
Minor
(Selected)
Railroads

criteria, which in turn can be derived from a synchronic field study.

THE AREA OF FIELD STUDY AND SELECTED SACRED PLACES

The study area comprises Himachal Pradesh and the Himalayan districts of Uttar Pradesh from which eleven sacred places were selected (see fig. 1-1). For comparative purposes Ujjain in Madhya Pradesh was also studied although not in detail.

The main reasons for the selection of Himachal Pradesh and Himalayan districts of Uttar Pradesh were as follows: (1) This relatively small area has numerous Hindu places of pilgrimage, many of which are of great antiquity and fame. (2) The large number of sacred places in this area facilitated selection. (3) The area has considerable linguistic homogeneity despite the variety of dialects. This, it was hoped, would result in relatively easy demarcation of the pilgrim fields. It turned out to be an erroneous assumption. (4) Since no special additional linguistic preparation was foreseen, it was hoped that interviewing would be relatively easy. This too proved only partially valid because at one place the majority of pilgrims were speakers of dialects of Tibetan—a language which I do not understand.

Two main considerations governed the selection of sacred places in the study area. First, the number of selected places was to be large enough to include at least one place well known throughout India, some places of presumably regional or subregional significance, and some of local importance. Second, the number had to be small enough that each place could be studied at least twice if there were more than one occasion or season of pilgrimage in a year.

The final selection of sacred places was the result of two steps: a preliminary selection from the available literature, and preliminary field investigation and interviews with the priests of these sacred places. The preliminary selection of sacred places was made from the information in the *Imperial Gazetteer*, the various district and state gazetteers, and the *Census of India*, 1961, vol. XIII, *Punjab*: part VII-B, *Fairs and Festivals*. Since the information in these publications is not uniform for all sacred places, and because the pilgrim fields cannot be determined from the literature, the selection of sacred places was perforce highly subjective.

If precise information about pilgrim fields had been available, there would have been no reason to make it a part of my field inquiry.

A preliminary field investigation was made for the following reasons: (1) To determine the exact dates of pilgrimage, particularly for those shrines about which information could not be obtained from the almanacs *(pañcāng* or *jantrī)*. (2) To carry out detailed interviews with the priests (except at Badrinath and Ujjain) in order to find their perception about the fields of respective sacred places, the caste composition of pilgrims, the legend regarding the chief deity of the place, and an examination of the records of pilgrims (when available) kept by the priests. These investigations were helpful in determining how much assistance I would need

TABLE 1-1
PILGRIMS INTERVIEWED AT SELECTED SACRED PLACES
(DURING 1968)

SACRED PLACE	*Occasion*	Number of pilgrims interviewed*
BADRINATH (Uttar Pradesh)	Annual *Yātrā*	400
BAIJNATH (Himachal Pradesh)	(1) *Śivarātri*	100
	(2) Monday of *Śrāvaṇa*	100
BHAGSUNAG (Himachal Pradesh)	*Śivarātri*	85
CHINTPURNI (Himachal Pradesh)	(1) *Navarātrās* of *Çaitra*	500
	(2) *Śrāvaṇa Aṣṭamī*	300
HARDWAR (Uttar Pradesh)	*Ardha Kumbha*	800
JWALAJI (Himachal Pradesh)	*Navarātrās* of *Caitra*	500
KANGRA (Himachal Pradesh)	*Navarātrās* of *Caitra*	450
NAINA DEVI (Himachal Pradesh)	(1) *Navarātrās* of *Caitra*	494
	(2) *Śrāvaṇa Aṣṭamī*	400
REWALSAR (Himachal Pradesh)	(1) *Sissoo* Fair	100
	(2) *Vaiśākhī*	100
SHIV BARI (Himachal Pradesh)	(1) *Śivarātri*	100
	(2) *Jātrā*	100
MANSA DEVI (Haryana)	(1) *Navarātrās* of *Caitra*	250
	(2) *Śrāvaṇa Aṣṭamī*	175
UJJAIN (Madhya Pradesh)	*Siṃhastha*	500
Total		5,454

NOTE: Figures in parentheses refer to the occasion number.

*Includes all pilgrims interviewed whether they answered some or all of the questions. Tables in individual chapters show the number of responding pilgrims for the specific questions analyzed there.

to carry out an adequate number of interviews with the pilgrims during the seasons of pilgrimage.[22] (3) To determine the exact number of places that could be studied within the constraints of time available for field research. Eleven places were selected in Himachal Pradesh and Uttar Pradesh, which, as my preliminary investigation showed, included sacred places of several levels, ranging from ones of all-India fame to the ones whose field extended to a few villages in the immediate vicinity.

A questionnaire was formulated which could give me the basic information about pilgrims and yet would not delay them unnecessarily while they were in a great rush to visit the shrine. It was found that the questionnaire must not take more than fifteen minutes even if the pilgrim was in no rush, because a longer time would mean fewer possible interviews if the fair was only of one day's duration. At places or in situations where it was expected that the pilgrims would be in a great hurry, only a few basic questions were selected : the district of origin of the pilgrim, his caste, his profession, and the purpose for undertaking the pilgrimage.[23]

The number of interviews carried out at each selected place and the occasions are shown in table 1-1.

[22]See table 1-1, on p. 12, for the number of interviews and the dates of festivals at each sacred place.

[23]See the Appendix for details.

Chapter I

A General Survey of the Literature on Places of Pilgrimage in India

The literature related to the study of Hindu places of pilgrimage is scattered, varies tremendously in the degree of scholarship and form of presentation, and excepting a few specific studies, is generally pedestrian in character. These characteristics seem to result partly from the nature of the subject, but largely from the lack of scientific approach. Contributions by geographers are relatively few. The neglect of this important cultural component of the Hindu religion by Indian geographers is easily explained by the general lack of development of historical-cultural geography in India until a few years ago. Non-Indian geographers, even those inclined toward cultural geography, have had, until recently, only a marginal interest in the Indian religions and their relevance to the cultural geography of India. Of those who have tried to understand the geography of India, most have unfortunately given only superficial attention to the significance of religion in India and have lacked, in general, an historical perspective; their inquiry has been, by and large, limited to the use of data provided by the census.[1]

The following pages of this survey present a short summary and evaluation of the pertinent literature relating to pilgrimages in India. For the purpose of the present study the following classification of the literature seems to be adequate: (1) Epic and Puranic material; (2) medieval works based on Puranic material; (3) travel literature coming largely from Christian missionaries; (4) specific studies of pilgrimages and places of pilgrimage by twentieth-century scholars: (*a*) noncritical or descriptive studies, (*b*) analytical and problem-oriented studies; (5) pilgrims' travel guides and related literature; (6) gazetteers and reports; (7) pilgrim registers and the records kept by priests at the sacred places.

[1]See, for example, O. H. K. Spate and A. T. A. Learmonth, *India and Pakistan* (1967), chap. 5; and John E. Brush, "The Distribution of Religious Communities in India" (1949).

EPIC AND PURANIC MATERIAL

Of the two great epics, the *Rāmāyaṇa* and the *Mahābhārata,* the latter is by far of greater importance for our study.[2] The *Āraṇyakaparvan* ("Book of the Forest") contains several sections devoted exclusively to the description of and merit attached to the visiting of a large number of *tīrthas* or sacred places (critical edition, vol. 3, secs. 80–88).[3] These sections consist of two narrations, the first being a recitation by the sage Pulastya. In this "dialogue" there seems to have been an attempt made to give a topographical account of the holy places throughout India (see chap. 2 for details). In the second narration (attributed to the sage Dhaumya) the sacred places are described in the four major divisions of India : East, South, West, and North, respectively. It may be noted that both descriptions lead the pilgrim in a clockwise direction. Despite the problem of interpolations at different times, the *Mahābhārata* (ca. 300 B.C.) remains the most important single source for the description of sacred places before the Christian Era. Chapter 3 shows that the details about place names become meager and confused in the area south of the Narmadā River. Furthermore, a number of place names mentioned in this epic cannot now be identified. But the very wealth of place names and the well-known locations make it the most valuable source for the geography of pilgrimage, apart from establishing the great antiquity of the institution of pilgrimage in Hinduism. No serious student of the cultural geography of India can afford to neglect this ancient source. It is surprising to find that pilgrim routes of the *Mahābhārata* have aroused only perfunctory interest among scholars.[4] The reconstruction of routes is a tedious task, but it

[2]There is no need to comment here on the nature of the *Mahābhārata*. For a concise and scholarly discussion of this, see A. D. Pusalkar, *Studies in the Epics and Purāṇas* (Bombay, 1963).

[3]*(The) Mahābhārata,* critically edited by Vishnu S. Sukthankar (Poona, 1941), Vol. 3. From here on this work will be referred to as the "critical edition." All references to the verses of the *Mahābhārata* are from the critical edition. For example, 3.80.41 means Volume 3, Section 80, verse 41. English quotations are from *The Mahābhārata* translated by Pratap Chandra Roy (Calcutta, n.d.). Wherever Roy's translation is used, only volume and pages are referred to.

[4]Shejwalkar has made a serious attempt to relate the sacred places of the Aryans, as described in the epic *Mahābhārata,* to the question of Aryan expansion in India. His two maps, however, cannot be reconciled with the text of the *Mahābhārata.* T. S. Shejwalkar, "The *Mahābhārata* Data for Aryan Expansion in India" (1944).

may be rewarding for an understanding of the early interaction between different parts of the country. The difficulties to be experienced in this type of reconstruction will be discussed in chapter 3.

The *Mahābhārata* not only is useful for a study of ancient sacred places, but also indicates places of greater or lesser sanctity, as is shown by the amounts of merit to be derived from visiting each of the sacred places. It is possible to get some idea about the relative sanctity of these places from the mere length of the laudatory descriptions in this epic.

The *Purāṇas* form an important source of our knowledge about the sacred places of India for the period approximately of the fourth through the eleventh century A.D. The Hindus traditionally recognize eighteen *Mahā-Purāṇas* (the greater *Purāṇas*) and a considerably larger and controversial number of the *Upa-Purāṇas*, or lesser *Purāṇas*. These important religious compendia contain vast and varied materials on the concepts and rituals of Hinduism, ranging from their cosmogonic concepts to the proper religious rites, rituals, and observances. There is a vast and growing literature on the *Purāṇas* for the study of which a start may be made with Pargiter's *Ancient Indian Historical Tradition,*[5] while recent trends in these studies are indicated by A.D. Pusalker,[6] and *The Purāṇa,* a journal solely devoted to Puranic studies.

For one concerned with the cultural geography of India, the importance of the *Purāṇas* lies in their preservation of a large number of place names. Of more specific value for the study of holy places of ancient and early medieval India are the descriptions of places of pilgrimage to be found in several of these *Purāṇas*. The chapters on places of pilgrimage in the *Purāṇas* have some similarities to the description in the *Mahābhārata*, but there are also differences.

The main similarity lies in mentioning the sacred places with the merit attached to visiting them. However, almost no details are given either in the *Mahābhārata* or in the *Purāṇas* about the physical setting of these places, their population, or relative distances in any form. In this respect these descriptions are indeed disappointing.

The main difference in descriptions of the two sources is that

[5]F. E. Pargiter, *Ancient Indian Historical Tradition* (London, 1922).
[6]*Studies In the Epics and Purāṇas* (Bombay, 1963).

while the *Mahābhārata* gives a description of sacred places in sequence, suggesting the general direction in which the pilgrim may proceed, the *Purāṇas* yield a very jumbled picture of the sacred places. The main reason for this seems to be that the *Purāṇas*, being of later composition than the *Mahābhārata*, may have found no need to suggest any sequence of *tīrthas*; the direction may have been presumed to be known to the pilgrims through word of mouth. Another possible reason is that the form of the verse in which these places are described may have dictated a different arrangement of the places just to maintain the quality of the verse. Whatever the reason, these kinds of descriptions show no regard for distance, direction, or any physical quality of the place.

Another difference in the descriptions of the *Mahābhārata* and those of the *Purāṇas* is the stress in the latter on the *māhātmyas* (the glories) of the sacred places. The more important ones are selected for the *māhātmyas*, which are more lengthy than the enumerative descriptions of sacred places (e.g., the *Matsya Purāṇa* devotes several small chapters to the *"Prayāga māhātmya"*). The *Purāṇas* also contain more information than the *Mahābhārata* on what religious rites and observances should be made at the sacred places. Thus, the *Purāṇas* are indispensable sources of information about the sacred places of ancient India. Sanskrit versions of *Purāṇas* have been edited and published by Bibliotheca Indica, and a number of critical studies concerning the *Purāṇas* have appeared in English.[7]

Since neither the approximate dates nor places of composition of the *Purāṇas* are at all certain, it is extremely difficult to relate the places mentioned in the *Purāṇas* with other historical events or cultural processes. Much more work on the *Purāṇas* needs to be done by Indologists before a geographer who lacks intimate knowledge of Sanskrit can make valid generalizations about the relative importance of places of pilgrimage in the early period.

MEDIEVAL SOURCES BASED ON PURANIC MATERIAL

In this class may be placed all the encyclopaedic, religious Sanskrit works which, in part, deal with the places of pilgrimage, the merit of visiting them, and the functions that can or must be

[7]See, for example, G. S. Gyani, *Agni Purāṇa, A Study* (Varanasi, 1964); and S. C. Kantawala, *Cultural History from the Matsya Purāṇa* (Baroda, 1964).

performed at these places. Apart from these we may also include works by such Muslim scholars as Alberuni (eleventh century) and Abu'l Fazl (sixteenth century).

The most useful medieval digest is *Kṛtyakalpataru* of Bhaṭṭa Lakṣmīdhara (early twelfth century). This work comprises several volumes, one of which, entitled *Tīrthavivecana Kāṇḍam,* deals exclusively with the sacred places of India. Rangaswami Aiyangar, the editor of this work, considers it one of the most comprehensive *nibandhas* (digests) of the age.[8] The fact that a whole volume has been devoted to the enumeration and *māhātmyas* (eulogies) of the *tīrthas* speaks for the significance of the institution of pilgrimage in medieval Hinduism. Aiyangar's long introduction to this work contains references to many other Sanskrit sources which can be helpful in the study of pilgrimages in medieval India.

Mazumdar, in his *Socio-Economic History of Northern India,* devotes one full chapter to the study of places of pilgrimage in the eleventh and twelfth centuries.[9] On the basis of many Sanskrit sources he has been able to show the probable decline of some sacred places and the ascendancy of others. Although his comparative analysis is praiseworthy, some conclusions he draws from his study are questionable. For example, he states : "Many bold and enterprising people sought an outlet for their energy in going out on pilgrimages, rather than engage themselves in constructive work for ameliorating the social and economic condition of their fellow beings."[10] We must observe that pilgrimage is not a lifelong occupation of people. *Gṛhasthas* (householders) engage in this activity for a limited time and then return to their normal work. Those people who did and do engage in pilgrimage for long periods, that is, *sādhus,* contribute little indeed to the economy but they were certainly important in the social order of Hinduism. It is, therefore, not proper for a scholar to pass unwarranted judgment on an institution without really being able to support his contentions.

The utility of the various Sanskrit sources is limited by the fact that their date of composition and authorship are usually uncertain.

[8]K. V. Rangaswami Aiyangar, ed., *Kṛtyakalpataru* of Bhaṭṭa Lakṣmīdhara, *Tīrthavivecana-kāṇḍam* (Baroda, 1942), Introduction, pp. xiv.

[9]B. P. Mazumdar, *Socio-Economic History of Northern India* (1030–1194 A.D.) (Calcutta, 1960).

[10]*Ibid.,* p. 349.

It will suffice here to say that a good deal of research is needed on these sources before their real significance for a study of places of pilgrimage can be realized. Apart from the Sanskrit sources, there are two Islamic sources of some importance which derive their knowledge of the sacred places of Hindus from Hindu scripture.

One of these is the eleventh-century work on India by Alberuni; the other is the sixteenth-century work of Abu'l Fazl. *Alberuni's India,* which has been translated into English by Edward Sachau, is a sort of compendium of Hinduism composed about 1030 A.D.[11] Its sub-title, "An Account of the Religion, Philosophy, Literature, Geography, Chronology, Astronomy, Customs, Laws and Astrology of India," gives a fair idea of the contents. Chapter 66 of the above work deals exclusively with pilgrimages and the visiting of sacred places. The mere mention of this institution in a separate chapter is an indication of its importance in "medieval" Hinduism. From his references it is clear that his knowledge about the sacred places, ponds, and mountains is based, in part, on the authority of *Vāyu Purāṇa* and *Matsya Purāṇa.* Unfortunately, his account of sacred places is limited to northern India and even there only a few places are referred to, for example, "Baranasi" (Varanasi), "Pukara" (Pushkar), "Kurukshetra," "Mahura" (Mathura), "Kashmir," and "Multan."[12] He also enumerates some sacred mountains and ponds. While his positive evidence is very important because it indicates the popularity of the above places of pilgrimage in the eleventh century, it is impossible to conclude anything from his silence about other sites. It is possible that Hardwar *(Māyāpuri),* which is now one of the most sacred places of India, was not so prominent in Alberuni's time; but nothing conclusive can be said about this. On the other hand, it is certain that Multan, which used to be an important sacred place, declined because of its destruction by foreign raids. His reference to Varanasi as the "Mekka of the Hindus" underscores the high status of this sacred city.[13]

The sixteenth-century work of Abu'l Fazl—*'Ain-i-Akbari*—is of greater value for us than *Alberuni's India* for two reasons. First, it describes a larger number of sacred places of the Hindus,

[11]Two vols., London, 1910.
[12]*Ibid.,* II, 142–148.
[13]*Ibid.,* p. 146.

and second, the descriptions are likely to be more authentic because of the author's more intimate knowledge of India.[14] *'Ain-i-Akbari* is the most important single source for the sixteenth-century place names of Hindu holy sites. This work reflects the author's knowledge of Hindu scriptures as well as his personal observations of contemporary India. Positive evidence about the popularity of several sacred places can be obtained from this work. This is probably the only non-Sanskrit source that attempts to classify the holy places according to an hierarchical scheme derived from the Hindu scriptures.

TRAVEL AND RELATED LITERATURE

In the nineteenth century a number of Christian missionaries and travelers wrote at length about Hinduism. Their presentation of ethnological data is of varying quality and degree of bias. It is hard to characterize this literature as scientific by any standard. The importance of this material for our study lies in the interesting descriptions of holy places that usually appear along with those of notable cities, castes, customs, and ceremonies of Hindus.

Examples of this class of literature include *The Orientalist*;[15] *The Travels of a Hindu*;[16] *A Description of the Character, Manners and Customs of the People of India*;[17] and *A View of the History, Literature and Religion of the Hindus*.[18] Often the authors of these works pretend to be objective and scholarly but actually are neither. Most descriptions are liberally sprinkled with derogatory remarks about Hinduism without any attempt to understand Indian culture. They notice the exotic and the remarkable, and delight greatly in noting what they believe is wrong, bad, or discreditable with the Indians. This class of literature can be called primitive ethnology with strong biases of Christian missiona-

[14]Bernard S. Cohn, following W. H. Moreland, believes that *'Ain-i-Akbari* is a compilation by various authors; see Bernard S. Cohn, "Structural Change in Rural Society," in Robert Eric Frykenberg, ed., *Land Control and Social Structure in Indian History* (Madison, 1969), pp. 55–56, and 114, n.6.

[15]Thomas Bacon, *The Orientalist* (Manchester : Ainsworth, 1842).

[16]Bholanauth Chunder, *The Travels of a Hindu,* 2 vols. (London, N. Trübner, 1869).

[17]Abbe J. A. Dubois, *A Description of the Character, Manners and Customs of the People of India* (Madras : Higgenbotham, 1862).

[18]W. Ward, *A View of the History, Literature and Religion of the Hindus,* 2 vols. (Serampore : Mission Press, 1815).

ries. Even though this literature is likely to infuriate the modern nationalistic Indians, it has its value for studying the places of pilgrimage in India. It is quite apparent that some of the writers consider pilgrimage an undesirable institution. For example, W. Ward says, "It is a deplorable circumstance that such a waste of time, of life, and of property, should be incurred through the fatal deception that the sight of a holy place will be accepted by the judge of Heaven and Earth, instead of repentance and conversion, instead of a contrite heart and a holy life."[19] Similarly, Abbe J. Dubois is usually hostile to Hindu religion as a whole. "A religion more shameful or indecent has never existed amongst a civilized people."[20]

To a slightly different category belong such works as Wright's *Lectures on India*,[21] and Hurst's *Indika*.[22] These are more popular descriptions of various places of interest including some places of pilgrimage. They reflect a shallow understanding of the philosophical underpinnings of Hinduism and are motivated largely by antiquarian interests.

Another category in the nineteenth-century literature which is of considerable importance for study of places of pilgrimage is the "gazetteer." One of the earliest gazetteers of India is *A Geographical, Statistical and Historical Description of Hindostan*.[23] This two-volume work gives a detailed description of a large number of places in India, including important places of pilgrimage. The descriptions are straightforward, without missionary or traveler's bias, and are therefore far more valuable than the studies referred to in this section previously. Much valuable information about the sacred places can also be gleaned from the various volumes of district gazetteers published in the early part of the twentieth century and their subsequent editions.[24]

TWENTIETH-CENTURY STUDIES

We shall now briefly review some of the twentieth-century publications related to places of pilgrimage. They may be divided

[19]*Op. cit.*, II, 320.

[20]*Op. cit.*, p. 308.

[21]Caleb Wright, *Lectures on India* (Boston 1851).

[22]John F. Hurst, *Indika* : *The Country and the People of India and Ceylon* (New York, 1891).

[23]Walter Hamilton, (London, 1820).

[24]For a detailed bibliography, see Henry Scholberg, *The District Gazetteers of British India*; *A Bibliography* (Zug : Interdocumentation Company, 1970).

into two broad categories : descriptive ; and analytical and problem-oriented.

Descriptive

For India as a whole there are but few studies on the places of pilgrimage. One of the earliest twentieth-century studies dealing specifically with the places of pilgrimage in India is Helmuth von Glasenapp's *Heilige Stätten Indiens*.[25] It is an excellent descriptive study of the important Hindu and Jain holy places of India (including what is now Pakistan) and Nepal, and includes a large number of photographs of temples in India. There is little attempt to account for the spatial distribution of these places. Every place is considered unique and is described with reference to its mythological basis. Glasenapp does not discuss either the philosophical aspects of pilgrimage or the historical development of the sacred places. B.C. Law's *Holy Places of India* is again a descriptive study of the major holy places of India.[26] As in Glasenapp's work, the holy places are described according to the provinces of India in a gazetteer fashion. Law adds a section on Buddhist sacred places, which Glasenapp omitted, describes more places, and shows locations on some maps. Some of the descriptions, however, are too brief. There is no uniformity of description by either of these authorities. In several cases no information is given about the deity, sect, or season of pilgrimage. The importance of both works lies in the fact that they represent a selection of holy places embracing the whole of India.

Wider in scope than either of the above studies is the description of holy places provided by Dave in his *Immortal India* (four volumes).[27] Some places described in the study are not holy places of pilgrimage as such, but the descriptions usually provide fairly detailed information about the origin of the place, its deity, and the season of festivals. Romain Roussel's *Les Pèlerinages* takes the institution of pilgrimages rather than the holy places as the basis of discussion.[28] He surveys this institution in various religions, including Hinduism, giving a list of sixty-seven of the more well-

[25]Munich, 1928.
[26]Calcutta, 1940.
[27]J. H. Dave, *Immortal India,* (Bombay, 1959–1961).
[28]*Les Pèlerinages à Travers les Siècles* (Paris, 1954).

known places of pilgrimage in India. Another work, very similar in scope, is a book of essays on the pilgrimages in various countries entitled *Les Pèlerinages*.[29] The chapter on Indian places of pilgrimage is by Claude Jacques of the Institut d'Indologie, Pondicherry (India).[30] While the description of places is sketchy, the concept of pilgrimage is very well described. The origin of pilgrimages, the concept of sanctity of the places, and the merit to be gained from pilgrimages are well outlined. In this respect it is better than all the four other sources mentioned above, where the usual emphasis (particularly in the first three) is on the description of places rather than on the concept of pilgrimage. Aiyangar's introduction to the *Tīrthavivecana Kāṇḍam* of *Kṛtyakalpataru* is an even better presentation of the traditional concept of pilgrimage in Hinduism.[31]

Analytical Literature

The greatest gap in the literature on places of pilgrimage occurs in the sector of analytical studies. There are some excellent studies of individual holy places, taking one or the other aspects of these places. The most valuable of these by far is Burton Stein's Ph.D. dissertation on Tirupati, "The Tirupati Temple: An Economic Study of a Medieval South Indian Temple."[32] The main concern of the author in that study was to view the South Indian temple as an institution for the redistribution of state resources. The wealth of the temple was derived from state grants and endowments, and these in turn were utilized by the temple for carrying out far-reaching economic improvements like irrigation. A more comprehensive but less analytical study is K. K. Pillay's *The Sucindram Temple*.[33] The chief limitation of Pillay's study is his lack of problem-orientation. His study includes the historical background as well as the intricacies of the religious observances and architecture. Stein's study, on the other hand, brings out the Tirupati temple as an important economic regional center. These studies, though concerned with sacred places, do not deal with the institution of pilgrimages as such; yet they take us far

[29]Sources Orientales, *Les Pèlerinages* (Paris, 1960).
[30]Claude Jacques, "Les Pèlerinages en Inde," in *ibid*, pp. 159–197.
[31]See n. 8 above.
[32]University of Chicago, Department of History, 1958.
[33]Adyar, Madras (Tamilnadu), 1953.

in the understanding of the significance of the sacred place for the mundane world. L. P. Vidyarthi, in *The Sacred Complex in Hindu Gaya,* has tried to show how from a sacred center a sacred complex grows up in time.[34] Unfortunately, the hypotheses he sets forth in his introduction are never fully substantiated, because he does not clearly identify the elements of the "little tradition" and the "great tradition."[35] The hypotheses are so broad that he finds it impossible to validate them on the basis of one particular sacred place. In spite of some of its failings, Vidyarthi's study is useful in understanding the dynamic aspect of Hindu culture.

Among anthropologists, Agehananda Bharati has shown a considerable interest in the institution of pilgrimages both from the conceptual and descriptive viewpoints.[36] His "Pilgrimage in the Indian Tradition" is a cogent, well-documented, and perceptive survey of the nature of pilgrimage, its growth, and its relationship with the Buddhist, the Hindu, and the Tantric traditions. Bharati delves into the question of pilgrimage essentially from the religious angle. Diehl, on the other hand, approaches the practice of pilgrimage from a more pragmatic perspective and suggests that pilgrims have definite objectives in view.[37] Among anthropologists of India, Diehl's analysis of the nature and motives of pilgrimage is perhaps one of the best even though it is constrained within one cultural region of India, namely, the Tamil area.

A good analytical understanding is provided by McKim Marriott in the study of "Little Communities in an Indigenous Civilization."[38] The author shows with great perceptivity how a local village cult eventually can be absorbed in the more universal Hindu tradition. Cohn and Marriott's insightful essay is, perhaps, one of the best, if short, analytical statements of "networks" and "centers" in traditional India.[39] The four levels of diversity set

[34]Bombay, 1961.

[35]The concepts "little tradition" and "great tradition" have been formulated in Robert Redfield and Milton Singer, "The Cultural Role of Cities." The formalization of these concepts specifically with respect to India is in McKim Marriott, "Little Communities in an Indigenous Civilization," in McKim Marriott, ed., *Village India* (Chicago, 1955), pp. 191–202.

[36]Agehananda Bharati, "Pilgrimage in the Indian Tradition" (1963), and "Pilgrimage Sites and Indian Civilization" (1970).

[37]Carl Gustav Diehl, *Instrument and Purpose, Studies on Rites and Rituals in South India* (Lund, 1956), p. 255.

[38]Marriott, *op. cit.*

[39]Bernard S. Cohn and McKim Marriott, "Networks and Centers in the Integration of Indian Civilization" (1958).

forth provide a framework for an analysis of the processes operative in Indian culture at varying levels of generalization. The authors recognize very clearly the significance of the networks of religions through pilgrimages, movement of professional religious entertainers, preceptors, holy men, and even beggars.

The concept of the city of "orthogenetic transformation" set forth by Redfield and Singer is a useful guide for the study of places of pilgrimage.[40] The orthogenetic city carries forward, develops, and elaborates a long-established local culture. Many places of pilgrimage are precisely such cities, whether their population is large or small. An interaction is established between this kind of city and the area from which people come to visit it. Thus, this interaction can be conceived as a direct connection between the rural and the urban—as well as the "little" and the "great" traditions.

The above analytical studies are largely by either historians or anthropologists. Geographers have shown relatively limited interest in the cultural processes of India. One of the vèry few geographers who has concerned himself with the general question of pilgrimages is Deffontaines.[41] Although some scholars (notably Isaac) regard Deffontaines' work as descriptive, at least the section on pilgrimages is more than that.[42] Deffontaines deals with several aspects of pilgrimage sites, for example, their localization, circulation generated by them, specialization, periodicity of pilgrimages. He thus attempts to discuss the significance of pilgrimages in the broader context of "circulation."

The only geographer who has attempted to account for the distribution of places of pilgrimage in India is Robert H. Stoddard in his Ph.D. dissertation. However, the three hypotheses that he sets forth later prove inadequate to account for the distribution of holy places.[43]

Of the few specifically geographic studies, Sopher's "Pilgrim Circulation in Gujarat" is by far the best, both for its recognition of the significance of pilgrim circulation and its analysis based upon field data.[44] Sopher's analysis brings out clearly, and not

[40]Robert Redfield and Milton Singer, "The Cultural Role of Cities" (1954).

[41]Pierre Deffontaines, *Gèographie et Religions* (Paris, 1948), pp. 295–338: "Géographie des Pèlerinages."

[42]For some comments on Deffontaines' *Géographie et Religions,* see Erich Isaac, "Religious Geography and the Geography of Religion" (1965).

[43]This work will be discussed in chapter 5.

[44]David E. Sopher, "Pilgrim Circulation in Gujarat" (1968).

unexpectedly, the validity of using caste groups as a basis of understanding social geographical problems in India. The relationship between the caste groups and pilgrim activity has been brought out. For example, above-average pilgrim activity is associated with the "high service castes." However, he throws relatively little light on such questions as: Why do certain pilgrims frequent certain specific places? What are the bases of pilgrimage as an institution? Is commitment more important than the caste or the economic level of the pilgrim? What are the pertinent factors associated with the varying sacred places? Many such questions could be raised regarding this study, but the fact remains that Sopher does break new ground in a neglected area of the cultural geography of India.

Sopher chooses to leave out from his analysis "chiefly sectarian places of pilgrimage" as well as "places of attraction for a single caste." By so doing he has amputated a vital part of the geographic expression of pilgrimage. This is somewhat surprising because he himself recognizes the importance of caste groups in relation to pilgrim activity.

PILGRIMS' TRAVEL GUIDES AND RELATED LITERATURE

The Department of Tourism of the Government of India publishes a number of pamphlets and small guides for the more well-known sacred places, obviously for the "tourist" pilgrims. From the viewpoint of pilgrims some private agencies, including religious organizations, publish guides for pilgrims; for example, the Sri Sita Rama Nama Sankirtana Sangham in Guntur, South India, publishes travel guides in regional languages as well as in English.[45] They give details of what religious ceremony should be performed at the sacred places and include other information about travel, board, and lodging. The Bharatiya Vidya Bhavan has published monographs on temples and legends of Bihar, Andhra Pradesh, Tamilnadu, and Maharashtra.[46] They usually give a detailed description of the legends about various important temples as well as historical and travel information, and are written by knowledgeable individuals. They are couched in a devotional tone and are thus different from the impersonal (ob-

[45] V. R. Ragam, *Pilgrim's Travel Guide,* 2 vols. (Guntur, 1963).
[46] See, e.g., R. K. Das, *Temples of Tamilnad* (Bombay, 1964).

jective?) attitude of the gazetteer writers. These booklets are valuable sources of information about a large number of sacred places. The *Tīrthāṅka* of *Kalyāṇa,* published by the Gita Press, Gorakhpur, in describing over 1,800 sacred places is perhaps the most nearly complete descriptive catalogue of the *tīrthas* available in India.[47]

GAZETTEERS

These are important sources of information about the sacred places of India. *The Imperial Gazetteer of India* 1908–9 (Provincial Series) gives the exact location and much, though unsystematic, information about a number of more well-known sacred places of India.[48] Additional data, also for places not mentioned in the *Imperial Gazetteer,* can be gathered from the district gazetteers and state gazetteers. Many of the district gazetteers of the British period are poorly indexed, and it is necessary to look for relevant information in various sections. The *U.P. District Gazetteers* give a list of places where fairs are held and have information about the deity, the time of the fair, and the approximate number of visitors. This type of table, however, is nonexistent in several other district gazetteers, which necessitates plowing through the arid, far from uniform descriptions.

The Census of India (1961) has published a series (not yet complete) of volumes on fairs and festivals of each state.[49] The published volumes provide extensive data about places where fairs are held. Information about the deities, times, and observances is also provided. It can serve as an excellent source for scholarly work on sacred places in India. Volumes on Gujarat, Punjab, Uttar Pradesh, and some districts of Andhra Pradesh have been published so far. When the series is complete, it may be possible to study the circulation pattern of pilgrims throughout India. Obviously these publications will not take the place of field work and further research, but the formulation of hypotheses and initial organization of research will certainly become easier than it is at present. From the geographical point of view the most

[47]*Kalyāṇa, Tīrthāṅka,* Vol. 31, no. 1 (1957). 704 pp.

[48]See volume 25 for an index of the sacred places.

[49]See, for example, *Census of India,* 1961, Vol. V, Gujarat: part VII-B, *Fairs and Festivals* (Delhi, 1965).

unfortunate omission in this series is that the places of origin of pilgrims cannot be established.

PILGRIM REGISTERS AND RECORDS KEPT BY PRIESTS

Various *dharmaśālās* (pilgrim rest houses) and lodging houses at important sacred places like Hardwar have pilgrim registers that, when properly maintained, show the origin of the pilgrim, his caste, and his profession. These registers can be useful for the study of pilgrim fields. Unfortunately, in most cases they are rather carelessly maintained and should be used with utmost care.

The *purohits* (priests) at many sacred places maintain *bahīs* (records) regarding the date and purpose of visits of their clients. These *bahīs* are of great value because they are firm evidence of the traditional relationship between the priests and their clients and have been maintained by generations of priests. Although they are difficult to consult, they can be of great value for social historians as well as for geographers. Professor B. N. Goswamy has used these records for research of fundamental importance to art history.[50]

From the general survey of the relevant literature it is evident that although there is abundant descriptive material, analytical studies are only in their inception. Clearly, it is in this direction that scholarly effort is most needed.

[50]The importance of these records is outlined in B. N. Goswamy, "The Records Kept by Priests at Centers of Pilgrimage as a Source of Social and Economic History" (1966). The use of these records has been excellently demonstrated in B. N. Goswamy, "Pahari Painting: The Family as the Basis of Style" (1968). Sometimes even relatively little known sacred places may yield most valuable documents bearing on the social and economic history. See B. N. Goswamy and J. S. Grewal, *The Mughals and the Jogis of Jakhbar* (Simla, 1967).

Chapter II

Distribution of Hindu Places of Pilgrimage According to the *Mahābhārata*

ANALYSIS OF THE DISTRIBUTION

It was noted in chapter 1 that the *Mahābhārata* is the oldest and the most important source of information about the places of pilgrimage in the ancient period. There is no unanimity on the date of composition of this epic. It is, however, almost certainly anterior to the *Purāṇas*.[1] If the approximate date of the composition of the *tīrtha-yātrā* sections of this epic is the same as that of the rest of the book itself, then there is no doubt that the institution of pilgrimages was well established at least a few centuries before the beginning of the Christian Era. The *Mahābhārata* clearly considers going on pilgrimages *(tīrtha-yātrā)* to be superior to sacrifice: "O thou best of Bharta race, sojourns in *tīrthas* which are meritorious and which constitute one of the high mysteries of the Rishis, are even superior to sacrifices."[2] Figure 2-1 shows the distribution of places of pilgrimage according to *Mahābhārata* and is based on both of the "dialogues" referred to in chapter 1.[3] About 270 places and sacred rivers are mentioned in the first dialogue, and about 60 are mentioned in the second dialogue.[4] The map shows only those places which I have been able to identify after comparison with the critical edition.[5]

[1]For detailed discussion of the dating of the *Mahābhārata*, see M. A. Winternitz, *A History of Indian Literature*, Vol. I, sec. 2, pp. 454–475. Also see P. V. Kane, "The *Mahābhārata* Verses and Very Ancient Dharmasūtras and Other Works," in *A Volume of Eastern and Indian Studies*, presented to Professor F. W. Thomas, edited by S. M. Katre and P. K. Gode (Bombay: Karnatak Publishing House, 1939), pp. 128: "But the time when original *Mahābhārata* was composed will probably remain an insoluble puzzle"; V. S. Sukthankar, "The *Mahābhārata* and Its Critics," in *On the Meaning of Mahābhārata* (Bombay: The Asiatic Society of Bombay, 1957), pp. 1–31; Franklin Edgerton, ed., *Mahābhārata, The Sabhāparvan* (Poona, 1944), p. XXVIII. Edgerton believes the first century A.D. is the probable date of composition of this epic.

[2]P. C. Roy, trans., *The Mahābhārata*, Vol. II, 175.

[3]Figure 2-1 is based on the Critical Edition of the *Mahābhārata*.

[4]*Mahābhārata*, Roy's translation, Vol. II, sec. 80–156.

[5]For identification of the place names, two most helpful sources are Nando Lal

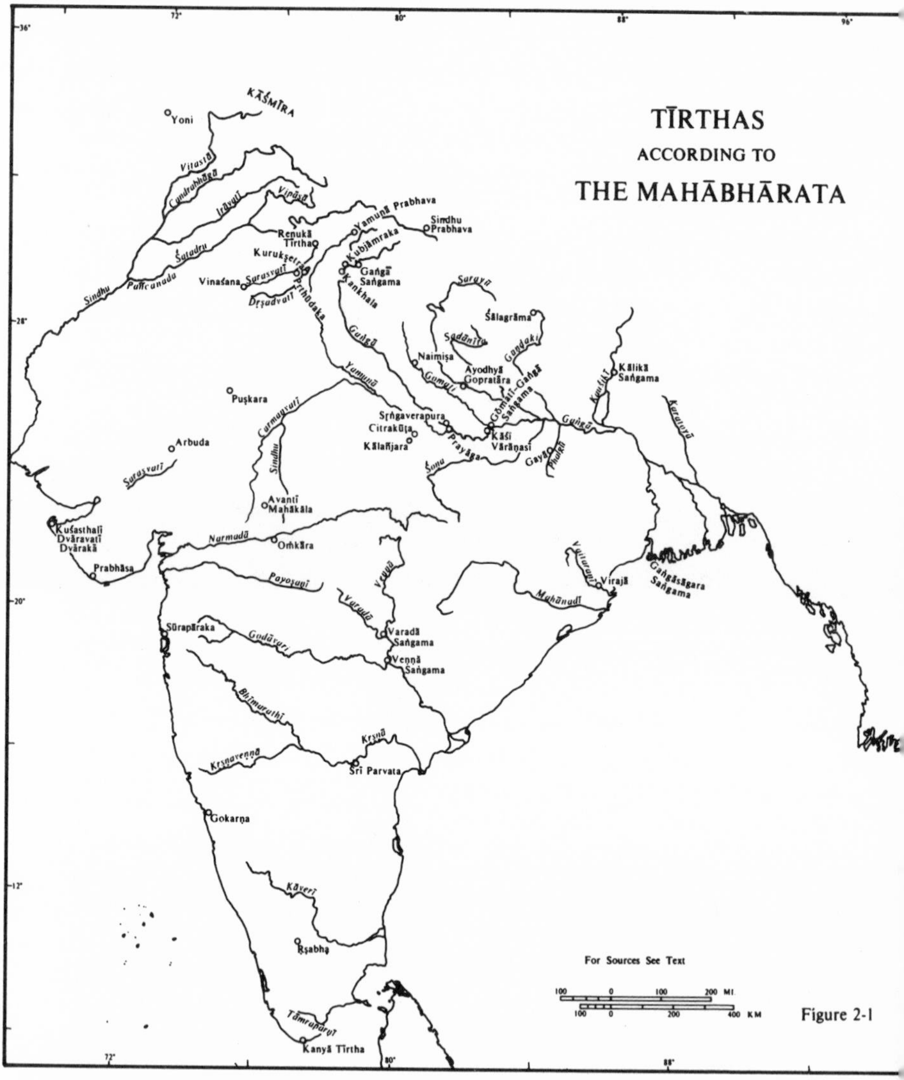
TĪRTHAS
ACCORDING TO
THE MAHĀBHĀRATA
KĀŚMĪRA
Yoni
Vitastā
Candrabhāgā
Irāvatī
Vipāśā
Yamunā Prabhava
Sindhu Prabhava
Renukā Tīrtha
Śatadru
Kurukṣetra
Kubjāmraka
Gaṅgā Saṅgama
Vinaśana
Sarasvatī
Pañcanada
Sindhu
Dṛṣadvatī
Pṛthūdaka
Kankhala
Sarayū
Śālagrāma
Sadānīrā
Gaṇḍakī
Gaṅgā
Naimiṣa
Ayodhyā
Gopratāra
Gomatī
Gomatī-Gaṅgā Saṅgama
Kauśikī
Kālikā Saṅgama
Karatoyā
Yamunā
Puṣkara
Carmaṇvatī
Śṛṅgaverapura
Citrakūṭa
Kālañjara
Prayāga
Kāśī
Vārāṇasī
Gayā
Phalgu
Śoṇa
Arbuda
Sarasvatī
Sindhu
Avantī
Mahākāla
Kuśasthalī
Dvāravatī
Dvārakā
Narmadā
Oṁkāra
Prabhāsa
Payoṣṇī
Veṇṇā
Vaitaraṇī
Virajā
Gaṅgāsāgara Saṅgama
Mahānadī
Varadā
Varadā Saṅgama
Śūrapāraka
Godāvarī
Veṇṇā Saṅgama
Bhīmarathī
Kṛṣṇā
Kṛṣṇaveṇṇā
Śrī Parvata
Gokarṇa
Kāverī
Ṛṣabha
Tāmraparṇī
Kanyā Tīrtha
For Sources See Text
100 0 100 200 MI.
100 0 200 400 KM
36°
28°
20°
12°
72°
80°
88°
96°
Figure 2-1

The identification of place names of so great an antiquity is a very tedious task because a large number of sacred spots were merely the abodes of one sage or another without any adjacent settlement of consequence. It would be a fruitless task to try to find the exact location of all the cottages and hermitages of the sages of antiquity. Even so, enough places have been identified on the map to give an idea of the sacred realm of the Hindus in the ancient period.

The list of sacred places in the first dialogue (in which *tīrthas* are described) is supplied by sage Pulastya, and that in the second dialogue by Dhaumya. The first list attempts to describe sacred places in a sequence along the routes of pilgrimage. However, it must not be concluded that the order of places is easily discernible; on the contrary, the list is extremely confused. Even so, I have tried to bring out the basic order in the description of *tīrthas* in the first dialogue, and this order will be discussed in the next chapter. The importance of this order lies in the fact that it has enabled me to map a grand sacred tour clockwise through the entire country some centuries before Christ.

The second dialogue in which Dhaumya supplies the list of major *tīrthas* of India is less satisfactory in the number of places mentioned; but the concept of clockwise pilgrimage is evident. This second list is a regional one. The sacred places of the East, South, West, and North are mentioned successively. This list repeats some of the most important *tīrthas* mentioned in the first, longer list. Because of its repetition and also because it immediately follows the first, more detailed list, I feel that it may be a later interpolation into the main body of the epic.[6] The critical edition of the *Mahābhārata,* however, retains this list, implying that it is a genuine part of the epic.

In the following discussion of the distribution of sacred places according to *Mahābhārata,* the main purpose is to see what this distribution suggests and what are the implications of this distribution. From the description of the *tīrthas* in the *Mahābhārata*

Dey, *The Geographical Dictionary of Ancient and Medieval India*; and B. C. Law, *Historical Geography of Ancient India.*

[6]Shejwalkar believes that the Dhaumya list of sacred places is the earlier one showing "a less advanced stage of Aryan Expansion." T. S. Shejwalkar, "The *Mahābhārata* Data for Aryan Expansion in India," p. 207. The available evidence is too meager for establishing the greater antiquity of Dhaumya narration.

and from the map of sacred places (fig. 2-1), the following observations may be made.

(1) Association of *tīrthas* with water is clearly brought out; most of the sacred spots lie either on riverbanks, at confluences, or on the seacoast. In the case of some *tīrthas* (for example, "Badri" (Badrinarain), Mahākāla (Ujjain), Vadava (Jwala Mukhi), no associated stream has been mentioned in the text of the *Mahābhārata.* Actually, however, all three of them have a riverbank site. Apparently the purificatory value of water was an important factor in locating *tīrthas.*[7] This simple fact alone is enough of a pointer to those who may be looking for either a random or an "optimally" ordered distribution of the places of pilgrimage in India without understanding the symbolic importance of water in the rituals of the Hindu religion.[8]

(2) The *Mahābhārata* mentions *tīrthas* and sacred rivers throughout much of the country, indicating that at least some dedicated people did travel far and wide to visit the holy places. In other words, there must have been some degree of commonality of religious concepts and beliefs over a large part of the subcontinent. It is impossible to say how large was the movement of pilgrims to various holy places. But at least a large number of focal points of religious beliefs existed which, being common to the religion as a whole, would have tended to provide some degree of unity in the religious sphere.

(3) The places of pilgrimage of the Hindus presumably existed in the areas effectively occupied by people practicing Hindu beliefs. There are, however, some sacred places, like Badrināth and Kedārnāth in the Himālayas, which, from the point of view of effective occupance, were and continued to be remote and inaccessible except in the summer season. Even though these and several other places were physically remote and difficult of access, they were sites that were deemed sacred from the viewpoint of the phenomenology of Hinduism. Their very remoteness may have been of special value. Being remote and isolated, they were, so to speak, away from the profane world and hence suitable places for the abode of gods. The greater the effort required to reach

[7]The word *tīrtha* means a ford. The symbolic meaning of ford is more pertinent than the literal meaning. To purify oneself at a *tīrtha* by bathing is to symbolize one's passage from the profane to the sacred world.

[8]See Robert H. Stoddard, "Hindu Holy Sites in India."

these places, the greater would have to be the conviction of the pilgrim and hence perhaps his expectation of religious reward. This attitude follows directly from the stress on austerity in Hinduism.

(4) The distribution of *tīrthas* according to the *Mahābhārata* clearly reveals certain clusterings of sacred places as well as large areas with but few holy spots. The largest number of *tīrthas* are situated in the Gaṅgā basin. Two distinct clusters can be identified, the first one comprising the upper reaches of Gaṅgā and Yamunā and the second one in the eastern part of modern Uttar Pradesh. Within the Gaṅgā basin Prayāga forms the focal point of the latter cluster. The region between the Gaṅgā and Yamunā, the Doāb, has been regarded as the "mons veneris" of the world and Prayāga as the foremost point of that region.[9] This appellation of the Gaṅgā-Yamunā Doab is suggestive both of the fertility and the preeminent sanctity of the region.

A third cluster of holy places is in the vicinity of the now truncated Saraswati river in the Kurukṣetra region. Only a few places can now be identified. Nevertheless, this region must have been one of major sanctity, as in fact it is today.

The clustering of holy places in the Gaṅgā plain and the Kurukṣetra region reflects the main foci of the domain of the Vedic Aryans. These were the regions sanctified by the Aryan sages and the fire god, Agni. The existence of sacred places suggests that these regions had been purified for the Aryan way of life. The acts of sanctification of the land may have been the prelude to the effective occupance of the land. Like many other ancient peoples, the Aryans also conceived of their ecumene as sacred space.[10]

The cluster of holy places in the upper reaches of the Gaṅgā and the Yamunā rivers can best be conceived as the spatial extension of the sacred ecumene. To be sure, the remote and difficult Himālayan headwater region of the Gaṅgā and the Yamunā could not have been "occupied" in the same fashion and with the same economy as the Gaṅgā plain, but then religion rather than economy may have been the underpinning of the Aryan ecumene.

Descriptions in the *Mahābhārata* suggest two other regions with some degree of clustering of *tīrthas,* although the problem of

[9]*Mahābhārata* (Roy's translation), II, 204.

[10]Cf. Fustel de Coulanges, *The Ancient City* (New York: Doubleday Anchor Books, 1955), chap. 6, "The Right of Property."

identification of place names makes it difficult to bring out the effect on a map. These two regions are modern Tamilnadu and Southern Andhra, and the Narmada-Ujjain area in Madhya Pradesh. The mention of many sacred places in these two regions, remote from the major foci of Aryan domination, raises the possibility that these areas were more intimately related to the religion of the North than other areas of Central or South India. What exactly were the circumstances favoring a greater degree of religious interaction between the Gaṅgā plain and these two far-flung areas is not clear.

It is interesting to note that some of the places in the South, which according to later tradition were so important, are not even mentioned in the *Mahābhārata*; for example, Rāmeśvaram, Śriraṅgam, and Tirupati. One probable inference is that these places had not yet attained the stature of sanctity that they now command. Or, that they may not have been sacred spots at all and that they developed only later. Another plausible inference is that the contact between the North and South on the basis of religion was not strong by 300 B.C. so that *Mahābhārata* selects only the more well-known sacred places from this southern region. If the intermingling of the religious lore and literature of the North and the South had been well established by about 300 B.C., then one would expect more places to have been selected from the South. However, even the mere mention of *tīrthas* in the far South suggests a degree of contact between the North and South at this remote period. In fact, Professor Nilakanta Sastri suggests that the Aryanization of South India had already been achieved during the period of the epics.[11] Some of the prominent and persistent themes of the epic, for example, the legend of the progressive southward movement of the Aryan sage Agastya, seem most likely to allude to the progressive Aryanization of the South during the period of the great epics.[12] If the Aryanization of the South at this early period is accepted, then the mention of sacred places of pilgrimage follows from it. The question still remains why more places are mentioned in the Tamilnadu than anywhere else in the South.

The nonuniform distribution of the places of pilgrimage raises further questions also. Why do some areas of India stand out clearly as deficient areas so far as recognized sacred places are

[11]K. A. Nilakanta Sastri, *A History of South India*, chap. 4.

[12]For a brief discussion of this legend see *ibid.*, pp. 67ff.

concerned? These areas include (1) a large part of Madhya Pradesh (Central India), (2) most of Southern Bihar, the plateau regions of Orissa and Andhra, (3) all of Bengal and Assam, and (4) the plateau regions between the Krishna-Bhima and the Kaveri rivers.

One way of approaching this problem is to correlate the non-Hindu population of the time of *Mahābhārata* with the areas deficient in pilgrimage sites. That, however, cannot be attempted at this stage of research because relevant material is not available. One would need to know the names as well as the locale of the non-Hindu or at least non-Aryan tribes in ancient India. B. C. Law has made an attempt to find references in the ancient literature about the various Aryan and other tribes of India.[13] However, the location of tribes is either uncertain or speculative. If some Indologists succeed in fixing the location of these tribes of ancient India, a step will have been taken to clarify the question of Aryan migrations inside India and the routes (or rather, preferred zones) of their southward movement.[14]

In the absence of knowledge about the exact locale of the ancient tribes, a simple though partial explanation is here proposed to account for the deficiency of sacred places in the regions mentioned above. The explanation rests on the assumption that the areas which at the time of the epic *Mahābhārata* (ca. 300 B.C.) had few Hindu sacred places were then occupied mostly by non-Aryanized tribes. As the latter gradually merged into the fold of Hinduism, Hindu sacred places would tend to emerge. If our assumption is to be valid, we should find only few recognized Hindu sacred places in the major tribal areas of today. Problems, however, arise immediately, because the modern term "scheduled tribe" includes such purely Hindu "tribes" as the Gaddīs of Chamba, as well as several other tribes reflecting varying degrees of Hindu influence. Furthermore, the cult spots of many of the tribes may have been incorporated into Hinduism. Questions can be raised regarding the existence of celebrated Hindu places like Amarkantak on the headwaters of Narmada, Nasik in Maharashtra, Abu in Rajasthan, and Kamakhya in Assam—all situated in areas where

[13] *Tribes in Ancient India.*

[14] I have made an effort to collate several sources and map the location of the "peoples" and places according to the *Vedas*, the *Rāmāyaṇa*, the *Mahābhārata*, and the *Purāṇas* in *South Asia Historical Atlas*. The latter is a project of the University of Minnesota and is nearing completion under the directorship of Professor Joseph E. Schwartzberg.

tribal population is considerable. A plausible explanation may be that many such places have been later incorporated into Hinduism —their former sylvan deities having been merged with the major Hindu deities. Of the above four sacred places the *Mahābhārata* mentions only one, Arbuda (Abu), fortifying our impression that the main tribal areas of today at least did not form part of the then sacred landscape of the Aryans.

West Bengal, Assam, and other eastern parts of India also were deficient in sacred places. Only a few districts of northern West Bengal have substantial tribal populations today, but further east tribal population is still large. The valley of Brahmaputra is basically nontribal, but the dense settlement of this region is relatively recent. The deficiency of Hindu sacred places in this eastern part of India, as revealed by the epic, thus seems to have been directly related to the non-Aryan tribal cultures of that time. In fact, the sacred literature strongly suggests that the eastward extension of Aryan culture of the central Gaṅgā basin encountered certain difficulties. The relatively late progress of the Aryan culture in Bengal and Assam seems to be reflected in the deficiency of sacred places at the time of the epic. The peripheral nature of Bengal and Assam with respect to the core areas of the Gaṅgā basin and their delayed contact with the latter is indicated by a legend in the *Śatpatha Brāhmaṇa* about the movement of the fire god, Agni, across the Gandak River to the east.[15] According to the legend, Agni initially stopped on the west bank of the Gandak River until he was carried by an Aryan chieftain across the river to the east. The cult of Agni not only is indicative of the purification of the land prior to the settlement of the Aryans but also brings into focus the need of clearing the denser forests as the expansion of Aryans led them toward the eastern, more humid climate.[16] The eastern kingdom of Videha, across the Gandak River, seems to have been the easternmost Aryanized domain in the late Vedic period. Beyond this kingdom Bengal and Assam were obviously in the non-Aryan tribal domain. The dominance of the non-Aryan people in the eastern parts of India seems to be the key factor in

[15]The *Śatpatha Brāhmaṇa* belongs to the late Vedic age and thus the above legend suggests a late expansion of Aryans toward far eastern parts of India. For more details, see A. L. Basham, *The Wonder That Was India*, p. 40. The chronology of the *Brāhmaṇas* is discussed in some detail in J. N. Farquhar, *An Outline of the Religious Literature of India*, 1967 ed., pp. 25–28.

[16]D. D. Kosambi, *The Culture and Civilization of Ancient India*, p. 91.

explaining why the *Mahābhārata* mentions but one sacred place in the whole area of Bengal and further east. The deficiency of sacred places in other regions may also be related to the dominance of non-Aryan cultures.

The distribution pattern of the sacred places of the epic on the Indian Peninsula as a whole is of considerable interest because I feel it can throw some light on certain aspects of culture contact between the then heartland of Aryan culture and the rest of the peninsula.[17] In the next chapter I have tried to identify some probable pilgrimage routes based on the epic text (fig. 3-1). For our present purpose it may suffice to observe that the pilgrim routes of which our knowledge is most reliable show a strong tendency to be peripheral in location. For example, the much traveled routes along the Orissa and Andhra coastal region, along the Kerala and Mysore coast, and finally in Malwa, Rajasthan, and Gujarat are far more clearly known than those in the interior of the peninsula. In other words, these may have been the general overland connecting corridors into peninsular India. The movements of peoples and trade may also have followed these generalized routes.

If the above outline of our argument is tentatively accepted, it follows that the more-frequented sacred places of the peninsula had locations on the margins of the cultures occupying the peninsula. A question can be raised here regarding the sacred rivers of the peninsula, most of which are mentioned in the epic.

Does the knowledge about the rivers mean that there was also corresponding intimate knowledge of the interior parts of the peninsula? I believe it is not a necessary condition, because the pilgrim routes clearly show that knowledge about the rivers could have been derived from the necessity to cross them while on pilgrimage to the more frequented places which lay on the margins of the peninsula.

We may now briefly explore the probable reasons for the location of sacred places on the margins of the peninsula. Avanti and Oṁkāra do not seem to fit this broad picture, and we shall make appropriate observations on their location.

Most of the scheduled-tribe population of India today lives in two major blocks in peninsular India (fig. 2-2), occupying, for the

[17]Peninsula here refers to the broad region designated by Spate as "the Peninsula." See O. H. K. Spate and A. T. A. Learmonth, *India and Pakistan,* fig. 13.1, p. 408.

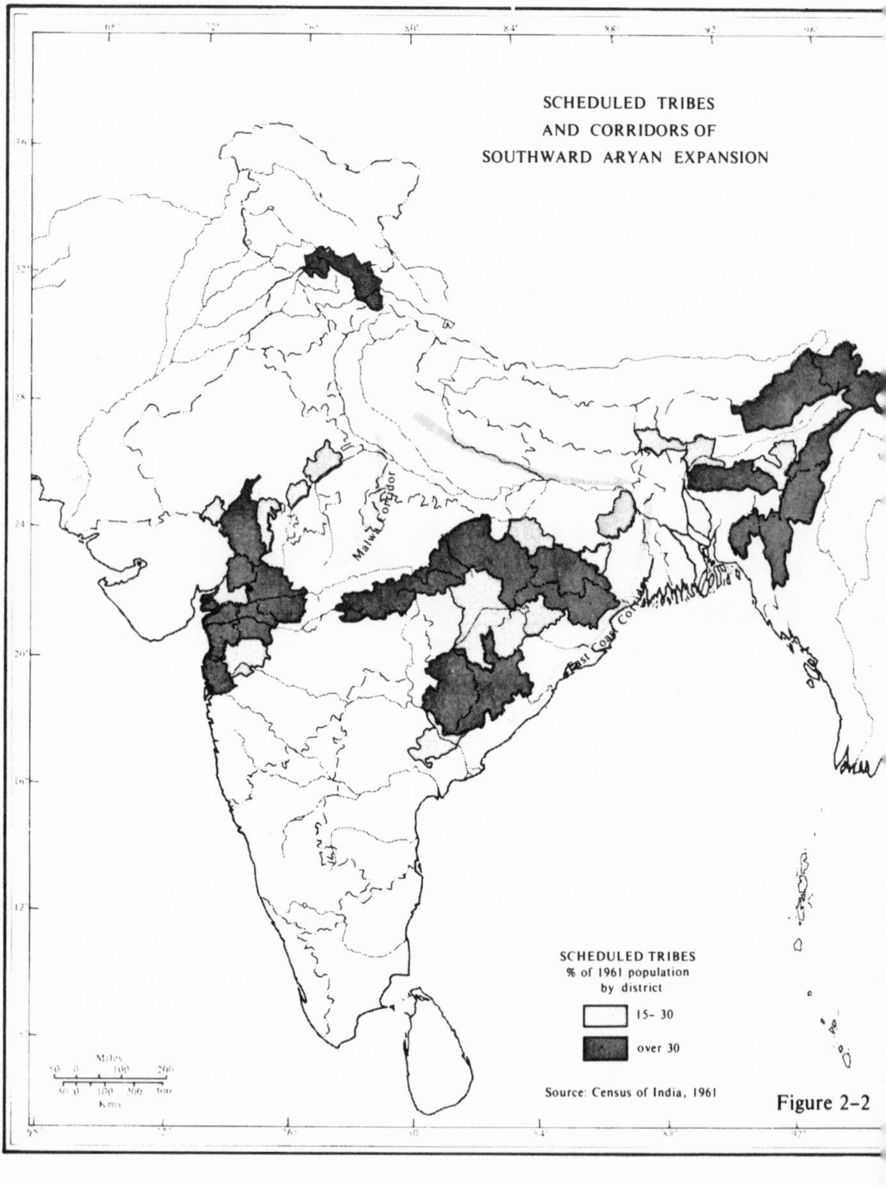

SCHEDULED TRIBES
AND CORRIDORS OF
SOUTHWARD ARYAN EXPANSION
Malwa Corridor
East Coast Corridor
SCHEDULED TRIBES
% of 1961 population
by district
15- 30
over 30
Miles
Kms
Source: Census of India, 1961

Figure 2-2

most part, areas of marginal agricultural value. Before the intrusion of Aryan culture these two blocks probably formed one continuous area of tribal population.

The Malwa plateau separates the eastern block from the western one, although further south a strong suggestion of the former link along the Satpura range remains. Despite problems of gully erosion, much of the Malwa plateau presents a sharp contrast (in its agricultural use) to the dissected uplands to the east and west.[18] In fact the Deccan lavas of the Malwa region "provide the only really extensive agricultural base in central India."[19] No wonder then that this region was attractive to the southward expansion of plow agriculture. In this Aryan or Aryanized kingdom of Malwa, Ujjain developed as a major sacred place. It may never be known whether it developed on the site of a former cult spot of the pre-Aryans, but the fact remains that its location on the trunk route from the Gaṅgā plain to the Arabian Sea may have made it a focus for pilgrimage as much as for trade. Archaeologists seem to agree that the impetus for the growth of Ujjain came from an iron-using culture of the Gangetic type about 500 B.C.[20] Ujjain thus lay, in the epic context, on a main highway of the southward-intruding Aryan culture.

Further south-southeast from Ujjain is another sacred place of the epic, namely Oṁkāra. Its location on the south bank of the Narmadā River and close to an important passageway (the "Burhanpur Gap") in the east-west trending Satpura hills suggests a crossing point on the Narmadā, hence a logical site for the growth of a *tīrtha*.

Fig. 2-2 clearly suggests a corridor of nontribal population along coastal Orissa and Andhra. Westward from this lies the eastern block of tribal population. Most of the rivers, from the Vaitaraṇī in Orissa to the Tāmraparṇi in Tamilnadu, are described in the epic as sacred rivers. The pilgrim route as derived from the epic follows the coastal zone. This seems to suggest very strongly that the coastal zone was an important corridor of movement from the Gaṅgā plain to Tamilnadu. Along this corridor the fords of rivers may have become sacred spots. It is true that relatively few holy

[18]The contrast between Malwa and the Vindhyas is well brought out by Spate and Learmonth, pp. 622–624.

[19]*Ibid.*, p. 624.

[20]Sir Mortimer Wheeler, *Early India and Pakistan*, p. 142.

"places" as such are given by the epic for the east coast, but the number of sacred rivers seems to fill that gap.

It seems quite probable that the tribal population was displaced or absorbed very early by the sedentary agricultural people expanding from the coastal areas, perhaps beginning with the introduction of plow agriculture. Archaeological evidence from Hastinapur suggests that "the cultivation of rice was a feature of the rise of Ganges civilization."[21] It is also believed that cultivation of rice spread through the peninsula during the Iron Age.[22] The question then arises, what were the favorable zones of diffusion of rice cultivation to the south from the Gaṅgā plain? The coastal zone seems to be a distinct possibility both because of its physical attributes and the relative ease of contact with the Ganga plain. The eastern coastal zone may have played a significant part in the spread of agriculture from the north, as well as in the exchange of ideas back and forth.

At the present state of our research it is not possible to put forth an explanation for the location of sacred places on the west coast, including Gujarat. They may have had their origin during the period of Indus Valley civilization, but archaeology is silent about the age of these sites despite the fact that several Harappan civilization sites have been found in Gujarat. The explanation of the location of sacred places on the west coast must remain for the future.[23]

RELATIVE IMPORTANCE OF *Tīrthas* AND CULTS ACCORDING TO THE *Mahābhārata*

It is not possible to clearly determine which of the numerous *tīrthas* mentioned in the epic commanded greater or lesser sanctity. Nevertheless, some sacred places stand out because of their eulogies or repeated references to them. Some of the sacred places that were prominent for the epic may no longer exist. On the other hand, minor places of the epic may now be preeminent.

[21]Bridget and Raymond Allchin, *The Birth of Indian Civilization*, p. 265.

[22]*Ibid.*, p. 265. Also compare Carl Whiting Bishop, "The Origin and Early Diffusion of Traction Plow," p. 277. Bishop believes that plow agriculture was common in India during the Vedic period.

[23]Shejwalkar believes that the "west coast was probably discovered by the sea-route" ("*Mahābhārata* Data," p. 219). Our reading of the epic *Mahābhārata* suggests that land routes were clearly available between the west-coast pilgrimage sites and those in Rajasthan and Malwa.

The description of *tīrthas* starts with Puṣkara (in Rajasthan) with hyperbolic statements about its sanctity. Why is Puṣkara taken as the starting point rather than, say, Vārāṇasī, clearly a celebrated holy place. Not only is Puṣkara taken as the starting point for the grand pilgrimage of the entire country, but also its merit is repeated at the end of the dialogue on pilgrimages. Both of these points indicate that Puṣkara in Rajasthan was perhaps the most prominent place of pilgrimage in the entire list of places supplied by the epic. Puṣkara is a *tīrtha* of Brahmā today and the *Mahābhārata* also recognizes it as a *tīrtha* of Brahmā. This leads to the supposition that Brahmā may have been a far more important deity during the epic period than today. The space devoted to eulogizing the merits of Puṣkara far exceeds that given to Vārāṇasī. Furthermore, the merit of visiting Puṣkara is considered in the epic to be equal to ten *aśvamedha yajñas,* that is, ten horse-sacrifices. On the other hand, the merit of visiting Vārāṇasī was merely a *rājasu yajña*—a normal ceremony of kingship and concomitant sacrifice much inferior to the horse sacrifice. These differences of relative merits attached to the two sacred places seem to indicate that Vārāṇasī had not yet attained the high relative sanctity that it enjoys today.

Today the cult of Brahmā is relatively insignificant in India since only one major holy place is associated with him, namely, Puṣkara. The epic, on the other hand, mentions several places or even regions (now hard to locate) associated with this deity, namely, Brahmakśetra, Brahmasthāna, Brahmayoni, Brahmodumvara, Brahmāvarta, and above all, Puṣkara. Obviously the cult of Brahmā has been eclipsed by the rise of other deities in the later period.

In the list of sacred places in the epic, no place is associated with Śiva by his name. There is a god by the name of "Rudra," or the "Husband of Uma," who is referred to several times in the course of the dialogue, but not "Śiva." It has been established that at a later stage in the development of Hindu religion "Rudra" was merged with Śiva, but in the epic this transformation is not evident.[24]

None of the sacred places in the epic has been associated with the currently prominent deities like Viṣṇu and Kṛṣṇa, and certainly no mention is made about the temples or icons of these deities.

[24]See, for example, K. A. Nilakanta Sastri, *Development of Religion in South India,* p. 19.

In other words, the kind of theistic worship we find in India today must have been almost totally lacking.

In the description of sacred places the *Mahābhārata* obviously shows a strong bias in favor of the place names of the Gaṅgā basin and a few other scattered areas. It is also clear that the names of almost all the large rivers and many small ones are mentioned throughout India. The actual sacred place names, however, are relatively few once the narration of regions outside the Gaṅgā basin begins. With so great an obsession for ritual purification by bathing, the emphasis on rivers as sacred entities is understandable.

The distribution of sacred places of the epic suggests an outline of the parts of the country which could be called the sacred space of Aryan culture. The areas deficient in sacred places indicate the habitat of the non-Aryan people. A more detailed identification of sacred place names of the epic may help in the understanding of the spatial dimensions and interpenetration of Aryan and non-Aryan cultures of ancient India.

The pattern of distribution of sacred places outside the Gaṅgā basin suggests certain preferred corridors or routes through which the expansion of Aryan culture may have occurred in the past. Archaeological and historical research in not too distant a future may be able to provide data on the basis of which the soundness of these corridors of cultural contact may be tested.

Chapter III

A Grand Pilgrimage of India According to the *Mahābhārata*

INTRODUCTION

The account of *tīrthas* given in *Tīrtha-Yātrā* (pilgrimage) section of the epic *Mahābhārata* suggests a grand tour of the entire country. Although several authors have noted the importance of the epic for a study of places of pilgrimage of ancient India, they have tended to overlook the point that the narrator of the sacred places suggests a clockwise circular pilgrimage of *India*.[1] This is understandable because the description of *tīrthas* becomes very confused at several points in the dialogue by Pulastya.[2] In the following pages of this chapter I have attempted to make some sense out of the scrambled account of *tīrthas* presented by Pulastya in the great epic.[3]

It must be a difficult task for anyone to enumerate, and even more to describe, systematically and successively, each holy place of the epic age. Therefore, let us accept, at the start, that errors are bound to occur in the order of sacred places in the epic. Other errors must have been introduced between the time these sections on pilgrimage were composed and the time when they were finally committed to writing. Interpolations and omissions may also have been numerous.

Given that there are errors, omissions, and interpolations, the underlying purpose nevertheless must have been to give an ordered account of all the known important places of pilgrimage of the entire subcontinent. Accepting this premise, an attempt has been made to reconstruct the pilgrim routes (see fig. 3-1). Although

[1]For example, K. V. Rangaswami Aiyanger, ed., *Kṛtyakalpataru of Bhaṭṭa Lakṣmīdhara,* Introduction. Also see Radha Kumud Mookerji, *Fundamental Unity of India,* p. 61.

[2]See *Mahābhārata,* Roy's translation, Vol. II, secs. 81–85, pp. 172–206; and critical edition, Vol. III, secs. 80–89.

[3]Cf. T. S. Shejwalkar, "The *Mahābhārata* Data of Aryan Expansion in India," his map facing p. 207.

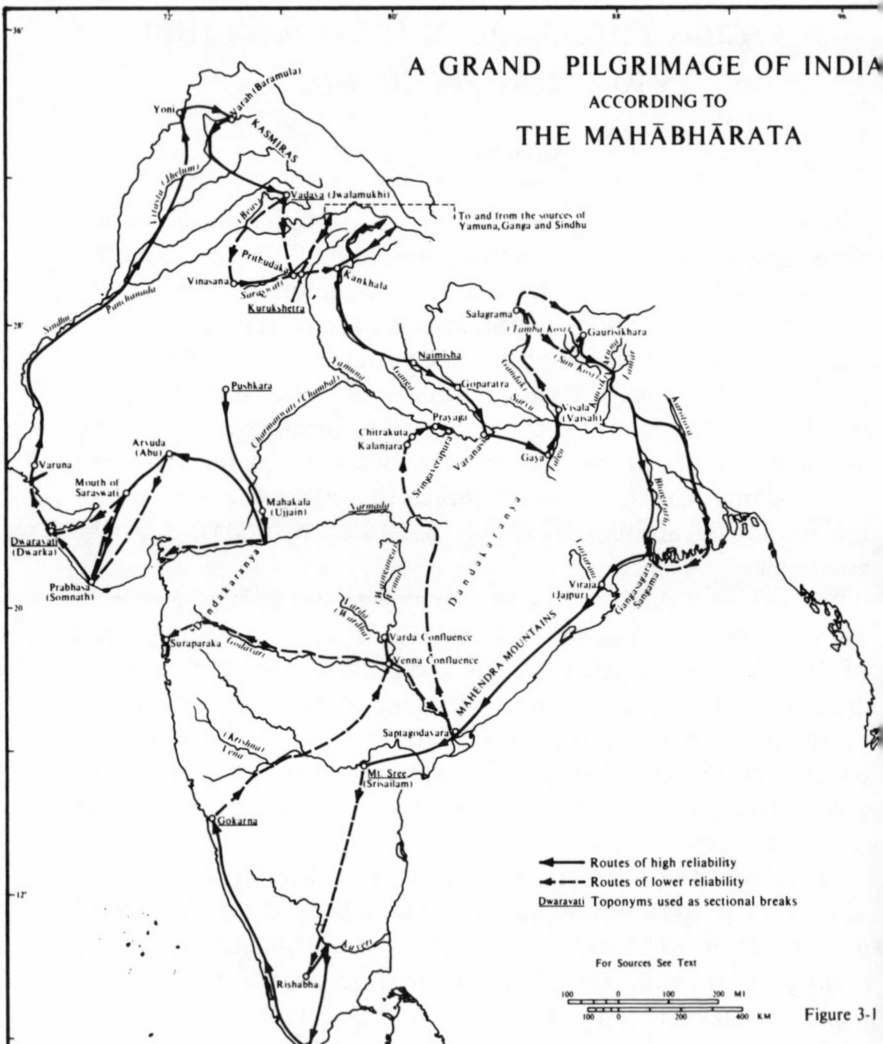
A GRAND PILGRIMAGE OF INDIA
ACCORDING TO
THE MAHĀBHĀRATA
Yoni
Varah (Baramula)
KASMIRAS
Vitasta (Jhelum)
Vadava (Jwalamukhi)
To and from the sources of
Yamuna, Ganga and Sindhu
Prithudaka
Vinasana
Saraswati
Kurukshetra
Kankhala
Panchanada
Sindhu
Salagrama
Gaurisikhara
Naimisha
Goparatra
Pushkara
Prayaga
Chitrakuta
Kalanjara
Varanasi
Gaya
Visala
(Vaisali)
Arvuda
(Abu)
Varuna
Mouth of
Saraswati
Mahakala
(Ujjain)
Narmada
Dwaravati
(Dwarka)
Prabhasa
(Somnath)
Dandakaranya
Viraja
(Jajpur)
Gangasagara
Sangama
MAHENDRA MOUNTAINS
Suraparaka
Godavari
Varda Confluence
Venna Confluence
Saptagodavara
Krishna
Mt. Sree
(Srisailam)
Gokarna
Rishabha
Kanya
Routes of high reliability
Routes of lower reliability
Dwaravati Toponyms used as sectional breaks
For Sources See Text
Figure 3-1

complete reconstruction is impossible, mainly because a large number of places cannot be identified, the general outline of the itinerary is clear. Interested scholars may refine or modify the reconstruction after identifying some more places. It may be said at the cost of repetition that, of the two dialogues about the places of pilgrimage in the epic (Roy's translation), the first one has been utilized because this is the one that suggests a grand sacred tour of holy places in India.[4]

For the sake of convenience and clarification, the itinerary has been divided into several sections. For each section, the place names that have been identified with a reasonable degree of certainty are designed as "sequential *tīrthas*." The identification of the general direction of the pilgrim route is based on these "sequential *tīrthas*." Once the most probable general direction of the route of a particular section was established, other places mentioned in the section were presumed to be on that route. In the case of these "other" places, there is usually a considerable confusion, probably resulting from an accumulation of errors, omissions, and interpolations. Identification of the general direction of the pilgrim route is followed by comments on each section. These comments are intended to further clarify the direction of the pilgrim route and to note alternate identification of some places by other scholars. In summary, the steps of the procedure are (1) division of the route into sections; (2) identification of important "sequential *tīrthas*" in each section, and listing of toponyms presumably en route in each section according to the epic;[5] and (3) commentary on each section.[6]

THE ROUTE OF THE PILGRIMAGE

Section 1. *From Pushkara to Narmada River*

Toponyms of Section 1

PUSHKARA, Jamvu Marga,*[7] Tandulikasrama,* Lake of

[4]*Mahābhārata,* Roy's translation, II, 172–206. Since Roy does not use diacritics, the place names taken from his translation conform to his spellings. The map showing pilgrim routes also conforms to Roy's spelling of toponyms.

[5]Sequential *tīrthas* are shown in capital letters in step 2 (toponyms); places that cannot be identified are starred.

[6]In this chapter the following abbreviations are used to facilitate references. Dey : Nando Lal Dey, *The Geographical Dictionary of Ancient and Medieval India.* Law : B. C. Law, *Historical Geography of Ancient India.* M. B. : *The Mahābhārata,* Vol. II, Roy's translation. V. P. : *Viṣṇu Purāṇa* (translated by H. H. Wilson).

[7]Located by Dey in Mount Abu (p. 80); by Wilson in V. P., Vol. II, ch. XIII,

Agastya,* Asylum of Kanwa,* Spot where Yayati fell,* MAHAKALA, Bhadravata,*[8] and finally NARMADA RIVER.

Comments

In the first section the pilgrim is directed to reach the Narmada from Pushkara. Some important sequential places, as noted above, clearly suggest this general direction (fig. 3-1). If the general direction of the route is accepted, then there is no reason to identify Jamvu Marga of *Mahābhārata* with Kalinjar as Wilson does.[9] Other places mentioned in this section must therefore lie on or close to the general direction from Jamvu Marga to Ujjain unless there are erroneous interpolations. This puts in question Dey's placing of Bhadravata in the Chanda district of Madhya Pradesh. It has to be somewhere south of Mahakala (i.e., Ujjain) and north of the Narmada River. I suggest that this place may be BARVAHA or near it, on the north bank of the Narmada and on the way from Ujjain to Omkara-Mandhata (a sacred place) on the south bank of the Narmada. It is suggested in the *Mahābhārata* that the pilgrim may proceed along the Narmada to the southern ocean.[10] Jamvu Marga should not be identified with Mount Abu,[11] but rather with some route between Pushkara and Mount Abu.

Section 2. From the Narmada to Dwaravati

Toponyms of Section 2

NARMADA, CHARMANWATI, ARVUDA, Asylum of Vasishta, Pinga,* PRABHASA, "the spot where Saraswati mingleth with the sea" (the mouth of Saraswati), Vardana,* DWARAVATI.

Comments

If in the above section we consider the places that can be identified without much doubt, then the general direction is quite clear. After the pilgrim has visited Narmada he presumably returns toward the headwaters of the present Chambal River and, pro-

as Kalinjar; by *Agni Purāṇa,* between Puṣkara and Mount Abu (Law, p. 42). The spelling conforms to M. B.

[8]Identified as Bhattaka ten miles north of Warora in district Chanda, by Dey, p. 31, or Bhandak, District Chanda.

[9]V. P., Vol. II, ch. XIII.

[10]Critical edition 3.80.72.

[11]Dey, p. 80.

ceeding in a general northwesterly direction, reaches the area of Mount Abu (or Arvuda, Arbuda). The asylum of Vasishta, or rather one of the various asylums of Vasishta, has been located by scholars in the area of Mount Abu.[12] The next two places after Pinga, namely, Prabhasa and "the spot where Saraswati mingleth with the sea,"[13] seem to be out of proper sequence, because going from Mount Abu toward Prabhasa (present Somnath) the mouth of the Saraswati should come before Prabhasa if a short route is taken. However, it is possible that the pilgrim route was intentionally the longer one, that is, from Arbuda (Abu) to Prabhasa (Somnath), then going north to the *then* mouth of the Saraswati and traveling again in a southwesterly direction toward Dwaravati.

Section 3. *From Dwaravati to Vitasta ("in the region of Kasmira") and then to Vadava*

Toponyms of Section 3

DWARAVATI, TIRTHA OF VARUNA, Drimi,* Vasudhara,* Sindhuttama,* Bhadratunga,* Kumarika,* PANCHANADA, YONI, Srikunda,* Vimala,* VITASTA, and VADAVA.

Comments

This section is quite confused in detail. A number of places mentioned above cannot be identified. However, since Varuna Tirtha (the place where the Indus falls into the Arabian Sea), Panchanada (where the Chenab and the Sutlej meet), and Vitasta (Jhelum) are in the correct sequence, the general direction of the route cannot be doubted. The general direction is obviously from present Dwarka to the then mouth of the Indus. From there the route presumably goes up along the river Indus to Panchanada and then follows the Jhelum River upstream toward Kashmir. Apart from the important sequential *tīrthas* above, the only other place that could fall near this route while proceeding to Vitasta is Yoni *tīrtha*.[14] If, as Dey and Cunningham suggest,[15] this *tirtha* is

[12]Law, p. 335.

[13]The Saraswati noted here is not to be confused with the Saraswati of Kurukshetra region. It is a small stream in Gujarat and empties itself in the little Rann of Kutch. See *Census of India,* 1961, Vol. V, *Gujarat,* Part VII-B, *Fairs and Festivals,* map between pp. 11 and 13.

[14]Identified by Dey, pp. 33 and 216.

[15]*Ancient Geography of India,* pp. 71–72.

associated with the ruined city of Takhti-Bahai, twenty-eight miles to the northeast of Peshawar, then the pilgrims may have proceeded from the Panchanada to Yoni *tīrtha,* thence eastward toward the Jhelum (i.e., Vitasta), and up the Jhelum to the Vale of Kashmir. This seems quite plausible. The next place beyond the Vitasta is Vadava. Since Vadava has been described in the *Mahābhārata* as presided over by the "deity of seven flames,"[16] it is plausible to identify Vadava with Jwalamukhi, which may be translated as "she of the flaming mouth." If we accept the above identification, the direction of the route becomes reasonably clear.

Section 4. *From Vadava to Kurukshetra*

Toponyms of Section 4

VADAVA, Raudrapada,* Manimat,* Devika,* Kamakhya,* Dirghasatra,* VINASANA, Shasayana,* Kumarakoti,* Rudrakoti, and KURUKSHETRA.

Comments

This section is even more confused than the preceding one, largely because most of the places mentioned cannot be identified clearly. The general direction, however, is suggested because the *tīrthas* on the extremities of this section, namely, Vadava and Kurukshetra, can be identified. It is possible that the other places referred to in this section can be reconciled to be in a sequence if the pilgrims moved from Jwalamukhi down the river Beas, then down the river Sutlej nearest to the place where the river Saraswati lost itself in the desert. From this point they would follow the Saraswati upstream toward Kurukshetra.

The occurrence of the place Kamakhya on this section of the route is impossible if it was meant to be the now famous shrine of the same name in Assam. The *Mahābhārata,* however, associates Kamakhya with the god Rudra rather than with a female deity, as is the case with modern Kamakhya. It is now difficult to determine whether this place has been named out of sequence or whether there was another place of the same name falling on this route.

[16] M. B., p. 179.

Section 5. The Kurukshetra Region

Toponyms of Section 5[17]

KURUKSHETRA, Soma,[18] Rama-hrada,[19] BRAHMAVARTA,[20] Rudrakoti,[21] DRISHADWATI,[22] Kanya,[23] PRITHUDAKA,[24] and SARASWATI.

Comments

The *Mahābhārata* leaves no doubt about the paramount sanctity of the Kurukshetra region by devoting an entire section to the sacred spots of this area. It is impossible to reconstruct the tangled pattern of routes in this region between the Saraswati and the Drishadwati. The task is made all the more difficult by the fact that many places of this region have the same names as other sacred places in different parts of the country. Clearly the epic indulges in hypostatization, which is so characteristic of Hinduism.[25]

Some *tīrthas* enumerated in the Kurukshetra region are clearly misplaced, while in some cases the *Mahābhārata* mentions other *tīrthas* simply for comparing the merits. Examples of the misplaced ones are *tīrthas* like Kapila,[26] Kedara in the Garhwal district of Uttar Pradesh, and Pundarika.[27] An example of the second type is Naimisha (or Nimsar near Misrikh in Uttar Pradesh), which has been mentioned in this section simply for comparing its merit with that of Kurukshetra.[28]

[17]There seems to be no need to write the names of the numerous sacred spots of the Kurukshetra region; section 83 of M. B. is entirely devoted to this region, indicating its great sanctity. A few selected sacred spots of this region are mentioned here. The exact location of most of the sacred spots is not even necessary for our prupose because they are, presumably, close to each other. The toponyms shown here have been identified to be in the Kurukshetra region; see relevant footnotes.

[18]Dey, p. 188.

[19]Dey, p. 166.

[20]S. G. Kantawala, *Cultural History from the Matsya Purāṇa*, p. 314.

[21]Dey, p. 171.

[22]Law, p. 75.

[23]Dey, p. 90.

[24]Dey, p. 160.

[25]There is only one *Gaṅgā* river, yet several streams may have the suffix *Gaṅgā*, indicating the transfer of sanctity of the sacred Gaṅgā to the local stream.

[26]Near the sources of Narmada (Dey, p. 147).

[27]Pandharpur in Maharashtra (Dey, p. 147).

[28]M. B., p. 192.

Section 6. From Kurukshetra to Naimisha

Toponyms of Section 6

KURUKSHETRA, Dharma,* Jnanapavana,* Saugandhikavana,* Saraswati,* Isanadhyaksha,* Trisulakhata,* Sakambari, Suvarana,* Dhumavati,* Rathavarta,* Dhara,* SOURCE OF THE GANGA, Koti Tirtha,* Saptaganga,* Triganga,* Sakravarta,* KANKHALA, Kapilavata,* Nagatirtha,* Lalitika,* Rudravarta,* Bhadrakaraneswara, KUVJAMRAKA, Arundhativata,* Brahmavarta, YAMUNA-PRABHAVA, Darvisankramana,* SINDHU-PRABHAVA, Vedi,* Rishikulya,* Vasishta, BHRIGUTUNGA, Virapramoksha,* Tirtha of Krittika and Magha,* Vidya,* Mahasrama,* Mahalaya,* Vetasika,* Sundarika,* Brahmani,* NAIMISHA.

Comments

There is hardly any doubt about the general direction of the route, which is from Kurukshetra to modern Nimsar via a number of *tīrthas* associated with the sources of the Yamuna, the Ganga, and the Sindhu in the Himalayan region of Uttar Pradesh and adjoining area of Tibet. There is, however, considerable doubt about the order of identifiable *tīrthas*. It is not clear, for example, whether the pilgrim is directed to proceed from Kurukshetra direct to the source of the Ganga, or first to that of the Yamuna. Clearly, if the pilgrim goes to the source of the Ganga first, then he has to pass Kankhala (near Hardwar) and Kuvjamraka.[29] It is possible that the sequence is incorrect in the *Mahābhārata*. However, since all important identifiable *tīrthas* of this section except Kurukshetra and Naimisha lie in the same general region (the Himalayas), there may not be any particular importance to the succession of *tīrthas* to be visited there.[30]

Section 7. From Naimisha to Gaya

Toponyms of Section 7

NAIMISHA, Gangodveda,* Saraswati,* Vahuda,* Kshiravati,* Vimalasoka,* GOPARATRA,[31] RAMATIRTHA,[32] Satasahasrika,* Bharthristhana,* VARANASI, Avimukta, Markandeya, and GAYA.

[29]Probably north of modern Rishikesh (Dey, p. 105).

[30]The usual order of the pilgrimage to the Himalayan *tīrthas* these days is from Hardwar to Rishikesh, Yamnotri, Gangotri, Kedar, Badri, and back to Hardwar (the pilgrimage to the sources of the Indus is now out of the question). There are, however, several variations of this sequence of *tīrthas* to be visited.

[31]Dey, p. 71.

[32]Very near Goparatra; not shown on the map of "A Grand Pilgrimage."

Comments

The outline of the route of this section is quite clear, and the sequence of the identifiable places is almost perfectly correct. Avimukta has been identified to be at the same place as Varanasi.[33] Markandeya is referred to in the *Mahābhārata* as situated on the "confluence of Ganges,"[34] and presumably this is the confluence with the Gomati.

Since this section is the least confused, our inference is that sacred places of the middle Ganga valley were well known and frequented during the epic period.

Section 8. *From Gaya to Gaurisikhara ("the peak of the great goddess Gauri") and from there to the Karotoya River*

Toponyms of Section 8

GAYA, Brahmasara,* Dhenuka,* Gridhravata,* Udyanta Mountain,* FALGU, Dharmaprishtha,[35] Brahmasthana,* Rajasuya,* Maninaga,* Vinasana,* GANDAKI, VISALA, Adhivanga,* Maheswari,* Somapada,* Salagrama,* Jatismara,* Maheswarapura,* Champaka,* Jyeshthila,* Kanya,* Nischira,* Maha-hrada,* Virasrama,* Agnidhara,* Kumara Dhara,* GAURISIKHARA ("Peak of the great goddess Gauri"), Stana Kunda,* Well of Tamraruna, Confluence of the Kirtika with the Kausiki and the Aruna, Uravasi,* Somasrama,* Kumbha-karnasrama,* River Nanda,* Rishava (Island),* Auddalaka,* Dharma,* Champa,* Bhagirathi, Lalitika,* and the KAROTOYA RIVER.

Comments

From Gaya to Visala (most probably Vaisali) the route is quite clear. Since the river Gandaki is mentioned en route from Gaya to Visala (Vaisali) it can only mean the confluence of this river with the Ganga. The pilgrim is then directed to go to Salagrama. Salagrama has been placed by Dey close to the source of the Gandaki.[36] If this identification is accepted, the next identifiable point on the itinerary, Gaurisikhara, might have been reached by two alternative routes. Either a trans-Himalayan route could have

[33]Kantawala, *Cultural History*, p. 326.
[34]M. B., p. 196.
[35]Four miles from Buddha Gaya (Dey, p. 36).
[36]Dey, p. 174.

been taken, or a route up the Tamba Kosi valley.[37] From Gaurisikhara to the Well of Tamraruna the only feasiblc route is along the Sun Kosi River. We may identify the Well of Tamraruna as close to or at the confluence of the present rivers Tamur and Arun. The next point on the itinerary is the confluence of the river Kirtika with the Kausiki and the Aruna. This can be identified with the present confluence of the three rivers Sun Kosi, Arun, and Tamur.[38] From this confluence the route was clearly southward toward the Bhagirathi and the present Karatoya rivers. The Karatoya forms the easternmost limit of the sacred places of the *Mahābhārata,* indicating perhaps the limit of Aryan expansion in this direction.

Section 9. From the Karotoya River (modern Karatoya) to Mountain Sree

Toponyms of Section 9

KAROTOYA, GANGASAGARA-SANGAMA, VAITARANI, VIRAJA, Confluence of the Sona and the Jyotirathi, Vanasagulma,* Rishava,* Kala,* Pushpavati,* Vadarika,* Champa* (on the bank of Bhagirathi), Lapetika,* MAHENDRA MOUNTAIN, Rama Tirtha, "Matanga's *tīrtha* called Kedara,"* MOUNTAIN SREE.

Comments

With one major exception, namely, "the confluence of the Sona and the Jyotirathi," the sequence of sacred place names is almost perfect. From the Karatoya River the pilgrims would proceed to the present Gangasagar Island (Gangasagara-sangama), onward to the Vaitarani River in modern Orissa and visit Viraja (modern Jaipur). The next point, that is, the confluence of the Sona (present Son) with Jyotirathi, does not fit the sequence at all. However, if this point can be disregarded, the next recognizable place name, Mount Mahendra or Mahendra Giri (a part of the present Eastern Ghats), is in proper order for the southwestward progress. Matanga's *tīrtha* cannot be identified on this route, but the next

[37]Shejwalkar suggests that a trans-Himalayan route was in constant use. See Shejwalkar, "*Mahābhārata* Data," p. 219.

[38]It may be noted that the confluence of the rivers Arun and Sun-Kosi and that of Tamur are within a very short distance from each other. See, for example, John Bartholomew's map of *India, Pakistan and Ceylon,* scale 1:4,000,000 (Edinburgh, 1966), Latitude 26°, 55′ N, Longitude 87°, 10′ E.

place, Mountain Sree, is very suggestive. It may be identified with Srisailam close to Krishna River. If these identifications are correct, and indeed they seem plausible, then the direction of the pilgrim route is clearly from the western part of Bengal toward Tamilnadu via coastal Orissa and Andhra. On the map showing the distribution of scheduled tribes (fig. 1-2), the coastal area is a corridor of nontribal population. It is, therefore, significant that the pilgrim route passes through this presumed corridor of early Aryanization.

Section 10. *Mountain Sree to Gokarna*

Toponyms of Section 10

MOUNTAIN SREE, RISHABHA, THE KAVERI, KANYA, GOKARNA.

Comments

On this part of the route few, but well-known, place names occur. This small number is somewhat surprising in view of the fact that from Srisailam (Mountain Sree) to Kanya Kumari and then up to Gokarna in north Kanara is a distance of several hundred miles. One may conclude that only the then most prominent sacred places of the south were known to anyone in the northern part of the country. Even so, the nearly correct sequence of *tīrthas* suggests that south India was far from being a terra incognita. Rishabha and Kaveri are not in sequence as one proceeds from Mountain Sree to Kanya Kumari.

Section 11. *Gokarna to Dandaka Forest (Ḍaṇḍakāraṇya)*

Toponyms of Section 11

GOKARNA, Gayatri,* THE VENA, GODAVARI, CONFLUENCE OF THE VENNA, CONFLUENCE OF THE VARADA, Brahmasthana,* Kusaplavana,* Deva-hrada, Jatismara-hrada,* Sarvadeva-hrada,* Payoshini, sacred forest of DANDAKA (Ḍaṇḍakāraṇya).

Comments

The general direction of this route presents several difficulties because the correct identification of even the important rivers is doubtful. The Vena River may be what Dey calls Bena and which he identifies with Wainganga.[39] The confluence of Venna is another problem. If the Venna River is taken to be what Ali calls Vena,

[39]Dey, p. 28.

then it has to be identified with a headwater tributary of Krishna.[40] If it is the same as Bena of Sircar, then it is one of three different rivers, namely, Wainganga, Penganga, or Vena (Bena). The "Confluence of Varada" is also not clear. The river Varada may be what is the present Wardha, a tributary of Wainganga (or Venaganga), or it may be a tributary of Tungabhadra, by the name of Varada.

The term Daṇḍakāraṇya (Dandaka forest) is applied not to a specific spot, but to a fairly extensive forested region. B. C. Law thinks that the Daṇḍakāraṇya of the *Rāmāyaṇa* "seems to have covered almost the whole of Central India from Bundelkhand region to river Krishna," but the *Mahābhārata* seems to limit Dandaka forest to the sources of the Godavari.[41] Dowson identifies it as lying between Godavari and Narmada.[42]

Since there is considerable confusion regarding the names of the rivers in this section, I am inclined to suggest such identifications as are in keeping with the sequence of the river names in the *Mahābhārata*.[43] The Vena (Veṇṇā in the critical edition) River of the *Mahābhārata* may be identified with the modern Krishna (known in the *Purāṇas* as Kṛṣṇaveṇṇa). The "confluence of Venna" may be identified as that of modern Wainganga with the Godavari. The "confluence of Varada" may have been the same as that of the modern Wardha with the Wainganga. In the region of the confluence of the Wainganga and the Wardha the pilgrim is already traveling in the Daṇḍakāraṇya. It is not necessary, therefore, to restrict the area of this forest.

It is once again clear from the description of places of southern India that only the most well-known names are referred to in the *Mahābhārata*. Yet it shows a degree of familiarity with this part of India which could arise only if sufficient numbers of people had visited these areas, mentally recorded their experience, and later passed it on into the literary tradition of Hinduism.

Section 12. *Dandaka Forest to Prayaga*

Toponyms of Section 12

DANDAKARANYA, Asylum of Sarabhanga,* SURAPARAKA, *tīrtha*

[40]S. M. Ali, *The Geography of the Purāṇas*, p. 122.

[41]Law, p. 280; and M. B., p. 202.

[42]John Dowson, *Classical Dictionary of Hindu Mythology and Religion, Geography, History, and Literature*, p. 80.

[43]*Critical edition* 3.83.19 through 3.83.31.

of Rama,* SAPTAGODAVARA, Deva-hrada, "forest of Tungaka"* (Tuṅgakāraṇya), Medhavika, KALANJARA, CHITRAKUTA, Bhartri-sthana,* Kotitirtha,* SRINGAVERAPURA, Mayuravata,* PRAYAGA.

Comments

The direction of the route is not clear in this section until Kalanjara is reached. Suraparaka has been identified by Ali as the western coastal plain drained by the river Surya, approximately coinciding with the Thana district of Maharashtra.[44] Law identifies this as Sopara in Thana district.[45] Sarabhanga was somewhere in the Dandakaranya but its location is not certain.[46] Kalanjara is the modern Kalinjar. Sringaverapura has been identified with a place twenty-two miles northwest of Allahabad.[47] Saptagodavara has been identified with the point at the apex of the Godavari delta.

Suraparaka lies on the west coast, while "Saptagodavara" is on the east coast of the Indian Peninsula. Therefore, it is unreasonable to expect that from the Dandaka forest the pilgrim could proceed to Suraparaka and then to Saptagodavara unless the *Mahābhārata* assumed a complete circumambulation of the Godavari River. The occurrence of Saptagodavara on this section of the route is odd, because the pilgrim had already passed close to this place while going southwestward (see section 9). Some authorities have identified Suraparaka with a seaport at the mouth of the Krishna River on the east coast.[48] Even if these authorities are correct, the question remains why Suraparaka, as identified by them, and Saptagodavara were "missed" on the southwestward pilgrimage (see section 9). If the postulate of the circumambulation of Godavari is accepted, then both Suraparka on the west coast and Saptagodavara near the east coast may be considered in order. Between Saptagodavara and Kalanjara there are only three toponyms, namely, Devahrada, forest of Tungaka, and Medhavika. The last place is very near modern Kalinjar itself.[49] The other two places cannot be identified. The problem of a link between

[44]Ali, *Geography*, p. 147–148.
[45]Law, p. 299.
[46]Dowson, *Classical Dictionary*, p. 282.
[47]Dey, p. 192.
[48]See the identification of Mitra and Yule referred to in Dey, p. 197, although Dey does not agree with this identification; also Ali, p. 147–148.
[49]Dey, p. 129.

"Saptagodavara" and "Kalanjara" of the epic therefore remains, and only a very tentative direction can be suggested on the map.

From Kalanjara onward to Prayaga there is no doubt about the general direction of the pilgrim route. The route was clearly from Kalanjara to Chitrakuta and Sringaverapura, then along the Ganga to Prayaga.

CONCLUSIONS

The *Mahābhārata* thus describes a grand pilgrimage of almost the whole of present India. It is approximately clockwise, beginning and ending with perhaps the two most important *tīrthas* of the time of the *Mahābhārata,* namely, Puṣkara and Prayāga (modern Allahabad). The preservation of this long itinerary of pilgrimage in the epic literature undoubtedly suggests long-distance movements of some motivated individuals throughout the country in ancient times. The awareness of the extent of the country resulting from the practice of pilgrimages over very long distances may have contributed materially to the recognition of a vast religious space.

It is noteworthy that the pilgrim routes of the epic seem to avoid the areas which even today contain most of the scheduled tribes' population of India. The paucity of sacred places in the central and northeastern plateau region, their uncertain identifications, and the confusion of routes give the impression that the knowledge about the interior was rather limited. Populated by the non-Hinduized tribes, much of the central and northeastern forested plateau regions may have been unfavorable areas for religious as well as commercial interaction. In chapter 2 we have suggested that the religious interaction between the North and the South may have progressed through a few corridors—the corridors of sedentary agriculture. These corridors lie in areas which may have been better suited for the diffusion of plow agriculture. The link between the early Aryanized North and the Dravidian South may have had its foundations on the sedentary nature of both societies to which religious circulation added a further dimension. The nonsedentary tribal societies seem to have been slow in interacting with the sedentary ones. This is clear from the fact that the tribal societies are still undergoing a process of Hinduization—a process far from complete despite the juxtaposition of these societies with their materially more advanced counterparts for over three millennia.

Our reconstruction of the pilgrim routes should be considered only a preliminary outline, because it may be subject to modifications and improvements by interested scholars. Despite the many shortcomings, it does suggest that the epic may be used for a deeper understanding of the geography of ancient India and for an elucidation of the religious circulation which has been continuous at least from the time of the epic.

Chapter IV

Sacred Places According to the *Purāṇas* and Some Later Sources

INTRODUCTION

The *Purāṇas* are, next to the epic *Mahābhārata*, the most important source of our information on places of pilgrimage in India. The *Purāṇas* as a body of Hindu literature not only possess great sanctity but also contain vast amounts of material for the study of cultural history, geography, ethnography, and many other aspects of ancient India. They provide us great insight into all aspects and phases of Hinduism.[1] The importance of the *Purāṇas* for an understanding about Hinduism was clearly realized by Alberuni as early as the eleventh century. The richness and variety of material of the *Purāṇas* drew considerable attention of Western scholars after the publication of the English translation of the *Viṣṇu Purāṇa*.[2] Credit, however, must go to Pargiter for arousing a scholarly interest in the study of ancient history based on the Puranic genealogies.[3] Literature on the *Purāṇas* has swelled to great proportions since then, and their significance for the understanding of ancient history as well as geography is now widely accepted.

Before discussing individual places of pilgrimage according to the *Purāṇas* it is necessary to state briefly the nature of this body of literature and some aspects of it which are especially pertinent to our study.

According to Winternitz[4] the word *Purāṇa* meant originally nothing but *Purāṇam akhyānam*, that is, old narrative.[5] Similarly Hopkins defined them as "Archaeologia" or ancient lore.[6] More

[1]For details, see M. Winternitz, *A History of Indian Literature*, p. 529.

[2]H. H. Wilson, *The Vishnu Purana*, London, 1840, more recently reprinted by Punthi Pustak, Calcutta, 1961.

[3]F. E. Pargiter, *The Purāṇa Text of the Dynasties of the Kali Age* (London, 1913).

[4]*History*, p. 529.

[5]*Ibid.*, p. 518.

[6]Edward Washburn Hopkins, *The Religions of India*, p. 436.

recently, A. L. Basham defined *Purāṇas* as compendia of legends and religious instructions.[7] These definitions can be misleading unless it is realized that this body of literature is far more inclusive than is suggested by etymology. For example, one of the *Purāṇas* is entitled the *Bhaviṣyat Purāṇa,* which, as Pargiter noted long ago, is a contradiction in terms because "*Bhaviṣyat*" means "of the future."[8] How can there be an ancient lore of the future? Obviously, the word *Purāṇa* must have lost its proper meaning rather early and become a specialized body of literature.

Several of the *Purāṇas* contain what is usually called *Bhuvanakośa* or geographical lists of tribes. Several Indologists have studied these lists and have tried to identify the location of the tribes as well as of the rivers, mountains, and cities.[9] Most of the *Purāṇas* also include in their text important information about the sacred places, sacred rivers, and mountains. This is the information used to identify the ancient places of pilgrimage in India on the maps (figs. 4-1 through 4-3) in this chapter. Because of regional, sectarian, and other biases of the *Purāṇas,* the lists of sacred places are by no means standard from one *Purāṇa* to the other.[10]

Primarily because of the wealth of material about the place names of India found in the *Purāṇas,* scholars interested in the ancient geography of India have made much use of the Puranic material. However, it may be said at the outset that almost all of these scholars have produced lists of place names without emphasizing the significance of these place names for the cultural geography of India. It certainly is true that, although an important first step long since has been taken toward the identification of place names, the significance of this research has not been fully appreciated by cultural geographers. What has usually been termed "geography" of ancient India still remains, by and large, the listing and identification of place names.[11]

[7]A. L. Basham, *The Wonder That Was India,* p. 299.

[8]F. E. Pargiter, *Ancient Indian Historical Tradition,* p. 50.

[9]See, for example, D. C. Sircar, *Studies in the Geography of Ancient and Medieval India,* chap. 2, entitled "Puranic List of Peoples," originally published in *Indian Historical Quarterly* (Calcutta), Vol. XXI (1945), pp. 297 ff.; C. A. Lewis, "The Geographical Text of the *Purāṇas*: A Further Critical Study," *Purāṇa* 4, (January 1962): 112 ff.

[10]Since the subject of *tīrthas* usually forms a well-defined chapter or series of chapters in the Purāṇas, for our purpose there was no need to read the whole work. Scholars proficient in Sanskrit may take further steps.

[11]Thus, for example, B. C. Law's *Historical Geography of Ancient India* is far

A professional Indian geographer who made a gallant, if highly speculative, attempt to reconstruct the geography of *Purāṇas* was Professor S. M. Ali.[12] His is perhaps the first serious effort to present the geographic horizons of the *Purāṇas*. Ali has given some consideration to the identification and mapping of the sacred places of India, which he calls Religious Centers.[13] Unfortunately, it is not clear from his maps whether the place names are derived from all the *Purāṇas* combined together or from just one. Furthermore, the symbols used on the maps are confusing. It is not always possible to distinguish between what he calls "Capital Cities," "Other important cities," and "Religious Centers."[14] For example, Kāmākhyā—a religious center—is shown as "other important city," while Madurāi and Mathurā, both of which were important religious centers as well as capital cities, are shown only as "capital city."

Some comments on the dating of the *Purāṇas* may be made before discussing the distribution of *tīrthas* according to the selected *Purāṇas*.

The determination of the date of composition of the *Purāṇas* is a most difficult and highly controversial question.[15] Authorities seem to agree that a long period of time must be assigned to the composition of this body of literature. During this period the texts grew through the addition of more religious material. However, none of the *Purāṇas* goes back earlier than the Gupta period.[16] Some authorities have postulated two distinct stages in the development of the extant *Purāṇas*.[17] The first stage, in which the *Purāṇas* contained ancient materials, including parts of the epics, is dated from the third through the fifth centuries A.D. The second stage—sixth century onward—was the one in which topics like the giving of gifts, *tīrthas*, rituals of worship, and the like were incorporated.

This later stage is characterized by a marked stress on theistic

from a geography, and may be more appropriately called a dictionary of ancient place names.

[12] *The Geography of the Purāṇas* (1966).

[13] *Ibid.*, figs. 16 and 17.

[14] *Ibid.*, fig. 17.

[15] See, for example, A. D. Pusalker, *Studies in the Epics and Purāṇas*, pp. 40–41.

[16] Basham, *The Wonder That Was India*, p. 299.

[17] For example, R. C. Majumdar (general ed.). *The History and Culture of the Indian People*: *The Classical Age*, p. 298.

worship. Since Alberuni, in the eleventh century, mentions eighteen *Purāṇas,* which is the number of *Purāṇas* currently accepted, it follows that all of them belong to an earlier period.[18] Thus, we must recognize the difficulty of assigning any precise dates to the contents of this literature. For our purpose we shall have to assume, therefore, that the sacred places described by the *Purāṇas* include several places of the epic period as well as others which may have come into prominence between the third and the eleventh centuries A.D. Unless more precision in the dating of individual sections of the *Purāṇas* is achieved, it is not possible to evaluate properly the rise or decline of sacred places. Several authorities have attempted to perform the tedious task of determining the dates of various sections of the *Purāṇas,* but the results are far from satisfactory.[19]

An additional difficulty is that the *Purāṇas* show sectarian as well as regional biases. Obviously, therefore, the omission of a certain sacred place by a given *Purāṇa* cannot be taken as sufficient evidence of the decline of that place, nor can the long eulogies of an otherwise obscure place be considered enough to raise it to the level of preeminence.

PLACES OF PILGRIMAGE ACCORDING TO THE *Purāṇas*

The maps of sacred places in this section are based on the information derived from three *Purāṇas,* namely, the *Garuḍa Purāṇa,*[20] the *Matsya Purāṇa,*[21] and the *Agni Purāṇa.*[22] Primarily because of the limitations of time and my inadequate knowledge of Sanskrit, the other *Purāṇas,* except the relevant portions of the *Vāyu Purāṇa,*[23] could not be studied. However, it was found that the information in the *Vāyu Purāṇa* was almost a repetition of the *Matsya Purāṇa.*[24] Even the rather limited number of the

[18]Edward C. Sachau, *Alberuni's India* (London, Trübner, 1910), I, 130–131. Alberuni gives two lists of the *Purāṇas.* These two lists do not completely agree in the names of the *Purāṇas,* although each of them lists eighteen *Purāṇas.*

[19]For discussions on the age of various parts of the *Purāṇas* see, for example: *Agni Purāṇa,* edited by Rājendralāla Mitra, Vol. III, Introduction; S. D. Gyani, *Agni Purāṇa, a Study*; S. G. Kantawala, *Cultural History from the Matsya Purāṇa*; *Purāṇa,* a semiannual publication of the Kashiraj Trust at Varanasi, devoted exclusively to Puranic research.

[20]*Garuḍa Purāṇa* (in Sanskrit), edited by Ramasankara Bhattacharyya.

[21]S. G. Kantawala, *Cultural History from the Matsya Purāṇa.*

[22]*Agni Purāṇa* (in Sanskrit), edited by Rājendralāla Mitra.

[23]*Vāyu Purāṇa* (in Sanskrit), edited by Rājendralāla Mitra.

[24]Cf. S. B. Chaudhry, in Kantawala, *Cultural History,* p. 295.

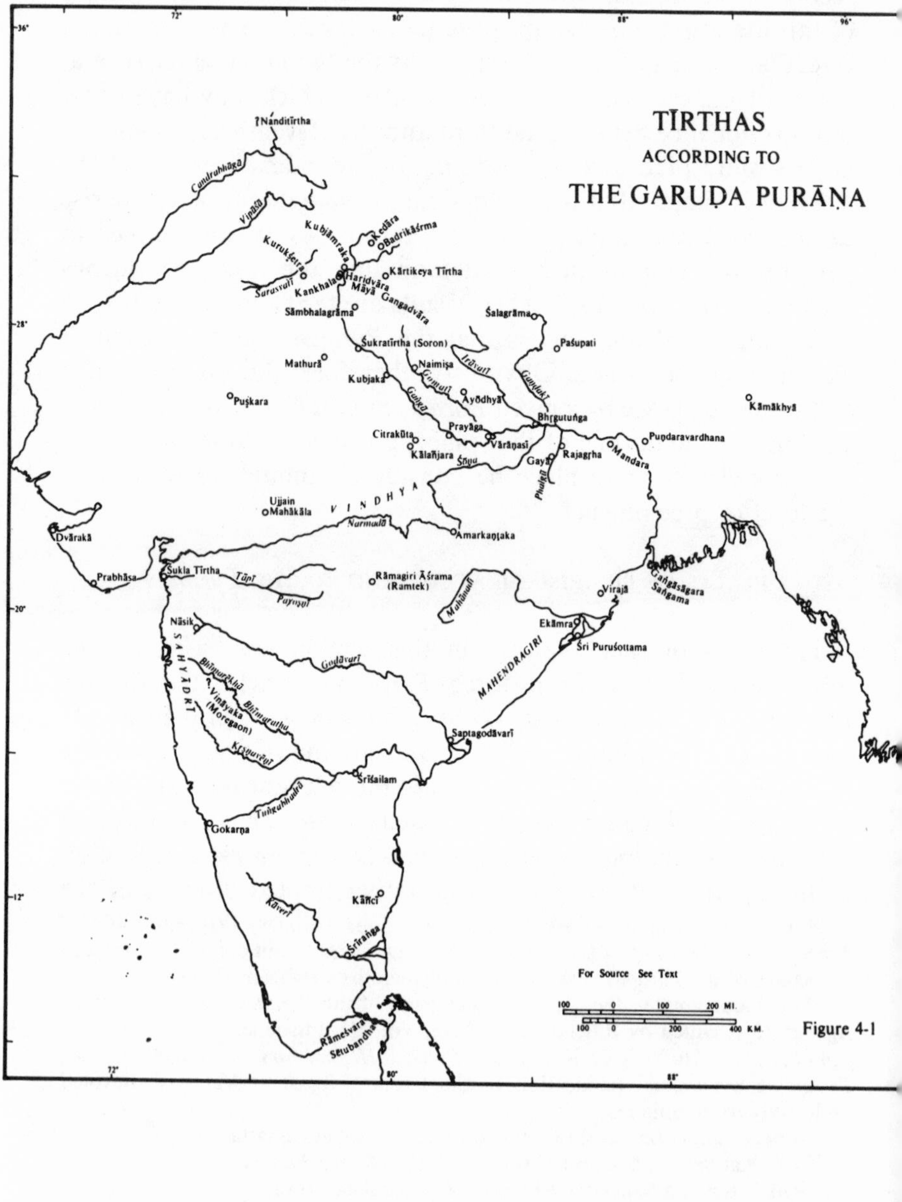
TĪRTHAS
ACCORDING TO
THE GARUḌA PURĀṆA
?Nanditīrtha
Candrabhāgā
Vipāśā
Kurukṣetra
Kubjāmraka
Kedāra
Badrikāśrma
Sarasvatī
Kankhala
Haridvāra
Māyā
Kārtikeya Tīrtha
Gangadvāra
Sāmbhalagrāma
Śalagrāma
Paśupati
Śukratīrtha (Soron)
Mathurā
Naimiṣa
Irāvatī
Gaṇḍakī
Kubjaka
Gomatī
Ayōdhyā
Puṣkara
Gaṅgā
Kāmākhyā
Bhṛgutuṅga
Prayāga
Citrakūṭa
Vārāṇasī
Puṇḍaravardhana
Kālañjara
Gayā
Rajagṛha
Mandara
Śoṇa
Phalgū
VINDHYA
Ujjain
Mahākāla
Narmadā
Amarkaṇṭaka
Dvārakā
Prabhāsa
Śukla Tīrtha
Tāpī
Payoṣṇī
Rāmagiri Āśrama
(Ramtek)
Mahānadī
Virajā
Gaṅgāsāgara
Saṅgama
Nāsik
Ekāmra
Śri Puruśottama
SAHYĀDRĪ
Godāvarī
MAHENDRAGIRI
Bhīmarathā
?Vināyaka
(Moregaon)
Saptagodāvarī
Kṛṣṇaveṇī
Śrīśailam
Tuṅgabhadrā
Gokarṇa
Kāverī
Kāñcī
Śrīraṅga
Rāmeśvara
Setubandha
For Source See Text
100 0 100 200 MI.
100 0 200 400 KM.
72°
80°
88°
96°
36°
28°
20°
12°

Figure 4-1

Purāṇas used in this study shows that variations in the lists of sacred places are likely to occur from one *Purāṇa* to the other. These variations may be the result of a regional bias, a sectarian bias, or both. Moreover, interpolations of sacred places cannot be ruled out. The *Garuḍa Purāṇa* seems to favor the sacred places of the Vaiṣṇavites. The *Matsya Purāṇa* shows a bias for Maharashtra. The *Agni Purāṇa,* although considered free from sectarian leanings, nevertheless leaves out most *tīrthas* of the Dravidian South. It must, however, be realized that in several cases the Vaiśṇavites and the Śaivites have the same sacred places, but different sacred spots at those places. For example, at Ujjain the temple of Mahākāl is especially sacred to the Śaivites, while the river Siprā and the Aṅkpāt area just outside Ujjain are venerated primarily by the Vaiṣṇavites. It is, therefore, a difficult task to portray these differences on the maps; only the texts of the *Purāṇas* can tell these differences. Thus, any interpretation of the sacred places of the *Purāṇas* must take these factors into consideration.

Tīrthas according to the Garuḍa Purāṇa

Like all other *Purāṇas,* the date of composition of the *Garuḍa Purāṇa* cannot be fixed with accuracy. The *Garuḍa Purāṇa* was compiled in its extant form perhaps between 800 and 1100 A.D.[25] It may, therefore, be tentatively taken to represent the places of pilgrimage of India in the early medieval period.

Figure 4-1 is an attempt to map the identifiable *tīrthas* of the *Garuḍa Purāṇa.* It is a common practice in the Hindu religious treatises—the epics as well as the *Purāṇas*—to regard sacred rivers also as *tīrthas.* Therefore, the common English expression "place of pilgrimage" is much too restrictive when applied to the sacred places of India. A *tīrtha,* therefore, may be an actual sacred "place"; but it may also mean sacred river, sacred mountain, or even sacred forest. Sometimes the word also means a sacred region, although the latter is more appropriately termed *kṣetra* (area or region) rather than *tīrtha.*[26]

The *Garuḍa Purāṇa* gives two separate lists of holy places or *tīrthas.*[27] This *Purāṇa* mentions, in all, eighty-one *tīrthas* through-

[25]*Garuḍa Purāṇa* (in Sanskrit), edited by Ramasankara Bhattacharyya, p. 12.
[26]The term *pīṭha* is usually applied to a sacred place of a female deity.
[27]*Garuḍa Purāṇa,* chaps. 66 and 81.

out India. In chapter 66 this *Purāṇa* lists sixteen *tīrthas,* which may be taken to mean sixteen important *tīrthas* of India. It is a very suggestive list, because none of these more important *tīrthas* is located south of the river Godāvarī. This *Purāṇa,* therefore, seems to emphasize the greater sanctity of the non-Dravidian *tīrthas*; this is perhaps indicative of its composition in northern India.

In chapter 81, however, where a longer list of *tīrthas* is supplied,[28] a number of sacred places in the Dravidian area of India are also given. The *tīrthas* of South India include the more important rivers as well as some places not mentioned in the *Mahābhārata* (see fig. 4-1). Examples of the latter are Kāñchī (Kāñcī), Rāmeśvara, Setubandha, and Śriraṅga (their modern names are Kanchipuram, Ramesvaram, Setubandha—or Adam's Bridge—and Srirangam). The obvious inference is that these sacred places may have arisen after the period of the epics. The reason for this emergence is not clear, but their importance may have come about as a result of the great religious revival which was at its peak in the seventh century A.D.[29] Also beginning with about the seventh century the Tamil language area, in which all the above-mentioned places are situated, enjoyed in general a period of political stability and economic prosperity. These factors may have helped the flow of government grants to the temples, making them powerful religious and social institutions. This process reached its climax in the Chola period, which began about the middle of the ninth century.[30]

Some *tīrthas* of the *Mahābhārata* are not given by *Garuḍa Purāṇa,* for example, Kanyā Kumārī, Tāmraparṇī (river), and Riṣabha (mountain). These places may have been dropped in the general process of selection which the *Garuḍa Purāṇa* apparently seems to follow (eighty-one *tīrthas* throughout India), or they may have actually become less important than the sacred places situated in the heart of Tamilnadu. At any rate, the *Garuḍa Purāṇa* seems to be a northern work, which would bias it against the enumeration of less well-known sacred places of South India.

Figure 4-1 clearly shows that the *Garuḍa Purāṇa* lists most of the prominent sacred places of northern India, and almost all of

[28]See verses 1–30.

[29]See K. A. Nilakanta Sastri, *A History of South India,* p. 412.

[30]For details, see Nilakanta Sastri, *History,* chaps. 8, 9, and 15. The most comprehensive study of the economic aspects of a South Indian temple remains that of Burton Stein, "The Tirupati Temple: An Economic Study of a Medieval South Indian Temple."

these places are considered sacred in modern literature (compare fig. 5-1 in chap. 5). This simple fact demonstrates the remarkable continuity of the sacred places of India. The demise of sacred places seems to be a rare occurrence associated largely with catastrophic events. Strong sectarian biases, which were by no means rare in the medieval period, also may have led to the omission of sacred place names of rival sects.

In the northwestern part of India the omission by the *Garuḍa Purāṇa* of some important places of the epic *Mahābhārata* needs comment. Some examples of these places are Vadava (Jwalamukhi), Pañcanada, Vārāha, Yonī, Vitastā, and Sindhu.[31] The reason for the elimination of these names is not clear. The writer feels that the omission of these sacred places was perhaps the result of growing control of the Indus River basin by the Muslims. There is good evidence for this view. Alberuni in the eleventh century observes that "in Multan there is a pond in which the Hindus worship by bathing, if they are not prevented."[32] Alberuni, again in reference to Multan, notes that the Hindus "*used* to visit Multan before its idol-temple was destroyed."[33] It is also noteworthy that Somnath (Prabhāsa), which was one of the major places of pilgrimage until plundered by Mahmud of Ghazna, is not included in the list of sixteen major *tīrthas* in chapter 66 of this *Purāṇa*. These observations suggest that perhaps the sanctity attached to places in northwestern India was considered to have been violated, resulting in their exclusion from the list of holy places.

The selected list of sixteen *tīrthas* of chapter 66 of the *Purāṇa* does not include such places as Badrināth, Kedārnāth, and Hardwār, which may not have attained celebrity until later times. On the other hand, Gayā was perhaps more important than even Vārāṇasī, as is indidated by the praise of this *tīrtha*.

All in all, the distribution of sacred places of the *Garuḍa Purāṇa* shows quite clearly that the major pattern of the sacred geography of India had been developed already and the events of many centuries to come would be unable to change that outline materially. The deficient areas of the epic age continued to be so in the early medieval period. These were largely the areas occupied by the pre-Aryan forest-dwelling tribes.

[31] Place names from Roy's translation of the *Mahābhārata*.
[32] Edward C. Sachau (trans. ed.), *Alberuni's India*, II, 145.
[33] *Ibid.*, p. 148. Italics mine.

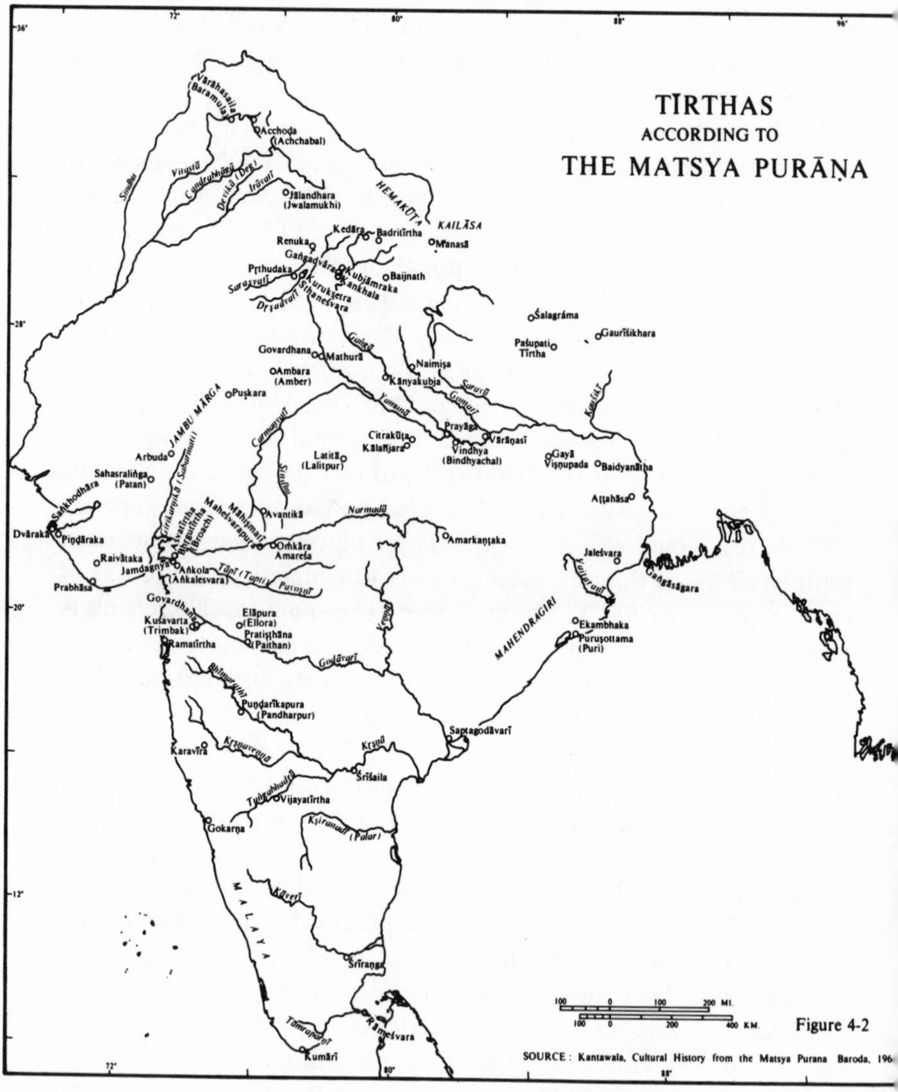

Figure 4-2

SOURCE: Kantawala, Cultural History from the Matsya Purana Baroda, 196

Tīrthas according to the Matsya Purāṇa

The *Matsya Purāṇa,* like other *Purāṇas,* is a composite work containing materials from ancient times down to perhaps the middle of the thirteenth century. The chapters in the *Purāṇa* relevant for the study of *tīrthas* are 22, 103 through 112, and 180 through 194.[34]

Figure 4-2 shows the places of pilgrimage according to the *Matsya Purāṇa*.[35] The number of *tīrthas* according to the *Matsya Purāṇa* is very much larger than in the *Garuḍa Purāṇa*.[36] This is particularly true in the area of the present state of Maharashtra. Because of the special attention given to enumeration of *tīrthas* in the Narmadā region, it is suspected that this *Purāṇa* was composed in this region. At least the chapters in this *Purāṇa* dealing with the *tīrthas* may have been composed especially with reference to the Narmadā region.

The above idea is further strengthened by the fact that the Narmadā River is exalted even more than the Gaṅgā. No less than six chapters (189–194) are devoted to the enumeration of *tīrthas* of the Narmadā. The *māhātmya* or glory of the Narmadā alone is sung in two chapters (186–187). While there is no chapter exclusively devoted to the Gaṅgā, several chapters (103–112) are devoted to the Prayāga *māhātmya*. Thus, we find the sanctity of the Narmadā being promoted through this religious compendium. Although there is a lot of controversy about the area of composition of the *Matsya Purāṇa*,[37] the fact that a large number of *tīrthas* in the Narmadā region are described and the sanctity of the Narmadā over all other rivers is stressed indicates strongly that the work was composed in the Narmadā region and not in South India as Dikshitar suggests.[38] To take just one example, the *Matsya Purāṇa* glorifies Oṁkāra on the Narmadā far more than

[34]See S.G. Kantawala, *Cultural History from the Matsya Purāṇa*. In appendix I, Kantawala gives a brief synopsis of the various chapters of the *Matsya Purāṇa*. In appendix III he gives a detailed gazetteer of "Geographical and Ethnic Data in the *Matsya Purāṇa*." Map 4-2 has been made using these data; the spelling of place names thereon follows the pattern used in transliteration by Kantawala.

[35]The identifications are largely based on Kantawala, *Cultural History,* and Dey, *Geographical Dictionary*.

[36]Many places, however, cannot be identified. Perhaps the *Purāṇa* tried to popularize the local places.

[37]See, for example, Kantawala, pp. 3–5.

[38]V. R. R. Dikshitar, *The Matsya Purāṇa, a Study,* p. 24.

Kurukṣetra and stresses that by bathing at Oṁkāra one gets a hundred times more religious merit than by bathing at Kurukṣetra.[39] An astronomical number of *tīrthas* are supposed to lie on the Narmadā in the proximity of Amarkaṇṭaka near the source of this sacred river.[40]

Apart from the extreme regional bias, the general outline of the sacred places of India is about the same as noted before, and the main deficient areas pointed out earlier continue to be so. The *Matsya Purāṇa* indicates that the worship of the Mother Goddess may have come into prominence during the medieval period of India. This is shown by the fact that this *Purāṇa* gives an account of the origin of *Śākta pīṭhas*, or places of Mother Goddess worship, and enumerates one hundred and eight names of the goddess, the places sacred to her, and the merit thereof.[41] It is, however, curious that the most important seat of Mother Goddess worship, Kāmākhyā in Assam, finds no mention, and much of Bengal and Assam, present-day stronghold of the Mother Goddess cult, continues to remain an area deficient in holy places. The *Matsya Purāṇa,* despite its comprehensive list of *tīrthas,* does not improve materially upon the number of places of the South as described in the *Mahābhārata.* On the other hand, it makes a concerted effort to shift the scene of sanctity from the Gaṅgā region to the Narmadā. Perhaps, it was an attempt to challenge the monopoly of sanctity enjoyed by the Gaṅgā *tīrthas* and their priestly class.

Tīrthas according to the Agni Purāṇa

The *Agni Purāṇa,* like the two *Purāṇas* referred to earlier (the *Garuḍa* and the *Matsya*), also supplies a list of *tīrthas* in chapter 109 entitled "Tīrtha Māhātmyam."[42] Apart from a general enumeration of *tīrthas* in this chapter, there are separate chapters devoted to the *māhātmyas* or glories of Gaṅgā (110), Prayāga (111), Vārāṇasī (112), Narmadā (113), and Gayā (114), indicating obviously the special sanctity of these places and rivers. In the general chapter of *tīrthas* sixty-two sacred places and rivers of India are described.

[39]*Matsya Purāṇa,* chap. 22, verses 27–28.
[40]Kantawala, p. 366.
[41]Kantawala, p. 263, *Matsya Purāṇa,* chap. 13.
[42]*Agni Purāṇa* (in Sanskrit), edited by Rājendralāla Mitra, Vol. III.

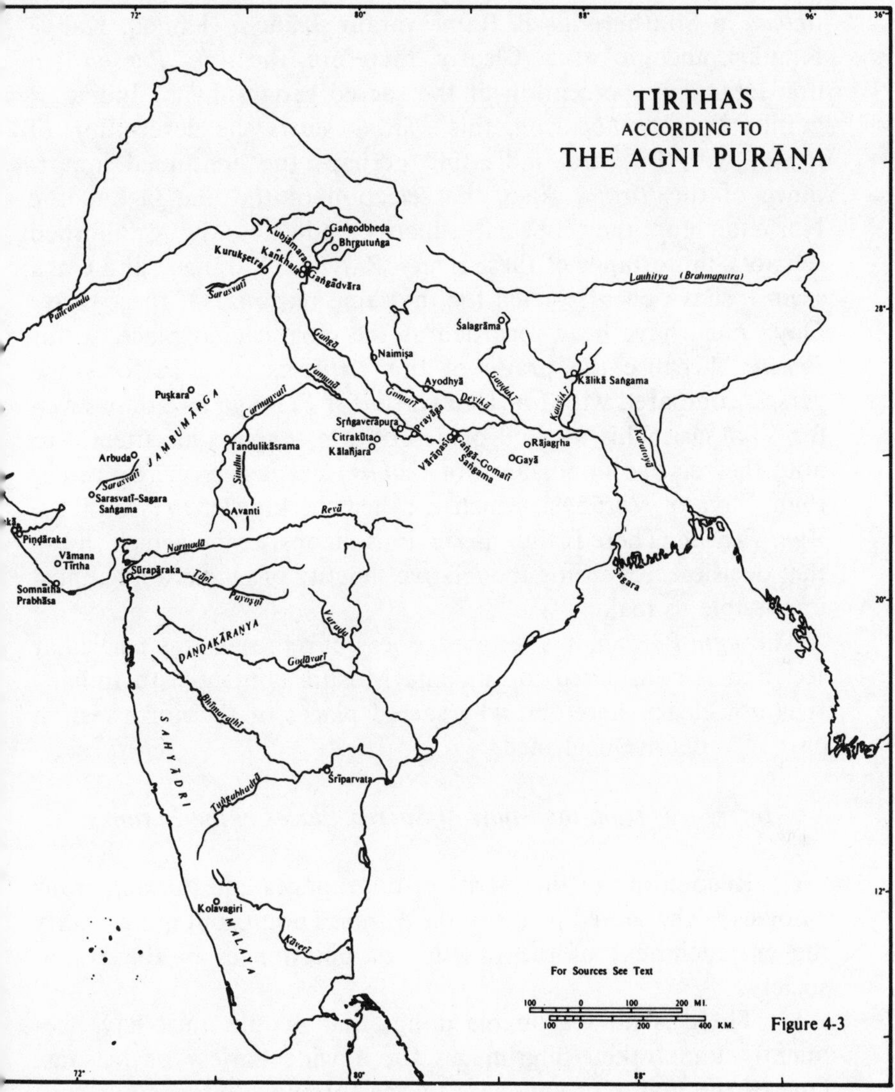
TĪRTHAS
ACCORDING TO
THE AGNI PURĀṆA
72°
80°
88°
96°
36°
28°
20°
12°
Gaṅgodbheda
Bhṛgutuṅga
Kubjāmra
Kurukṣetra
Kaṅkhala
Gaṅgādvāra
Sarasvatī
Pañcanuda
Lauhitya (Brahmaputra)
Śalagrāma
Gaṅgā
Naimiṣa
Yamunā
Ayodhyā
Gomatī
Devikā
Gaṇḍakī
Kālikā Saṅgama
Kauśikī
Karatoyā
Puṣkara
JAMBUMĀRGA
Carmaṇvatī
Śṛṅgaverapura
Prayāga
Citrakūṭa
Kālañjara
Vārāṇasī
Gaṅgā-Gomatī Saṅgama
Rājagṛha
Gayā
Tandulikāśrama
Arbuda
Sindhu
Sarasvatī
Sarasvatī-Sagara Saṅgama
Avanti
Revā
Piṇḍāraka
Narmadā
Vāmana Tīrtha
Sūrapāraka
Tāpī
Payoṣṇī
Somnātha Prabhāsa
Sāgara
Varadā
DAṆḌAKĀRAṆYA
Godāvarī
Bhīmarathī
SAHYĀDRI
Śrīparvata
Tuṅgabhadrā
Kolavagiri
MALAYA
Kāverī
For Sources See Text
100 0 100 200 MI.
100 0 200 400 KM.
72°
80°
88°
Figure 4-3

Most of the sacred places enumerated in the *Agni Purāṇa* are situated in northern India (see fig. 4-3). In South India sacred places enumerated are very few, but the major rivers of South India occur in the list. There is no mention of such important *tīrthas* in South India as Rameśvaram, Kāñchī (Kāñcī), Kanyā Kumārī, and Gokarṇa. Clearly, therefore, the *Agni Purāṇa* is a non-Dravidian perception of the sacred geography of India.

Like the *Mahābhārata,* this *Purāṇa* starts the description of *tīrthas* with Puṣkara, indicating perhaps the continued importance of this *tīrtha.* Also, the selection of the Gaṅgā and the Narmadā for their special sanctity indicates the established religious importance of these rivers. Prayāga, Vārāṇasī, and Gayā seem to have been selected for the same reasons. Of these three, Gayā must have been regarded as the most sacred place in this *Purāṇa,* because the praise of this *tīrtha* is sung in forty-one verses, compared with fourteen verses for Prayāga and only seven for Vārāṇasī. This method of description suggests an attempt to note the relative importance of *tīrthas.* Yet it is Prayāga, rather than Gayā or Vārāṇasī, which is called the king of *tīrthas* by the *Agni Purāṇa.* There is thus an obvious inconsistency, which shows that decisions regarding the relative sanctity of places were almost impossible to make.

The *Agni Purāṇa*, it is believed, does not represent any particular sect and is considered to antedate Muslim contact with India.[43] It is not clear, therefore, why sacred places of the northwestern part of India are neglected.

Inferences from the Study of Sacred Places in the Purāṇas

(1) Recounting of the merits of pilgrimages and the numerous eulogies of the sacred places in the *Purāṇas* points out quite clearly the entrenchment of the practice of pilgrimages in the Hindu society.

(2) There is no reasonable doubt that people must have frequently undertaken pilgrimages for a wide variety of reasons. One of the major reasons was the performance of religious rites and rituals for the deceased. Thus, the *Purāṇas* not only enumerate *tīrthas* for the general purificatory rites but also implicitly *recommend* specialized places where sacrifices for the manes could

[43] *Agni Purāṇa,* p. xxxvi. Comments of the editor.

be performed. The most important of these sacrifices was the *śrāddha*, and perhaps the most desirable *tīrtha* for its performance was Gayā.[44] It is largely because of this that Gayā appears in the *Purāṇas* as the most popular *tīrtha* of India.

(3) The establishment of the pattern of the sacred geography of India, as shown by the places of sanctity, must have been achieved very early, long before the beginning of the Christian Era. This outline has tended to persist with minor changes.

(4) Since the *Purāṇas* seem to have fixed the major lineaments of the sacred geography of India, additional important sacred places had meager prospect of developing. Thus the deficient areas have tended to persist. These areas are the ones occupied even to this day by a considerable proportion of the pre-Aryan tribes.

(5) It follows from the preceding observation that the process of Aryanization, rapid in its early phases, may have slowed down as Hinduism became more codified. The process of Aryanization included, it seems, the concomitant expansion of plow agriculture. Thus, it may be postulated that areas least desirable for plow agriculture were least Aryanized. Brāhmaṇic Hinduism thus seems to have developed largely in the more desirable areas of plow agriculture.

(6) Within the major areas of Aryanization, pilgrimages must have continued to provide religious connectivity. This may have resulted in a degree of uniformity in the major religious practices and rituals despite a great variety in the local practices.

(7) The *Purāṇas* do seem to have regional biases, as shown by the efforts to promote the sanctity of certain *tīrthas*. This may have been done by the priests in order to attract more pilgrims and thereby to benefit from the fee paid by the pilgrims for the performance of rituals. This process may have ultimately resulted in the establishment of vested interests of the class of religious specialists called the *tīrtha purohits* or *paṇḍās*.[45]

[44]Even today Gaya is accepted by the Hindus as the most desirable sacred place for the performance of *pitri-śrāddha*, a propitiatory rite for the deceased male ancestors.

[45]Not only the priests but also the Indian princes and rajahs seem to have had important vested interests in the *tīrthas*, because of the revenue received from taxing the pilgrims. The National Archives of India (New Delhi) contain several documents that establish the economic importance of certain sacred places to the princes in whose jurisdiction these places fell. According to one document the

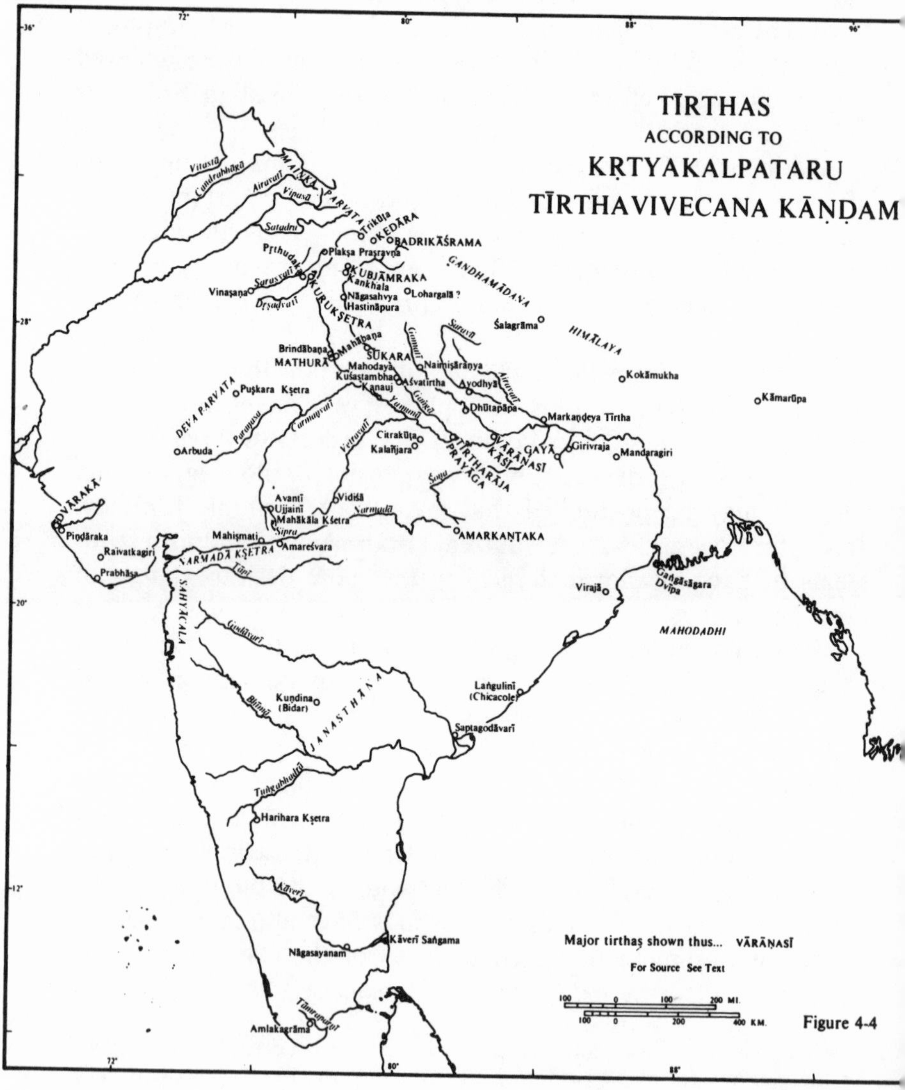
TĪRTHAS
ACCORDING TO
KṚTYAKALPATARU
TĪRTHAVIVECANA KĀṆḌAM
Vitastā
Candrabhāgā
Airavatī
Vipāsā
Śatadru
MAINĀKA PARVATA
Trikūṭa
KEDĀRA
BADRIKĀŚRAMA
Pṛthudaka
Plakṣa Prasravṇa
Sarasvatī
Vinaśana
Dṛṣadvatī
KURUKṢETRA
KUBJĀMRAKA
Kankhala
Nāgasahvya
Hastināpura
Lohargalā ?
GANDHAMĀDANA
Śalagrāma
HIMĀLAYA
Brindābana
MATHURĀ
Mahābana
SŪKARA
Mahodaya
Kuśastambha
Kanauj
Aśvatirtha
Naimiṣāraṇya
Ayodhyā
Dhūtapāpa
Kokāmukha
Kāmarūpa
Gomatī
Sarayū
Airavatī
Gaṅgā
Yamunā
DEVA PARVATA
Puṣkara Kṣetra
Arbuda
Parṇāśā
Carmaṇvatī
Vetravatī
Citrakūṭa
Kalañjara
TĪRTHARĀJA
PRAYĀGA
VĀRĀṆASI
KĀŚI
GAYĀ
Girivraja
Markaṇḍeya Tīrtha
Mandaragiri
Śoṇa
DVĀRAKĀ
Piṇḍāraka
Raivatkagiri
Prabhāsa
Avantī
Ujjainī
Mahākāla Kṣetra
Vidiśā
Narmadā
Śiprā
Mahiṣmati
Amareśvara
NARMADĀ KṢETRA
Tāpī
AMARKANṬAKA
SAHYĀCALA
Gaṅgāsāgara
Dvīpa
Virajā
MAHODADHI
Godāvarī
Kuṇḍina
(Bidar)
Bhīmā
JANASTHĀNA
Laṅgulinī
(Chicacole)
Saptagodāvarī
Tuṅgabhadrā
Harihara Kṣetra
Kāverī
Kāverī Saṅgama
Nāgasayanam
Tāmraparṇī
Amlakagrāma
Major tīrthaṣ shown thus... VĀRĀṆASĪ
For Source See Text
100 0 100 200 MI.
100 0 200 400 KM.
36°
28°
20°
12°
72°
80°
88°
96°

Figure 4-4

DISTRIBUTION OF HINDU PLACES OF PILGRIMAGE IN THE EARLY PART OF THE TWELFTH CENTURY A.D.

In the religious literature of medieval India, if there is any treatise on the sacred places whose date and authorship are reasonably certain, it is the formidable nine-volume digest entitled *Kṛtyakalpataru* of Bhaṭṭa Lakṣmīdhara, compiled about 1110 A.D.[46] This digest is based largely on the Puranic authority. The eighth part of this work, entitled *Tīrthavivecana Kāṇḍam,* lists a large number of *tīrthas* over the entire country. Since, however, the author was a resident of North India, his list contains comparatively few sacred places of South India.[47]

Figure 4-4 shows the distribution of *tīrthas* in India according to the above authority. There are some limitations of this map, however. A large number of *tīrthas* given in the *Tīrthavivecana Kāṇḍam* cannot be shown on the map either because they cannot be identified now or, and more important, because a large number of *tīrthas* are subsumed under one particular *tīrtha* or a sacred *kṣetra* (area). For example, Lakṣmīdhara enumerates 275 different sacred spots in the Vārāṇasī *kṣetra* alone. Similarly, a number of *tīrthas* are subsumed in Prayāga *kṣetra* and Gayā *kṣetra.* With these limitations in mind, we may extract the following observations from our reconstruction of the distribution pattern of sacred places described in the *Tīrthavivecana Kāṇḍam* (fig. 4-4).

(1) There is an obvious attempt in the *Tīrthavivecana Kāṇḍam* to separate and eulogize, at length, the glories (*māhātmyas*) of the more important *tīrthas*: Vārāṇasī, Prayāga, Gaṅgā, Kurukṣetra, Pṛthūdaka (modern Pehoa), Puṣkara (modern Pushkar), Ujjaini, Narmadā, Kubjāmraka (near Hardwar), Sukra (Soron), Kokāmukha (in Nepal), Badrī, Mandar (not identified), Śalagrāma (in

Rajah of Gaya used to receive a sum of over 300,000 rupees as *malikana* (proprietary rights) of the temples at Gaya. The same document accepts the claims of the Rajah of Gaya to receive *malikana.* The collusion between the princes and priests to enhance the religious importance of sacred places is a distinct possibility and needs attention from the social historian. See Home Department, Land Revenue Branch, Document No. 29–37 f, dated November 25, 1839, in the National Archives of India, New Delhi.

[46]For a more detailed discussion of the nature, the purpose, and the authorship of this digest, see K. V. Rangaswamy Aiyangar, ed., *Kṛtyakalpataru, Tīrthavivecana Kāṇḍam,* Introduction, pp. xix ff.

[47]Bhaṭṭa Lakṣmīdhara was the chief minister at the court of King Govindacandra belonging to the Gahadvala dynasty of Kanauj. *Ibid.,* p. xvii.

northern Nepal, but cannot be precisely identified), Stutsvāmī (not identified), Kedāra (modern Kedarnath), and Naimiṣa (modern Nimsar).

Apart from the above prominent *tīrthas* there is a category of "nānātīrthāni," or miscellaneous *tīrthas,* whose praise is sung in one or more verses in chapter 23 of *Tīrthavivecana Kāṇḍam.* The major *tīrthas* above must have been the ones which Lakṣmīdhara considers most notable. Four of these cannot now be identified, but the rest continue to be among the premier sacred places today.

(2) None of the major *tīrthas* of Bhaṭṭa Lakṣmīdhara is located south of the Narmadā River, which indicates that the southern places of pilgrimage were of limited importance for the North Indian pilgrims. In fact, most of the major *tīrthas* are placed in the Gaṅgā basin or very near it. The placement of major *tīrthas* in the Gaṅgā basin merely underscores the sanctity attached to *tīrthas* in this general region for a very long time on the basis of established tradition preceding the times of Bhaṭṭa Lakṣmīdhara.

(3) A large area bounded in part by the Narmadā-Son trough, the Eastern Ghats, and the Godavari River contains an insignificant number of *tīrthas.* This forested and tribal region once again emerges as an area of very limited sanctity. Similar is the case with much of Bengal and Assam. In fact, the main deficient areas of sanctity still continue to be as they were in the early twelfth century, excepting modern Bengal.

(4) The sanctity of flowing water is again stressed, as was the case with the description in the epic and the *Purāṇas.* Most streams of the Indus-Gaṅgā plains, as well as the major rivers of the peninsula, are in the sacred fold except for the curious exception of the Mahānadī.

(5) A large part of the *Tīrthavivecana Kāṇḍam* is devoted to the praise of Vārāṇasī, which leaves little doubt that this site by the twelfth century had become the most popular sacred place of the Hindus, surpassing Puṣkara and Gayā, which attracted much greater attention in the epic and the *Purāṇas.*

(6) If the digest of Lakṣmīdhara is any guide, then it seems that there was some retrogression in the sanctity of various regions of India as viewed from the Gaṅgā basin. The *Mahābhārata* and the *Purāṇas* describe more sacred places in the northeastern part of the country as well as on the west coast than Lakṣmīdhara does. The causes of this retrogression are difficult to determine,

but the main reason seems to be an aversion on the part of Lakṣmīdhara to call places "sacred" which had already passed under the the then "foreign" culture, namely, Islam. According to Aiyangar, when these areas "passed under hostile occupation, tracts which had been the homes of ancient sages had to be omitted even in the comprehensive accounts of places of Hindu pilgrimages."[48] However, this does not explain the omission of South Indian holy places.

(7) Lakṣmīdhara omits, without giving any reason, such important South Indian *tīrthas* as Rameśvaram, Kāñchī (Kāñcī), Kanyā Kumārī, and Gokarṇa. Since there are references to these in the *Mahābhārata* as well as in the *Purāṇas,* it is rather surprising that they have not been mentioned in the presumably comprehensive list in the *Tīrthavivecana Kāṇḍam.* It certainly reflects a bias against the South Indian shrines, which in the twelfth century were flourishing religious places.[49] The reasons for this bias are far from clear.

DISTRIBUTION OF HINDU PLACES OF PILGRIMAGE BASED ON SOME NON-HINDU MEDIEVAL SOURCES

Three non-Hindu sources stand out as the most informative ones about the Hindu places of pilgrimage, from the seventh through the sixteenth centuries. These are (1) the accounts of Hsüan-tsang's travels in India between A.D. 629 and 645;[50] (2) Alberuni's *Kitāb-ul-Hind* written about A.D. 1030;[51] and (3) Abul Fazl's *'Ain-i-Akbari* of the late sixteenth century.[52] Apart from the above non-Hindu sources there are several others, of limited value for our purpose, which can be used to elucidate some minor points.

Although it is not the primary purpose of the above sources to enumerate Hindu places of pilgrimage, the importance of the institution of pilgrimage in Hinduism compels these authors to take note of it and describe some of the most important places.

[48]Aiyangar, *op. cit.,* p. xliii.

[49]See K. A. Nilakanta Sastri, *Development of Religion in South India,* chap. 6.

[50]Thomas Watters, ed., *On Yuan Chwang's Travels in India* (629–645 A.D.).

[51]Edward C. Sachau, *Alberuni's India* (London, 1910), Vol. II. This is a translation of *Kitab-ul-Hind.*

[52]Abul Fazl-i-'Allami, *'Ain-i-Akbari,* translated by H. S. Jarrett, revised and further annotated by Sir Jadu Nath Sarkar. This work was submitted to the Mughal emperor Akbar in A.D. 1593.

The seventh century account of Hsüan-tsang provides, among other things, one of the earliest foreign accounts of the institution and places of pilgrimage in India. Its significance for our purpose is not only that it gives perhaps the most methodical first-hand "regional" account of early medieval India, but also that the author was traveling from one holy place to the other gathering information about the state of Buddhism in India. Although his main concern was Buddhism, he could not help observing the state of affairs of Hinduism and particularly the sacred places of the Hindus.[53] It may be noted here that by the seventh century orthodox Hinduism was in a period of resurgence against Buddhism as a religion in India.

From the travels of Hsüan-tsang it is quite evident that Hindu places of pilgrimage were spread over the entire length and breadth of the country. The Buddhist traveler noticed the practice of bathing in the sacred rivers, particularly in the Gaṅgā River. He also commented on the merit of drowning in this river as well as the tradition of consigning the ashes of the dead to the Gaṅgā.[54] Hsüan-tsang's remarks on some of the non-Aryanized areas of India are extremely valuable. His account suggests that Buddhism never spread in Kāmarūpa (Assam) and this area continued to have a wild tribal population.[55]

The itinerary of Hsüan-tsang in India shows quite clearly his general avoidance of areas without contemporary or former allegiance to Buddhism. And, since Buddhism was merely an overlap on Hinduism, both in the religious and areal sense, the areas avoided by him are by and large the less Hinduized areas of the seventh century A.D. The outline of Hsüan-tsang's pilgrimage in India seems to resemble broadly the pilgrimage route described in the *Mahābhārata*.[56]

Alberuni in the third decade of the eleventh century A.D. noticed the institution of pilgrimage and the significance of ritual bathing

[53] See "Index of Chinese Names of Places" in Watters, II, 319–328. A detailed map of the places visited by Hsüan-tsang has been recently prepared by Shiva G. Bajpai for the South Asia Historical Atlas Project, University of Minnesota, Minneapolis (not yet published).

[54] *Ibid.*, I, 319, 364. The latter practice still continues.

[55] *Ibid.*, II, 185–186.

[56] Alexander Cunningham, *The Ancient Geography of India* (London, 1871), frontispiece. A more detailed and informative map has been prepared by the South Asia Historical Atlas Project, University of Minnesota, Minneapolis (not yet published).

in Hinduism. Since Alberuni remained in the northern part of the country, he mentions the more important sacred places of northern India only. On the authority of the *Vāyu* and the *Matsya Purāṇas,* Alberuni mentions a number of holy ponds in the cold mountains around Meru.[57] Alberuni clearly notes the significance of ritual bathing in Hinduism: "In every place to which some particular holiness is ascribed, the Hindus construct ponds intended for the ablutions."[58]

The important *tīrthas* noticed by Alberuni were Baranasi (Varanasi), Pukara (Puskara), Taneshar (Thanesar), Mahura (Mathura), Nandagola (near Mathura), Kashmir, and Multan. The most venerated of the sacred places was, of course, Varanasi, which he compares to Mecca.[59] Similarly Mahura (Mathura) "is a holy place, crowded with Brahmans."[60]

One particular Hindu holy place which was commented upon by an Arab geographer of the tenth century is Multan. Ibn Haukal in his work *Kitab ul Masalik wa-l Mamalik* notices Multan (now in Pakistan) and pilgrimages to it: "There is an idol there held in great veneration by the Hindus, and every year people from the most distant parts undertake pilgrimages to it, and bring vast sums of money, which they expend upon the temple."[61] The description of Alberuni, however, shows that the temple at Multan had been destroyed and consequently pilgrimage to it had ceased.[62]

An important list of major Hindu places of pilgrimage is supplied by Abul Fazl in his celebrated digest on administration entitled *'Ain-i-Akbari* and written in the last quarter of the sixteenth century. Abul Fazl gives a concise view of the basic philosophy of the institution of Hindu pilgrimages and attempts to classify and enumerate the more important of these places, particularly in reference to northern India. In his work we once again find the importance of ritual bathing in Hinduism and consequently the sanctity of the rivers. Since Abul Fazl was a minister at the court of Akbar the Great, he emphasizes the sacred places of that part of India which was under the Mughal administration. Therefore,

[57]Most of these ponds are in Himalayan and trans-Himalayan areas of the sources of Ganga, Yamuna, Indus, etc. See Sachau, *Alberuni's India* II, 142–143.

[58]*Ibid.,* p. 144.

[59]*Ibid.,* p. 146.

[60]*Ibid.,* p. 147.

[61]Ibn Haukal as quoted in H. M. Elliott, *Early Arab Geographers,* pp. 35.

[62]Sachau, II, 148.

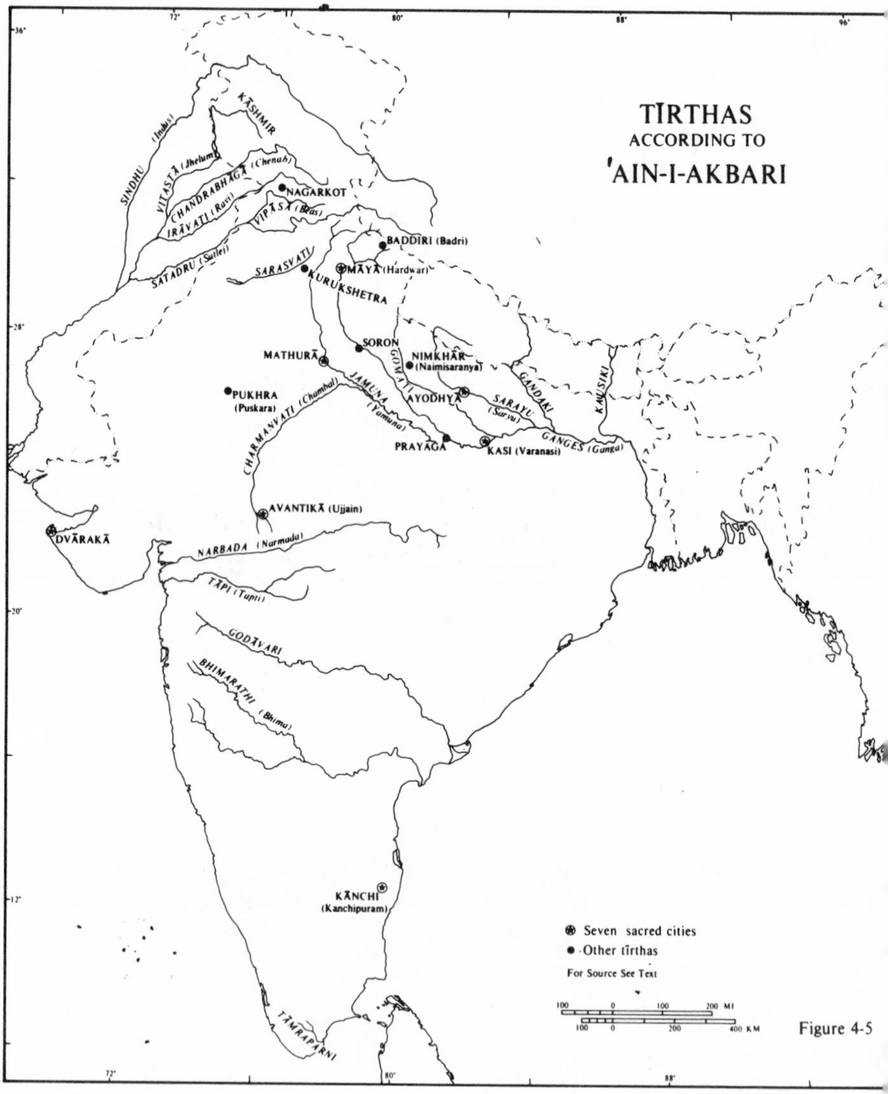

TĪRTHAS
ACCORDING TO
'AIN-I-AKBARI
KĀSHMIR
SINDHU (Indus)
VITASTĀ (Jhelum)
CHANDRABHAGĀ (Chenab)
IRĀVATI (Ravi)
VIPĀSĀ (Beas)
SATADRU (Sutlej)
NAGARKOT
BADDIRI (Badri)
SARASVATI
MĀYĀ (Hardwar)
KURUKSHETRA
SORON
MATHURĀ
NIMKHĀR (Naimisaranya)
GOMATI
PUKHRA (Puskara)
JAMUNA (Yamuna)
CHARMANVATI (Chambal)
AYODHYĀ
SARAYU (Saryu)
GANDAKI
KAUSIKI
PRAYĀGA
KASI (Varanasi)
GANGES (Ganga)
AVANTIKĀ (Ujjain)
DVĀRAKĀ
NARBADA (Narmada)
TĀPI (Tapti)
GODĀVARI
BHIMARATHI (Bhima)
KĀNCHĪ (Kanchipuram)
TĀMRAPARNI
Seven sacred cities
Other tīrthas
For Source See Text
100 0 100 200 MI
100 0 200 400 KM
72°
80°
88°
96°
36°
28°
20°
12°

Figure 4-5

he virtually disregarded sacred places in South India. Given this limitation, his list may be considered a reliable guide to determine the more venerated places in India in the last quarter of the sixteenth century.

Figure 4-5 attempts to show the sacred places and rivers of India as described in *'Ain-i-Akbari*. Some of the sacred places and rivers mentioned by this author cannot be identified, but the emphasis on the North is quite clear. Gayā, which is so much eulogized in the epic *Mahābhārata* as well as in the *Purāṇas*, is not mentioned in the selected places noted by Abul Fazl. No sacred place is stated in Bengal or Assam, nor in the northeastern forested and tribal area. While several sacred rivers of South India are recognized, no place except Kanchi (Kāñcī) is noted. The selection of this place from amongst all others reflects, perhaps, its popularity among the pilgrims of northern India.

CONCLUSIONS

By the use of some selected sources, both from the Hindu sacred literature and from the non-Hindu accounts of India, it has been possible to present a broad outline of the distribution of places of pilgrimage. Despite the possible sectarian biases of the Puranic literature and the personal biases of individual writers, it is clear that sacred places and visits to them have constituted an important element of the Hindu religious tradition from very ancient times.

Most of the sources used reflect a North Indian bias. The only way to correct this is to incorporate literary and other sources from South India. Researchers with intimate knowledge of South Indian languages may take up such a task. Current interest in the religious literature may eventually open ways and means to fix the dates of various portions of the *Purāṇas*, which will be a significant step forward to relate the development in the religious realm to the broader social and cultural aspects of India.

The distribution of sacred places, as viewed through the religious and other literature, shows that despite the remarkable continuity of the institution of Hindu pilgrimage, certain regions of India have remained culturally peripheral to this circulatory aspect of Hinduism.

Chapter V

Tīrthas : Their Relative Importance, Site Characteristics, and Principal Deities

DISTRIBUTION OF SACRED PLACES

The distribution of modern Hindu sacred places of pilgrimage is based largely on a consensus of seven different sources.[1] These sources were selected largely because all of them have attempted to describe or list sacred places for the whole of India. There are also a number of regional monographs which usually give a detailed description of the sacred places of the regions in question including the legends attached to these sacred places.[2] Figure 5-1 includes all the places considered sacred by at least three of the seven sources referred to above. A number of other sacred places are also shown on this map, selected solely on the merit of the description given by the relevant author of the regional monographs and *Kalyāṇa, Tīrthāṅka.* Thus the map (fig. 5-1) shows eighty-four places considered sacred by at least three authorities and another fifty-eight derived from *Kalyāṇa* and various regional monographs.

Scholars dealing with the places of pilgrimage in India are likely to be faced with the problem of selecting a manageable number of sacred places from among hundreds of them scattered all over the country. This difficulty will be easily appreciated by any scholar who cares to go through scores of district and state gazetteers of India, let alone the numerous religious treatises. Robert Stoddard has discussed this problem admirably in his Ph.D. dissertation.[3] After considering some other alternatives to be

[1]The sources used for arriving at a consensus are *The Imperial Gazetteer of India*, Vol. XXV; *Encyclopaedia of Religion and Ethics*; Glasenapp, *Heilige Stätten Indiens*; B. C. Law, *Holy Places of India*; R. Roussel, *Les Pèlerinages a travers les Siècles*; *Kalyāṇa, Tīrthāṅka,* Vol. 31, No. 1, 1957; J. H. Dave, *Immortal India*.

[2]For example, R. K. Das, *Temples of Tamilnad*; N. Ramesan, *Temples and Legends of Andhra Pradesh*; Pranab Chandra, Roy Chaudhury, *Temples and Legends of Bihar* (Bombay : Bharatiya Vidya Bhavan, 1965); and M. S. Mate, *Temples and Legends of Maharashtra.*

[3]"Hindu Holy Sites in India," p. 26–33.

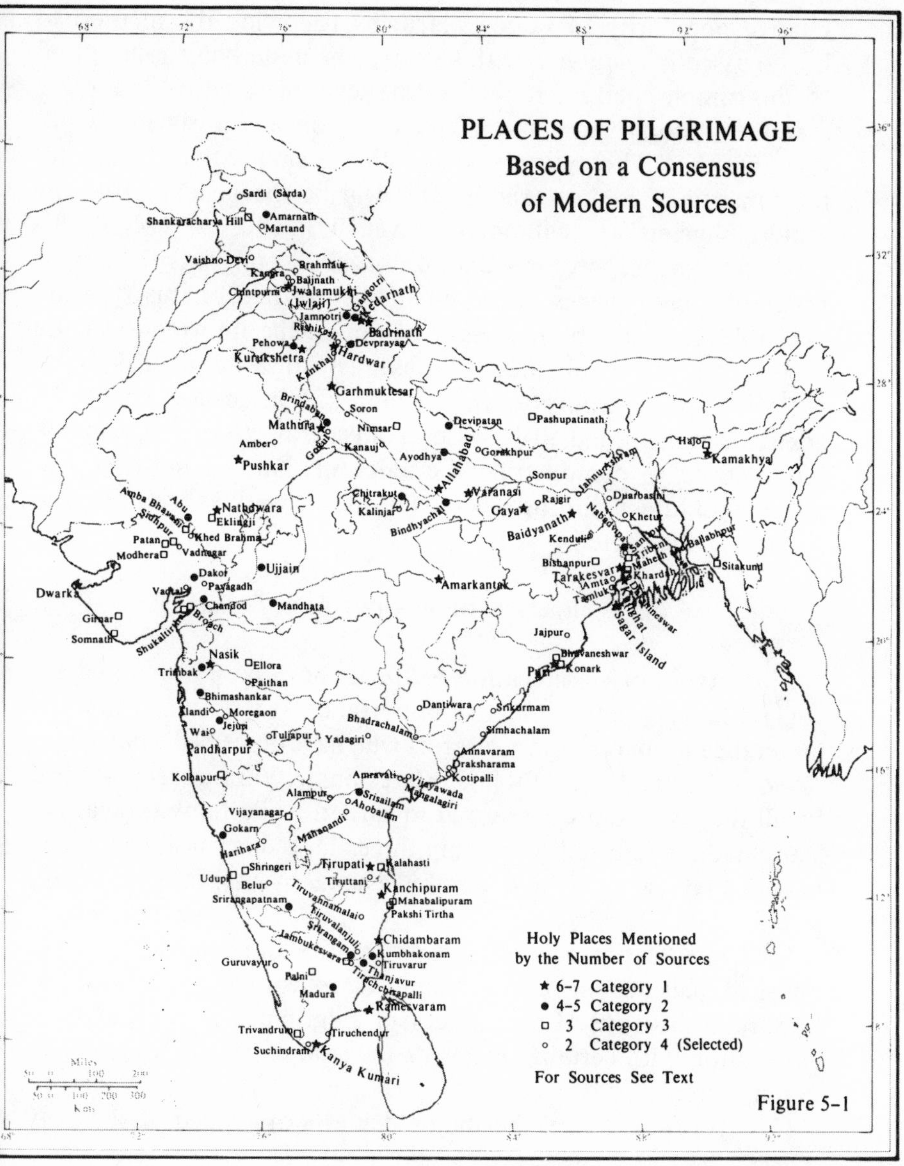
PLACES OF PILGRIMAGE
Based on a Consensus
of Modern Sources
Sardi (Sarda)
Shankaracharya Hill
Amarnath
Martand
Vaishno-Devi
Brahmaur
Kangra
Baijnath
Chintpurni
Jwalamukhi
(Jwlaji)
Gangotri
Kedarnath
Jamnotri
Rishikesh
Badrinath
Pehowa
Devprayag
Kurukshetra
Hardwar
Kankhal
Garhmuktesar
Brindaban
Soron
Mathura
Gokul
Nimsar
Devipatan
Pashupatinath
Amber
Kanauj
Ayodhya
Gorakhpur
Hajo
Kamakhya
Pushkar
Allahabad
Sonpur
Jahnu Ashram
Chitrakut
Varanasi
Rajgir
Duarbasini
Amba Bhavani
Abu
Nathdwara
Kalinjar
Bindhyachal
Gaya
Baidyanath
Nabadvipa
Khetur
Sidhpur
Eklingji
Kenduli
Patan
Khed Brahma
Ballabhpur
Modhera
Vadnagar
Bishanpur
Sitakund
Dakor
Ujjain
Tarakesvar
Amta
Khardah
Dwarka
Pavagadh
Amarkantak
Tamluk
Vadtal
Chandod
Mandhata
Dakshineswar
Girnar
Broach
Kalighat
Sagar Island
Somnath
Shukaltirth
Jajpur
Nasik
Ellora
Bhuvaneshwar
Trimbak
Paithan
Puri
Konark
Bhimashankar
Dantiwara
Srikurmam
Alandi
Moregaon
Simhachalam
Wai
Jejuri
Tuljapur
Bhadrachalam
Yadagiri
Pandharpur
Annavaram
Draksharama
Kotipalli
Kolhapur
Amravati
Vijayawada
Mangalagiri
Alampur
Srisailam
Ahobalam
Vijayanagar
Gokarn
Mahanandi
Harihara
Tirupati
Kalahasti
Udupi
Shringeri
Tiruttani
Belur
Kanchipuram
Srirangapatnam
Tiruvannamalai
Mahabalipuram
Pakshi Tirtha
Tiruvalanjuli
Chidambaram
Srirangam
Jambukesvara
Kumbhakonam
Tiruvarur
Guruvayur
Thanjavur
Palni
Tiruchchirapalli
Madura
Rameswaram
Trivandrum
Tiruchendur
Suchindram
Kanya Kumari
Holy Places Mentioned
by the Number of Sources
★ 6–7 Category 1
● 4–5 Category 2
□ 3 Category 3
○ 2 Category 4 (Selected)
For Sources See Text
Miles
Kms
68°
72°
76°
80°
84°
88°
92°
96°
36°
32°
28°
24°
20°
16°
12°
8°
Figure 5-1

inadequate, he uses the method of consensus of several authorities.

The method of consensus, however, is adequate only for a broad overview. It is possible to establish, more objectively, the relative popularity of sacred places by following the method to be discussed in chapter 7 of this study. The underlying assumption of this simple method is that as the level of sanctity of a place increases, people from more and more diverse areas make pilgrimages to it. Theoretically, this notion is simply that the greater the sanctity of a place, the greater will be the distance that the Hindu pilgrims are willing to travel. The effective use of this method, however, requires data on origins of pilgrims for a wide range of sacred places. Since no published data of this type are available, it would be necessary to obtain the information from each sacred place individually—obviously an arduous task.

For the present purpose the method of consensus seems to be adequate at the broad all-India level of generalization. In chapter 9, I have tried to demonstrate the value of data on the origin of pilgrims obtained through personal interviewers as well as from records at the sacred places.

CLASSIFICATION OF PRESENT-DAY *Tīrthas*

Three types of classification of *tīrthas* have been attempted.[4]

(1) Classification by relative importance. It is assumed that the larger the number of commentators who have described a particular *tīrtha,* the more prominent it is. For example, Varanasi is described by all the seven sources referred to earlier, while Jambukesvara in Tamilnadu is referred to by only three. Thus Varanasi is included in the first category and Jambukesvara in the third category (see fig. 5-1).

(2) Classification according to association of *tīrthas* with certain physical features or other diagnostic phenomena. This seems important because Hindu places of pilgrimage appear to have association with certain objects of the landscape which are considered sacred.

(3) Classification by the major deities worshipped at the holy places.

[4]Bharati gives a threefold typology, which is useful for descriptive purposes. See Agehananda Bharati, "Pilgrimage Sites and Indian Civilization," p. 97.

Classification of Tīrthas *by Their Relative Importance*

A general idea of the relative repute of sacred places of Hindu pilgrimage may be gained from figure 5-1. At an all-India level of generalization the holy places noted by at least six "authorities" may be considered the most popular, while those mentioned by only two may be considered the least popular. The method of consensus used here merely reflects the relative eminence of sacred places at an all-India scale and there is no intention to suggest their relative *sanctity* for a specific cult or a specific region. Certain biases will remain, no matter how many authorities or other individuals are consulted. The number of sacred places in each category—from the most to the least renowned—is shown below.

First category	(6–7 authorities)	: 28 places[5]
Second category	(4–5 authorities)	: 26 places
Third category	(3 authorities)	: 30 places
Fourth category	(2 authorities)	: 58 places

Classification of Tīrthas *according to Their Site Characteristics*

The classification of the site characteristics of the sacred places is not merely an academic exercise, but rather has a deeper meaning in the geography of religion. As a student of geography I am interested in the character of the sacred place. In the realm of Hindu religion certain sites are selected as holy. Beyond the mere physical appearance of the site, it is accorded sacred quality. Thus, the Hindu religion, by bestowing sacred qualities to specific localities, has created a differentiated space. At the chosen sites of sanctity the power of the deity repeats itself, and by this reaffirmation of the supernatural (which we call the deity), the place assumes a sacred character.[6]

The physical phenomena that give character to a holy place are to be understood in their symbolic sense.[7] It is in this sense that river sources, hot springs, prominent hilltops, and certain forests and woods assume a sacred character. Kristensen asks a very

[5]Ujjain has been placed in the first category despite the fact that it has been noted by five sources. Tradition as well as my own field investigation suggests its inclusion in the first category.

[6]Cf. G. van der Leeuw, *Religion in Essence and Manifestation: A Study in Phenomenology*, II, 393.

[7]For a masterful analysis of Symbolism, see Mircea Eliade, *The Two and the One*, chap. 5, "Observations on Religious Symbolism."

pertinent question in this regard, namely, what makes a place holy or sacred? And he believes that "it is certainly not the fact that a sacred act is performed there such as the utterance of a prayer, the swearing of an oath or performance of ritual purification. It is rather that this is the place where God dwells and where he reveals himself."[8] Thus, at the sacred places, the god who is worshipped there is conceived to reveal himself in the nature of that place. That is why the classification of sacred places based on their site characteristics becomes pertinent to a student of the geography of religion.

It may be imagined that a deity can manifest himself wherever he chooses to do so. This is only theoretically possible. In fact, each society conceives the deities in the framework of its religion, and it is ultimately the society which selects the holy places where its deities manifest themselves. Thus, a classification of the sites of holy places is in fact a means to understand that characteristic space or those localities which the religion selects from the rest of space and calls sacred. The credit of manifestation is always given to the deity because, by definition, he is more powerful than man.

Some writers have suggested that the mystery and wonder of remote places may have been the original basis of their sanctity.[9] Others, particularly Indian scholars, are inclined to believe that places of fascinating beauty and grandeur, by providing supreme peace and consolation, are conducive for meditation and thus become holy places.[10]

The *Mahābhārata* itself suggests a variety of reasons why certain places are sacred: "Just as certain limbs of the body are purer than others, so are certain places on earth more sacred—some on account of their situation, others because of their sparkling waters, and others because of the association or habitation of saintly people."[11] It seems clear that no single variable can explain the distribution of sacred places.

[8]W. Brede Kristensen, *The Meaning of Religion*: *Lectures in the Phenomenology of Religion*, pp. 359–360.

[9]See, for example, David E. Sopher, *Geography of Religions*, p. 52; and Rudolph Otto, *The Idea of the Holy*, chap. 4, "Mysterium Tremendum."

[10]See, for example, Haridas Bhattacharyya, ed., *The Cultural Heritage of India*, IV, 495; Bhakat Prasad Mazumdar, *Socio-Economic History of Northern India*, p. 316.

[11]*The Mahābhārata, Anusāsan Parvan*, chapter 108, verses 16–18, as translated in J. H. Dave, *Immortal India*, I, xiv.

The distribution of sacred places today represents the cumulative effect of the process of sanctification of certain selected locales over more than two millennia. Since the process of sanctification may have consisted of numerous elements, a single hypothesis cannot be expected to explain satisfactorily the distribution of sacred places.

The formulation of explanatory hypotheses is made all the more difficult by the fact that the pattern of distribution of Hindu holy places, particularly the more eminent ones, shows a high degree of conservatism. The outline of this pattern, as we have observed in the preceding chapters, was established as early as the epic period. Thereafter, the *Purāṇas,* by according sacred status to several other places, helped to evolve a pattern that came to be accepted, by and large, as given. Although several local and subregional shrines and a few regional shrines may have come to prominence despite the Puranic traditions, the fact remains that the Puranic tradition fixed the sacred status of the prominent religious places. The sanctity is not randomly distributed but is bestowed upon certain chosen localities particularly associated with sacred streams and their confluences, with the coast, and with the hilltops.[12]

In the process of the spread of Hinduism, partly through actual spatial expansion and partly through absorption of non-Hindu tribal populations, those areas which came to be sanctified early have, therefore, a large number of sacred places associated with the sacred streams, the coast, or the hilltops. As the process continued, more of such places could be expected to be consecrated. As observed earlier, once the major sacred points had been selected and became accepted as such through the religious lore and literature common to Hinduism over the country, the further addition of places of sanctity, one surmises, encountered some opposition from priests with vested interests in the established ones. Therefore, new candidates for the rank of major sacred places would not be able to join the accepted lists unless the religious authority recognized them as such. The newcomers might be accepted if due efforts were made by the priests or the rulers. Often the priests had to invent or manipulate a legend and write a *sthala purāṇa*

[12]Cf. David E. Sopher, *Geography of Religions,* p. 49. "The distribution of Hindu holy places thus shows some correspondence with selected features of the physical landscape."

(a sacred book of legend of the place) to promote the recognition of their sacred place in the existing religious literature. Sacred places without the authority of a *sthala purāṇa* would be disregarded in the literature of sacred places, even though people from nearby areas might make pilgrimages to them. As the *Purāṇas,* and the *sthala purāṇas,* achieved the status of being the sacred word (hence true) the place considered sacred by them would be accepted as such without question.[13]

So far I have merely suggested a process whereby the sanctity of many eminent places may have continued and some "new" places may have been accepted in the sacred fold. The question still remains why important Hindu sacred places are found at the river sources, at the confluences, on the coast, and on the hilltops. It has been suggested earlier that ritual purification by bathing is extremely important in Hindu religion, which may be an important reason for the fluvial association of many sacred places. However, it does not explain the special sanctity attached to bathing at the source of a river (e.g., Gangotri, Yamnotri, Amarkantak) or at a confluence (e.g., Allahabad) or at places marking land's end (e.g., Cape Comorin, Ramesvaram, Dwarka). The answer to such questions may be partly sought in the symbolic meaning that the various physical features have in Hinduism. The Ganga, for example, is not merely any river, but acquires its sanctity because it is supposed to issue forth from the very locks of Śiva's hair. To reach the origin of the Ganga is to reach the abode of Śiva. The abode ot Śiva is the Himalaya, more particularly Mount Kailas. The quality of sanctity of the Ganga and of the Himalaya seems to have been transferred in part to other rivers and other mountains respectively. Every mountain top can be a local abode of Śiva or his consort Śakti. Every river can be a local Ganga. This transferring of sanctity is a quite frequent phenomenon in India.[14] We need to know much more about the symbolic signi-

[13]The *sthala purāṇa,* in many instances, is merely a legitimating device used by the priests to popularize the allegedly ancient origin of a sacred place. During my field work at Bhagsu Nag (popularly called Bhagsu Nath) near Dharmasala in Himachal Pradesh I found that the priest had published handbills in which the "history" of this place is described and it is claimed that the place was established 5,077 years ago! See Shri (Swami Mahant) Ganesagiri, "Mandir Bhagsunag, Sahitiya" (Dharmasala : Desh Press, n.d. [circa 1967]).

[14]See Agehananda Bharati, "Pilgrimage in the Indian Tradition," *History of Religions,* Vol. 3, no. 1 (1963), p. 165. This article is one of the best that I know on the subject of pilgrimage.

ficance of physical objects before an explanation of this type can be formalized.

TABLE 5-1
ASSOCIATION OF *Tīrthas* WITH SITE CHARACTERISTICS (I)
(142 *tīrthas*)

	River bank	River sources	Confluence of rivers	Coast	Hilltop	Others	Total
Total	60	6	7	11	21	37	142
Percent of total	42.3	4.2	4.9	7.7	14.8	26.1	100

NOTE : All water-associated sites = 84, or 59.2 percent of total of 142.

TABLE 5-2
ASSOCIATION OF *Tīrthas* WITH SITE CHARACTERISTICS (II)
(84 *tīrthas* mentioned by at least three authorities)

Category	River bank	River sources	Confluence of rivers	Coast	Hilltop	Others	Total
First	16	1	1	5	3	2	28
Second	9	4	2	1	3	7	26
Third	13	1	1	4	6	5	30
Total	38	6	4	10	12	14	84

NOTES :
All water-associated sites = 58, or 69 percent of a total of 84.
All hilltop sites = 12, or 14.3 percent of a total of 84.
Water-associated sites in the first category = 23, or 82 percent of places.
Water-associated sites in the second category = 16, or 61 percent of places.
Water-associated sites in the third category = 19, or 63.3 percent of places.
Water-associated sites in the fourth category (derived by subtraction from data of table 5-1) = 26, or 44.8 percent of places.

Tables 5-1 and 5-2 show the major site associations of the sacred places of India. The first table comprises all of the 142 places of figure 5-1; the second includes only the 84 places mentioned by three or more sources.

From these two tables some observations may now be made.

(1) When all the 142 sites are considered, more than half show association with water, particularly rivers.

(2) When the selection is reduced to 84 sites, mentioned as sacred by at least three authorities, the association with water increases, so that 69 per cent of all sites are associated with rivers or the coast.

(3) When the selection is further reduced to sites considered sacred by at least six authorities, the association with water is even more apparent: about 82 per cent of these sites are associated with running water (including the sea).

(4) When the sites considered sacred by only one or two authorities are examined, the association with water is much reduced, so that out of the 58 sites in the fourth category less than half are associated with running water.

(5) From the above four observations it is clear that proximity of running water is an important characteristic of the more popular Hindu holy places. This is very much in keeping with the significance in Hinduism of ritual bathing for purification. It must be emphasized that bathing at sacred places is not an act of physical purification, it is an act of symbolic purification of the soul.[15]

(6) If the sites associated with either water or hilltops are considered, they account for 70 of the 84 sites (over 83 per cent) noted by three or more of our sources. Thus, we find that certain elements of the physical landscape tend to be selected as the favored sacred spots.

Classification of Tīrthas *according to Their Chief Deities*

Most places of pilgrimage in India are associated with a specific chief or presiding deity (fig. 5-2).[16] Usually more than one deity is worshipped at these places, but theoretically there is one major deity to whom the place was devoted originally, with other deities added later on.[17] Association of places of pilgrimage with presiding deities can be a useful initial step for the understanding of the spatial aspects of religious evolution in India. In this way the sacred places can indicate the areal spread of the cult of a particular

[15]The Sipra River at the time of the *Siṃhastha* fair in 1968 was a foul-smelling stream covered with thick scum over which the birds could walk! Yet thousands of devout individuals were bathing, unmindful of the physical state of the stream. Obviously, hygiene and ritual purification by bathing are two widely different concepts.

[16]The most complete source for information regarding the deities at each sacred place is *Kalyāṇa, Tīrthāṅka*, Vol. 31, no. 1.

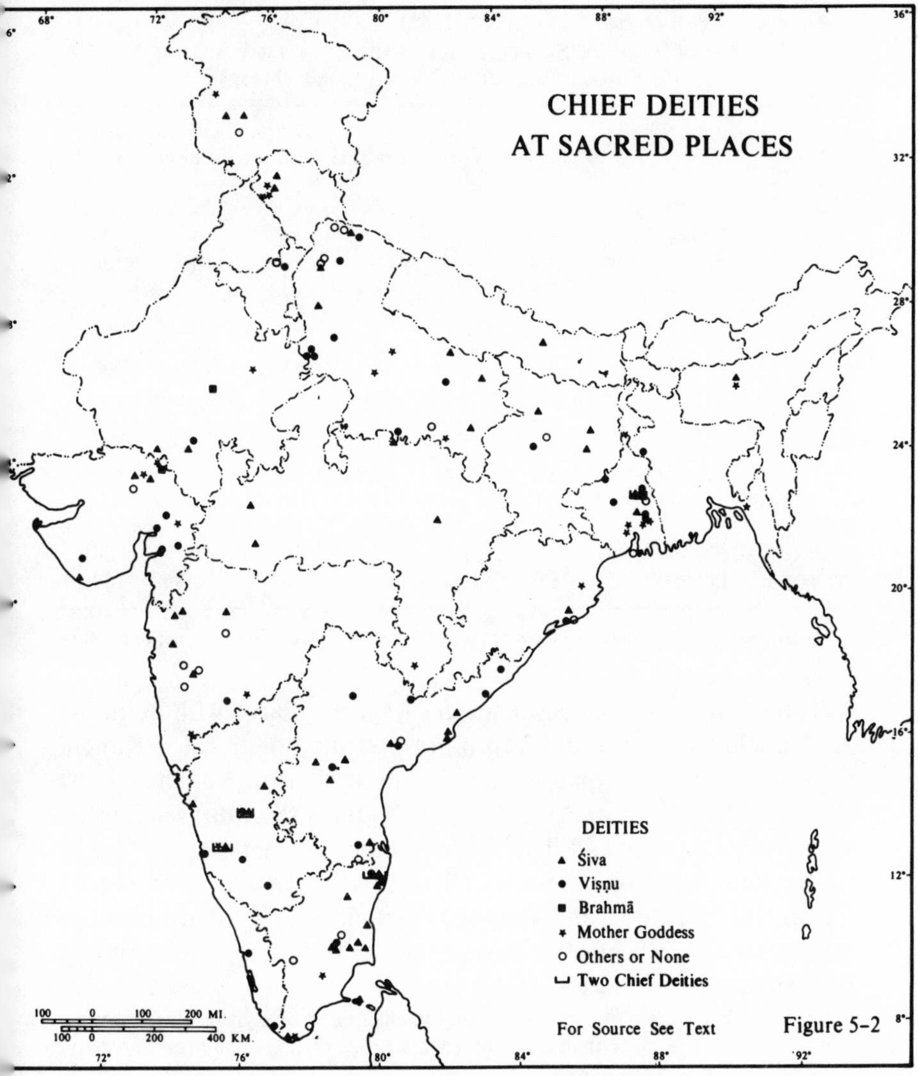

For Source See Text

Figure 5–2

deity. The classification of sacred places on the basis of presiding deities may bring out the relative importance of various deities in the Hindu religion.

TABLE 5-3
ASSOCIATION OF SACRED PLACES WITH CHIEF DEITIES (I)
(84 *tīrthas* of categories One, Two, and Three)

Category		Śiva	Viṣṇu	Brahmā	Mother Goddess	Others or none	Total
One							
	Places	11	10	1	4	3	29
	Percent	37.9	34.5	3.4	13.8	10.4	100
Two							
	Places	11	9	0	3	3	26
	Percent	42.4	34.6	0	11.5	11.5	100
Three							
	Places	11	8	0	7	5	31
	Percent	35.5	25.8	0	22.6	16.1	100
Total* of three	Places	33	27	1	14	11	86
categories	Percent	38.4	31.4	1.1	16.3	12.8	100

*Total exceeds the number of places because at two places there is more than one "chief deity."

Table 5-3 shows the association of sacred places with deities.[18] At Kanchi both Śiva and Viṣṇu are presiding deities, for Kanchi is divided into a "Śiva-Kanchi" and a "Viṣṇu-Kanchi."[19] At Shringeri both Śiva and the Mother Goddess (Sharda) seem to be of equal importance.[20] The total number of deities therefore is more than the actual number of places. There are some sacred places like Hardwar and Prayag where no specific deity presides because the significance of these *tīrthas* is not associated with any particular cult or deity.[21]

[17]It is not always possible to determine the chief deity of a given place, because it may be sacred to more than one cult, each with its own specific presiding deity.

[18]Eighty-four selected places.

[19]*Kalyāṇa, Tīrthāṅka*, pp. 355–356.

[20]*Ibid.*, p. 317.

[21]One of the priests at Hardwar suggested to me a simple twofold classification of sacred places: *Jal-tīrtha* and *Mandir-tīrtha*. At the former, purificatory bath is the chief activity, and at the latter, visit to a specific deity is the chief goal of the pilgrim.

It should be pointed out that on figure 5-2 and in table 5-3 the places where Viṣṇu is considered the presiding deity include all the places where the various incarnations of Viṣṇu are the presiding deities. Thus, places sacred to Kṛṣṇa, who is an incarnation of Viṣṇu, are included under Viṣṇu. If the various incarnations of Viṣṇu were treated separately, the table would have shown an overwhelming dominance of Śiva. Similarly, the various forms of Mother Goddess have been included in one category.

An examination of table 5-3 shows that when places mentioned as sacred by at least three of our sources are considered on an all-India scale, there are more places sacred to Śiva than to any other deity.

TABLE 5-4
ASSOCIATION OF CHIEF DEITIES WITH PLACES OF PILGRIMAGE (I)
(142 *tīrthas* as shown on maps 5-1 and 5-2)

	Śiva	Viṣṇu	Brahmā	Mother Goddess	Others or none	Total
Places*	53	43	2	27	21	146
Percent	36.3	29.5	1.3	18.5	14.4	100

*Total exceeds 142 because at four places two deities are equally important.

The overall leading position of Śiva as a deity of the Hindus is confirmed if we take all the 142 places shown on the map (fig. 5-1). Table 5-4 shows the association of deities with these places.

From a comparison of the above tables it is clear that whether all the 142 places or the 84 sacred places mentioned by three or more authorities are taken, the relative importance of the deities is Śiva, Viṣṇu, Mother Goddess, and Brahmā, in descending order. When only the fourth category is taken (see table 5-5), the relative importance of Śiva and Viṣṇu is reduced, while the Mother Goddess shows up much more prominently than is the case when 84 places are examined (compare table 5-3).

Since the selection of the sacred places of the fourth category (58 places) is based on a consensus of only two sources for each place, the resulting list may be more biased when compared with the first three categories. Such biases will remain unless a catalogue of all the possible sacred places is available. The list of the largest

TABLE 5-5

Association of Chief Deities with Places of Pilgrimage (II)
(of the Fourth Category)

	Śiva	Viṣṇu	Brahmā	Mother Goddess	Others or none	Total*
Places	20	16	1	13	10	60
Percent	33.3	26.7	1.6	21.7	16.7	100

*Total exceeds 58 because at two places two deities are equally important.

number of sacred places so far available is in *Kalyāṇa, Tīrthāṅka,* which describes 1,820 places in the whole of India. A 10 percent random sample from this list shows that the relative order of association of sacred places with deities remains the same as in table 5-5, although their proportion varies (see table 5-6).

TABLE 5-6

Association of Sacred Places with Chief Deities (II)
(10 percent random sample from *Kalyāṇa, Tīrthāṅka*)

	Śiva	Viṣṇu	Brahmā	Mother Goddess	Others or none	Total
Places	64	29	1	22	66	182
Percent	35.1	15.8	0.5	12.1	36.5	100

Note : Number of sacred places in the sample = 182.

In the above random sample there were only 14 sacred places included in the first three categories in figure 5-1. In other words, most sacred places in the sample are of relatively minor importance. We can conclude on the basis of this sample that the cult of Śiva in India is considerably more widespread than that of Viṣṇu. Second, the association of sacred places with minor deities of Hinduism greatly increases at lower-level shrines. Third, the Mother Goddess becomes much more prominent in relation to Viṣṇu at the lower-level sacred places (compare tables 5-3 and 5-6).

Places exclusively sacred to Brahmā are rare at the present time. In fact, out of the 84 places of categories one, two, and three there is only one place—Pushkar—which is exclusively sacred to this deity. The reason for the minor role of Brahmā lies perhaps in the very early decline of the popularity of this deity. Brahmā represents the principle of creation of the universe, Viṣṇu that of preservation, and Śiva that of ultimate dissolution. Within this cosmogonic schema the function of Brahmā has long been accomplished, that of Viṣṇu continues, while Śiva's function—destruction—has yet to come. The latter two functions give force to the propagation of the cult of Viṣṇu and Śiva by arousing reverence and fear respectively. On the other hand, Brahmā's function, which no longer has relevance to the physical order of the universe, lacks force whether of reverence or of fear. A. L. Basham sums up the decline of Brahmā's cult thus: "Brahmā . . . had a history of slow decline. In the early Buddhist scriptures he and Indra were the greatest of the gods, and in the *Mahābhārata,* he was still very important; but though depicted in medieval sculpture, sometimes with four faces, he was little worshipped after Gupta times."[22] Apart from the four main deities there are a number of others who have a restricted importance in the all-India context, but are prominent at the regional or subregional levels. Such deities are Gaṇeśa, Subrahmanya, Kārtikya, Sūrya, and some minor ones.

The data presented in tables 5-3 through 5-6 suggest that the main deities of Hinduism, which most probably are of pre-Aryan origins, namely, Śiva and the Mother Goddess, are together associated with more sacred places, at the all-India scale, than the major deities having clearly Aryan origins (Viṣṇu and Brahmā). This observation, combined with the ancient bases of the present pattern of sacred places, indicates that at least part of the explanation of the distribution of these sites may be sought in the spatial spread and the religious concepts of the ancient Dravidians. A recent report about the partial decipherment of the script of the Indus Valley civilization by Asko Parpola and his associates suggests that "important aspects of modern Indian civilization, like the pollution concept within the caste system, may be traced to the society and religion of the Proto-Dravidian Indus people with their huge public and private baths and complex drainage system."[23] It is possible that the Hindu concept of ritual purification by bathing is a contribution of the Dravidian civilization of the Indus Valley.

[22]*The Wonder That Was India,* p. 312.

[23]Association for Asian Studies, "The Proto-Dravidian Inscriptions of the Indus Civilization Being Deciphered," p. 87.

STODDARD'S ATTEMPT TO ACCOUNT FOR THE DISTRIBUTION OF HOLY PLACES

Stoddard is the only geographer who has made a full-fledged scientific attempt to account for the distribution of sacred places of the Hindus.[24] A brief discussion of his hypotheses is necessary here in order to bring out the difficulties involved in this problem.

Stoddard poses three hypotheses to account for the distribution of major Hindu holy sites and after analysis of his data comes to the conclusion that "in essence the three hypotheses pertaining to the distribution of holy sites and their relationship to other phenomena were found inadequate as stated" (p. 143). His first hypothesis is that "the major Hindu holy sites are distributed optimally relative to the Hindu population where optimality is defined in terms of minimizing aggregate travel distance" (p. 140). The second hypothesis states that "the distribution of the major holy sites is similar but not coincident to that of largest urban centers" (p. 142). The third hypothesis "explores the possibility that the distribution of certain social characteristics of the population might indicate the location of holy sites" (p. 142). For the last hypothesis he selects three social variables that may be related to the location of holy places: percent of caste Hindus, female literacy rate, and sex ratio. Data for each are presented by district as of 1961.

To this writer the first hypothesis appears to be intuitively unsound for two reasons. First, it is well known that some of the most renowned sacred places of the Hindus lie on the margins of dense population—for example, Badrinath, Kedarnath, Pushkar, Dwarka, Ramesvaram, and Puri. Second, and more important, the formulation of the hypothesis seems to go against the concept of *tīrtha-yātrā* (pilgrimage), which is essentially an austerity rather than an effort to minimize aggregate travel distance.

The second hypothesis can, in fact, be considered a corollary to the first one. Since the idea of optimality of spacing of urban settlements within economic space is derived from the postulated need to minimize aggregate travel, Stoddard's second hypothesis entails the same presumed explanatory factor as his first one. This can be regarded as one case of an urban system. However, we know that there are numerous sacred places, including many

[24]Stoddard, "Hindu Holy Sites in India."

renowned ones, which are not urban at all. Stoddard himself concluded that "the distribution of the holy sites is neither coincident nor similar to that of the major urban centers" (p. 142).

Having found his first two hypotheses inadequate, Stoddard turned to the possible association of sacred places with certain social characteristics of population as noted earlier. The social characteristics chosen by him are based on recent data, but the basic pattern of sacred places was established as early as the epic period. The present writer, therefore, finds it difficult to understand Stoddard's bases for seeking the possible relationship between holy sites and the selected social characteristics of population.

Even though Stoddard finds all three of his hypotheses inadequate to explain the distribution of Hindu holy sites, his study is valuable. His rigorous testing of these hypotheses suggests that future work ought not to ignore some of the basic concepts of Hinduism as well as the very early development of the pattern of the Hindu sacred places.

CONCLUSIONS

The modern spatial pattern of holy places is the result of a cumulative process of sanctification of sites, many of which have been considered sacred for at least two millennia. Explanation of this pattern, which has ancient religious moorings, cannot be fruitfully accomplished by relating it only to the modern distribution of Hindu population.

Our study shows a fairly strong association of Hindu sacred places with certain elements of the physical landscape, namely, flowing water and hilltops, and points to the symbolic meaning of these elements in Hindu religion. This, however, is far from a full explanation because Hinduism has absorbed many characteristics and sacred spots of Buddhism, of Jainism, and of several former tribal groups.

At the all-India scale, it appears that the major deities, whose origin is most probably pre-Aryan, are associated with more sacred places than the deities of Aryan origin. This observation points to the need for a deeper study of the religious concepts of pre-Aryan people, particularly the proto-Dravidians, because the sacred places of ancient origin may have been the cult spots of the proto-Dravidian people of the Indus civilization. At the present status of our research, however, it is not possible to advance a single theory which can satisfactorily explain the very complex spatial distribution of the Hindu sacred places.

The town of Mandi (Himachal Pradesh) as seen from a Siva temple. In the foreground is the symbolic mount of Siva, Nandi (the bull). In the center of the town, another temple provides the religious focus.

Circumambulation (*pradakṣinā*) is an important practice at the goddess shrines. P grims from Uttar Pradesh and Punjab perform the *dandavat pranām* at the *Vajreśv* temple, Kangra, in Himachal Pradesh, as they circumambulate the sanctum.

Priest-Pilgrim ties. A priest at Chintpurni showing the record of earlier visits of pilgrim and his ancestors. These records are used to establish the continuing prie pilgrim ties. The priests help the pilgrims in performing religious rites and ceremoni and in turn receive appropriate fees from the pilgrims.

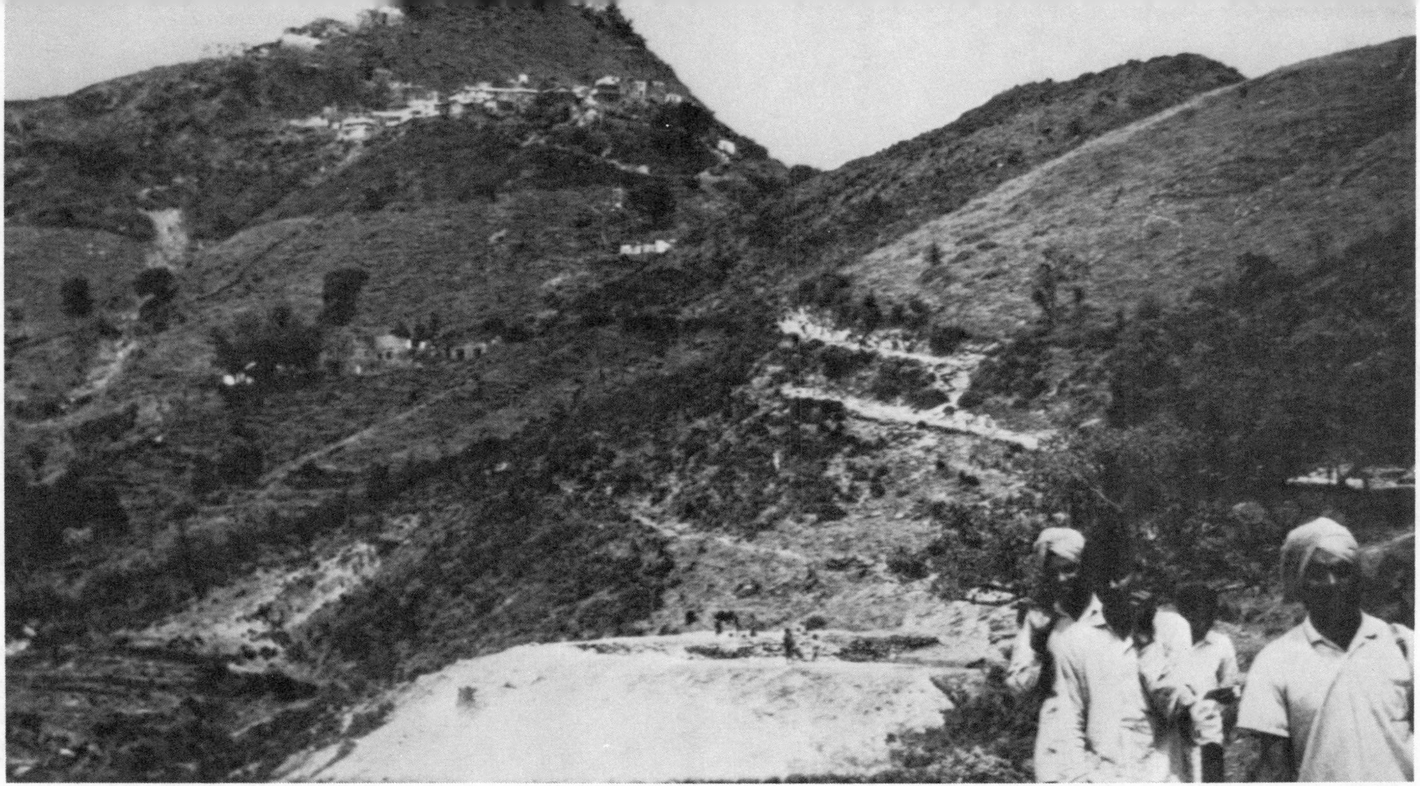

Pilgrims returning from the Naina Devi temple, situated on a pinnacle of the Siwalik hills.

Young boys clad in the garb of *sādhus* sing devotional songs (*bhetā*) on way to Naina Devi.

Family Planning Exhibition at Hardwar. Such exhibitions by the government are becoming increasingly useful for disseminating new ideas among pilgrims.

At Shiv Bari pilgrimage to the Siva temple is combined with fun and social gathering of relatives outside the temple precincts.

Badrinath. Deep in the Himalayas lies the picturesque temple of Badrinath, visited by pilgrims from all over India. The traditional high priest of the temple, called "Rāwal," is always from the State of Kerala.

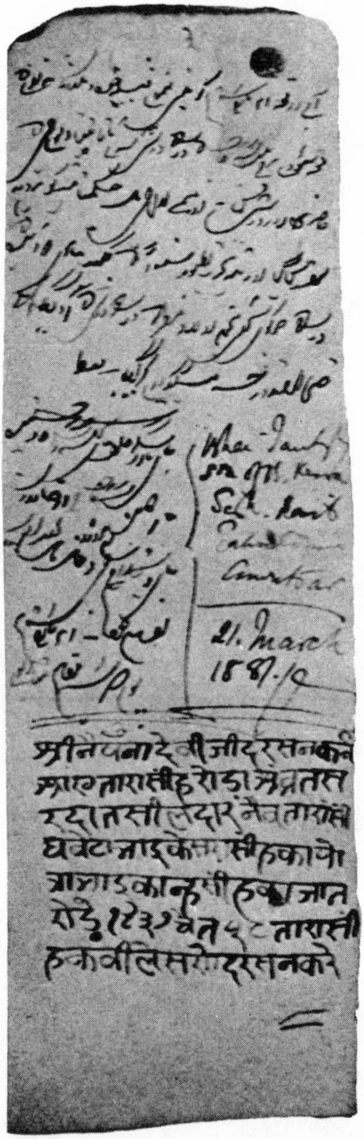

Pilgrim Records. A page from the *bahī* of a priest of Naina Devi. Such records are kept by priest families, and in some instances go back several generations. Social historians are beginning to realize the importance of these records.

Chapter VI

Perception of the Ranks of Sacred Places

INTRODUCTION

Hindu religious literature implicitly recognizes the fact that some holy places are more sacred than others, but no single system defines which particular sacred place is "the most sacred" for all times, for all regions, and for all the diverse sects. In a complex religion like Hinduism it is futile to look for a single system that classifies or ranks sacred places. Yet, religious tradition gives some of them special importance. This chapter gives a brief survey of attempts in the religious literature to provide a basis for ranking sacred places on a "scale of sanctity." Following this discussion, the writer presents his observations on the perception of ranks of sacred places by pilgrims interviewed at some shrines. The idea was to find out if there is any clear recognition of the rank of sacred places, and if so, what factors pilgrims take into account when ranking the sacred places.

RANKING OF SACRED PLACES IN TRADITIONAL HINDUISM

The Concept of Ranking the Sacred Places in the Purāṇas

The Puranic tradition classifies the *tīrthas* into four basic categories:[1] (1) the *Daiva Tīrthas,* (2) the *Āsura Tīrthas,* (3) the *Ārṣa Tīrthas,* (4) the *Mānuṣa Tīrthas.* This simple fourfold classification is not merely for convenience, but seems to have a hierarchical basis, as becomes evident from the following descriptions.

(1) The *Daiva Tīrthas*: These sacred places result directly from the benevolent divine acts of the three major deities of Hinduism, namely, Brahmā, Viṣṇu, and Śiva—all male deities. As Aiyangar states: "If the three gods have sanctified a *tīrtha* it is of utmost sanctity."[2] Illustrations of these provided by Aiyangar are Kāśī

[1] *Brahmapurāṇa,* Chapter LXX, Verse 16ff. as quoted in Aiyangar, ed., *Kṛtyakalpataru,* lix.

[2] *Ibid.*

(Varanasi), Puṣkara, Prabhāsa (Somnath). Similarly, these three major male deities have caused the most sacred rivers. Brahmā by his action created the Sarasvati, Śivā, the Gaṅgā and the Narmadā. Some springs and lakes associated with the three major deities are called *Daivakhāta*, or "dug by gods."[3]

(2) The *Āsura Tīrthas*: These sacred places are "associated" with demons, or *Asuras*. This association does not mean that demons created them. Instead, their sanctity derives from acts of the three major gods, who destroyed the demons, thus restoring moral order. The destructive acts of gods that result in the *Āsura Tīrthas* obviously differ from the benevolent divine acts related to *Daiva Tīrthas*. They are clearly of a lower order than the acts of creation, hence belong not only to the second class but also to the second order. Gaya illustrates such a sacred place, where Viṣṇu subdued the demon Gaya.[4] It is to be noted that although the place name Gaya derives from the name of the demon, the presiding deity at the sacred place is the god Viṣṇu, who vanquished the demon.

(3) The *Ārṣa Tīrthas*: The third type of *tīrthas* has been consecrated by the human actions of saints and sages through their austerities, penances, and sacrifices. One of the most important of such *tīrthas* is Naimiṣa in Uttar Pradesh.[5] However, not the actions of all kinds of people, but rather those of the religiously superior individuals, bestow sanctity. From the actions of gods in the first two categories we have moved down to the consecrating action of the saintly humans.

(4) The *Mānuṣa Tīrthas*: The fourth type of sacred places are those that have been sanctified theoretically by the rulers of solar and lunar dynasties.[6] These are the *tīrthas* where the rulers established a temple and duly consecrated it. Etymologically, the expression *mānuṣa tīrtha* should mean the "human sacred place." Here temporal authorities, not gods or holy men, are solely responsible for creating a sacred place. These acts are of a lower order than the acts of holy men; in turn, the acts of holy men are of lower order than those of the gods. Further, godly acts of

[3] *Ibid.*

[4] For Gaya mythology, see L. P. Vidyarthi, *The Sacred Complex in Hindu Gaya*, appendix I, pp. 113–117.

[5] For citations from ancient religious literature regarding Naimisa, see *Kalyāṇa, Tīrthāṅka*, pp. 109–110.

[6] Aiyangar, *op. cit.*, p. lix.

creation are of a higher order than godly acts of destruction. Thus, the fourfold "classification" in fact attempts to *rank* the orders of places that result from the orders of actions.

The Puranic ordering can by no means include all kinds of sacred places. For example, none of the above categories provides room for the sacred places of the Mother Goddess. The elaborate religious literature that has arisen around the goddess worship clearly attempts to recognize such major and minor *Śākta pīṭhas.*

The Concept of Major and Minor Śākta piṭhas

The recognized number of the *Śākta piṭhas,* or the seats of the Mother Goddess, is very large, as is evident from the excellent index of *Śākta pīṭhas* prepared by Sircar.[7] *Śākta pīṭhas* are traditionally associated with the various dismembered parts of the body of *Sati*—the consort of Śiva.[8] Sircar's comparison of the various traditions regarding the *Śākta pīṭhas* shows that four major and forty-six minor sacred places are usually recognized. The more venerated shrines are associated with the magically more potent organs of the goddess.[9] Thus the most important of the Śākta shrines—Kamakhya—is associated with the pudenda of the goddess.[10] Similarly, the skull of the goddess is venerated at the temple of Kalighat in Calcutta, and the tongue at Jwalamukhi in Himachal Pradesh. Other seats of the goddess are associated with her less potent organs. Evaluating the sanctity of the goddess's shrine according to the magical qualities of the different organs is obviously an attempt to rank in order the sacred places of the Mother Goddess. However, with the passage of time, numerous sacred places of the Mother Goddess have arisen, making the possible original ranking a matter of vague conjecture.

Traditional sectarian literature attaches special significance to the sacred places of the deity that the sect favors. Thus, although there are more holy and less holy places, it is impossible to find one accepted literary source that ranks all places for the entire body of Hinduism. Considering this, how do present-day pilgrims perceive the ranking of holy places?

[7]D. C. Sircar, "The Śākta Pīṭhas," *Journal of the Royal Asiatic Society* (B), Vol. XIV, No. 1, Appendix V.

[8]For details, see Sircar, pp. 10–41.

[9]See Agehananda Bharati, *The Tantric Tradition,* p. 90.

[10]Sircar, p. 36.

PERCEPTION OF THE RANK ORDER OF SACRED PLACES

The pilgrims' perception of the rank ordering of holy places is based on actual interviews with pilgrims at the selected sacred places. Interviewees were asked: "Which in your opinion are the three most sacred *tīrthas* in the whole of India?" It was hoped that the responses of pilgrims would indicate whether there was a high degree of consensus among the Hindu population regarding their sacred places. Although the question may appear to be a rather simple one, most respondents had to think hard to come up with an answer. The answer to this question naturally depended on many factors—for example, the names of other sacred places known to the individual, the opportunity of visiting them, the pilgrim's view of sanctity, perhaps his caste affiliations, or his familiarity with a particular region. Moreover, the mere fact that a pilgrim has chosen to come to a given place introduces a bias in favor of that place. Thus, although many biases and preferences may be built into the choices, yet certain useful observations can be made from these data.

The Most Sacred Place

Table 6-1 shows the perception of pilgrims regarding the most sacred place in the whole of India.[11] Several inferences can be made from this table.

(1) There is no absolute opinion regarding the holiest place. This simple fact underscores the basic differences between Hinduism on the one hand and Christianity, Islam, and Judaism on the other. It is possible that our results would have been different had the sample been taken in the villages and cities rather than at the place of pilgrimage. However, I feel that even then there would have been a great diversity of opinions. At Badrinath—one of the chief places of pilgrimage of India—as many as thirty-five different sacred places were mentioned by different pilgrims as the most sacred. The fact that only about 17 percent of the pilgrims *at* Badrinath consider it the most sacred place in India shows very clearly that even though they may have a bias in favor of this place, yet many find it impossible to consider it *the holiest* place.

[11]It was assumed that the place which a pilgrim named first was his first choice, that is, the most sacred place in the whole of India according to the pilgrim.

TABLE 6-1
PERCEPTION OF PILGRIMS REGARDING THE MOST SACRED PLACE IN THE WHOLE OF INDIA

Place of interview and number of responding pilgrims[1]	Most frequent choice, and percentage of pilgrims making this choice	Second most frequent choice, and percentage of pilgrims making choice	Third most frequent choice, and percentage of pilgrims making choice
Badrinath 400	Badrinath 17.25	Hardwar 9.25	Varanasi 7.00
Baijnath 100	Hardwar 37.00	Baijnath 7.00	(Amritsar) (Chamunda) (Vaishno Devi) 6.00
Bhagsunag 85	Hardwar 30.59	Bhagsunag 17.65	Jwalaji 10.59
Chintpurni 250	Chintpurni 22.80	Hardwar 20.00	Jwalaji 9.20
Hardwar 300	Hardwar 38.33	Varanasi 9.00	Badrinarain 8.67
Jwalaji 248	Hardwar 23.39	Jwalaji 10.48	Amritsar 10.08
Kangra 200	Hardwar 21.00	Kangra 14.50	Jwalaji 5.00
Naina Devi 122	Hardwar 32.79	Naina Devi 13.90	Anandpur Sahib 9.84
Rewalsar (i)[2] 100	Rewalsar 9.00	Hardwar 8.00	Buddha-Gaya 6.00
Rewalsar (ii) 100	Hardwar 43.00	Manikaran 5.00	Badrinath 5.00
Shiv Bari 100	Hardwar 30.00	Amritsar 14.00	Chintpurni 7.00

NOTE : Each of the places in parentheses had equal value.
[1]Only those of whom the question was actually asked, irrespective of the response.
[2]Because of markedly different composition of the pilgrims at the *Sissoo* Fair (i) and at *Vaiśākhī* (ii) it was necessary to show comparative data for the two occasions.

Similarly, although Varanasi is often spoken of as the "Mecca of the Hindus," our data show that such an appellation does not reflect the perception of pilgrims.

(2) Pilgrims to the Himachal shrines, with the exception of Chintpurni and Rewalsar,[12] consider Hardwar to be the most sacred place although the highest ranking of Hardwar is not due to an absolute majority rating. The bias for Chintpurni is clear in its highest rating, but at other places pilgrims select Hardwar rather than the place of their visit as the most sacred place. The special sanctity of Hardwar lies perhaps in the fact that this is the place where most Hindus from Punjab, Himachal Pradesh, and western Uttar Pradesh consign the ashes of the dead to the Ganga. Hardwar has intimate association with the ceremonies of life cycle and of the life after death. Such associations naturally are reflected in the choice of Hardwar. Since most pilgrims to the Himachal shrines are from Punjab, Himachal Pradesh, and western Uttar Pradesh, and since it is these regions which are intimately connected to Hardwar for the life-cycle rites, the high rank of Hardwar is easily understandable.

(3) The pilgrims to Hardwar, who should have had every reason to consider Hardwar the most sacred place in the whole of India, in fact named thirty different places in response to our question. The interviews at Hardwar were carried out on one of the holiest occasions—the *Ardhakumbha Melā*—and yet there was a great diversity of opinions about the most sacred places in India. It shows that even though pilgrims have a bias for a sacred place, this is not sufficiently strong to ignore other sacred places. Thus we can infer that in India as a whole the idea of sanctity is diffuse.

(4) Table 6-1 shows that at five sacred places the place of interview itself was the *second* most frequently mentioned as "the most sacred place in the whole of India." The bias of the pilgrims is much more clearly reflected in favor of the place of their visit.

The Second and Third Most Sacred Places

The most general inference is that pilgrims at any given sacred place are keen to give *it* high praise, but select also other places which they know best—usually in Himachal Pradesh, Punjab, or western Uttar Pradesh. These places mean more to them than distant ones whatever their national repute. In other words, the

[12]At Rewalsar, the *Sissoo* fair attracts large numbers of Buddhist pilgrims for whom Hardwar, a purely Hindu sacred place, has less meaning.

pilgrims seemed to select sacred places not primarily on the basis of their repute in religious literature or their national importance but rather because of the relationships these places may have with *their* lives. In any case, it is very difficult for pilgrims to neatly rank sacred places because there is no single clear system for the ranking of sanctity in Hinduism.

Other Answers of Pilgrims about Ranking Sacred Places

A significant proportion of pilgrims at all sacred places either regarded all sacred places as equally holy or expressed their inability

TABLE 6-2
PROPORTION OF PILGRIMS WHO BELIEVE ALL SACRED PLACES ARE EQUALLY SACRED OR ANSWER "DON'T KNOW" (first choice)

Place of interview	Number of responding pilgrims	Percentage replying "All equal"	Percentage replying "Don't know"	Total of percentage columns
Badrinath	400	28.75	2.25	31.00
Baijnath	100	1.00	5.00	6.00
Bhagsunag	85	0	0	0
Chintpurni	250	16.40	2.40	18.80
Hardwar	100	5.00	3.00	8.00
Jwalaji	248	8.06	6.45	14.51
Kangra	200	7.00	6.50	13.50
Naina Devi	122	8.20	7.38	15.58
Rewalsar (i)[1]	100	3.00	53.00[2]	56.00[2]
Rewalsar (ii)[1]	100	3.00	14.00	17.00
Shiv Bari	100	2.00	7.00	9.00

[1]Because of marked ethnic differences at Rewalsar, comparison of two occasions is necessary.

[2]This high percentage is due to the aversion of many Buddhist pilgrims to this question. Moreover, in several instances the Tibetan speakers could not understand us or were not willing to talk to us. In some cases we were thought to be government officials checking the passes of Tibetan refugees.

to answer the question positively. Table 6-2 shows the result of these responses.

At most of the sacred places the pilgrims did, even if somewhat reluctantly, come up with their choice of the most sacred place. At Badrinath and Chintapurni the "all equal" answer does assume importance, perhaps because of a relatively larger proportion of those classes of people who have traveled considerably and visited many places of pilgrimage. Therefore they are less sure which place ranks first. In fact, many pilgrims questioned why it is even necessary or desirable to rank sacred places.

The answer "do not know" may be due to a variety of reasons. It may mean that some pilgrims actually do not know the names

TABLE 6-3
PERCENTAGE OF PILGRIMS WHO RESPONDED "DO NOT KNOW" TO THE QUESTION REGARDING THE THREE MOST SACRED PLACES IN THE WHOLE OF INDIA

	First choice	Second choice	Third choice
Badrinath	2	10	15
Baijnath	5	5	6
Bhagsunag	None	5	12
Chintpurni	2	11	18
Hardwar	3	8	15
Jwalaji	6	12	21
Kangra	6	11	22
Naina Devi	7	17	24
Rewalsar (i)[1]	53[2]	57[2]	68[2]
Rewalsar (ii)[1]	14	19	31
Shiv Bari	7	11	19

NOTE : Number of total respondents is the same as in table 6-2. All percentages are rounded to the nearest whole number.

[1]See table 6-2, note 1.

[2]See table 6-2, note 2.

of sacred places. More probably it means either a reluctance on the part of pilgrims to rank sacred places or the difficulty of ranking sacred places. We feel that unless the ranking of sacred places over the entire country has some clear meaning in the life of pilgrims the question itself becomes insignificant. Since even minor nearby shrines may be more intimately related to the life of the people than the far-flung ones, it makes no sense to them to consider the value of their sanctity.

It is interesting to compare the "do not know" response (table 6-3) of pilgrims for the "three most sacred places in the whole of India." Although most pilgrims in our sample were usually able to tell us their three choices, the fact that in many instances the second and third choices were not made needs some explanation. The first choice was easy for all pilgrims except at Rewalsar.[13] However, in all cases the second and third choices became progressively more difficult for the pilgrims (table 6-3). Excluding Rewalsar (*Sissoo* fair), between 6 percent and 31 percent of the pilgrims at different places could not think of their third choice of a sacred place. The conclusion is obvious. Among the relatively few sacred places with which the pilgrims interact they may have one favorite shrine. The others become progressively remote from their sphere of interaction, hence their impression is faint, making it difficult for the pilgrims to recall and compare them at a moment's notice.

PERCEPTION OF "THE MOST SACRED PLACE" AS RELATED TO CASTE[14]

Procedure and Empirical Observations

Caste in India is one of the most pervasive variables in the study of social and religious phenomena. Therefore, intuitively it is felt that caste may have significant bearing on the ranking of sacred places by the pilgrims. Such a study, however, is complicated by the fact that widely different numbers of individual castes may be present at different sacred places. For example, only 2 members of the scheduled castes were encountered at Badrinath in a total pilgrim sample of 400 (table 6-4). On the other hand, at Jwalaji the comparative figures were 44 in a sample of 248 pilgrims

[13]At Rewalsar the difficulty of communicating with Tibetan speakers resulted in unusually large negative response.

[14]For explanations of caste groupings, see the appendix.

(table 6-8). Furthermore, even though the total sample of pilgrims may be adequate for certain purposes (e.g., determining the field of a sacred place), the sample for individual castes or caste groups may not be adequate for comparing their perception of the most sacred place.

With such limitations in mind, I shall examine below the possible relationship between the caste groups of the pilgrims (at selected sacred places) and their perceptions of "the most sacred place." The criterion for the selection of sacred places for this analysis is that there should be a total of at least twenty-five pilgrims in two or more caste groups who considered the given place as "the most sacred."[15] This leaves us with Badrinath, Baijnath, Chintpurni, Hardwar, Jwalaji, and Kangra. The pilgrims' responses to the question of "the most sacred place" were compared at each place. The data are presented in tables 6-4 through 6-9. (All percentages

TABLE 6-4
PILGRIMS OF SELECTED CASTE GROUPS AT BADRINATH WHO CONSIDER BADRINATH OR HARDWAR OR VARANASI THE MOST SACRED PLACE

	BADRINATH		HARDWAR		VARANASI	
Selected castes	Number	Percentage of caste group	Number	Percentage of caste group	Number	Percentage of caste group
Brahman	23	19	12	10	9	7
Khatri-Arora	6	10	8	13	5	8
Other mercantile castes	24	18	10	7	8	6
Total of all castes	60		37		28	

NOTE: Total pilgrims of all castes 400*
Brahman 120
Khatri-Arora 63
Other mercantile castes 82

*These figures represent those pilgrims who replied to our question "Which in your opinion are the three most sacred *tīrthas* in the whole of India?"

[15]Thus Bhagsunag, Naina Devi, Rewalsar, and Shiv Bari are eliminated because less than twenty-five pilgrims at each of these places regarded any given place as "the most sacred." Mansa Devi and Ujjain are excluded too because the question related to three most sacred places was not asked there. For details regarding the caste groupings, see the appendix.

are rounded to the nearest whole number.) With the help of these data the following observations may be made regarding each

TABLE 6-5
PILGRIMS OF SELECTED CASTE GROUPS AT BAIJNATH WHO CONSIDER HARDWAR THE MOST SACRED PLACE

Selected castes	Number	Percentage of caste group
Brahman	19	46
Rajput	11	35
Total of all castes	37	

NOTE : Total pilgrims of all castes 100*
Brahman 41
Rajput 31
All others 28
*See table 6-4.

TABLE 6-6
PILGRIMS OF SELECTED CASTE GROUPS AT CHINTPURNI WHO CONSIDER CHINTPURNI OR HARDWAR THE MOST SACRED PLACE

	CHINTPURNI		HARDWAR	
Selected castes	Number	Percentage of caste group	Number	Percentage of caste group
Brahman	18	28	17	27
Rajput	5	16	9	29
Khatri-Arora	10	22	7	16
Other mercantile castes	7	23	7	23
Scheduled castes	7	27	3	12
Total of all castes	57		50	

NOTE : Total pilgrims of all castes 250*
Brahman 64
Rajput 31
Khatri-Arora 45
Other mercantile castes 30
Scheduled castes 26
All others 54
*See table 6-4.

selected place. These observations will be discussed at the end of this section.

(1) At Badrinath (table 6-4): The pilgrims at Badrinath considered Badrinath, Hardwar, and Varanasi to be "the most sacred places in the whole of India," in descending order. The Brahmans and the "other mercantile castes"[16] seem to favor Badrinath much more than the Khatri-Arora caste group, which is itself a very important mercantile caste group of the Punjab and adjoining areas. On the other hand, the Khatri-Arora caste group seems to rate Hardwar higher than do the Brahmans or the mercantile castes. The opinion of the three caste groups regarding Varanasi shows little difference.

(2) At Baijnath (table 6-5): Thirty-seven percent of the pilgrims at Baijnath considered Hardwar to be the most sacred place. The Brahmans seem to favor Hardwar more than do the Rajputs. The reasons for this preference are far from clear, but with total samples of only 41 and 31 in those two groups respec-

TABLE 6-7
PILGRIMS OF SELECTED CASTE GROUPS AT HARDWAR WHO CONSIDER HARDWAR OR VARANASI OR BADRINATH THE MOST SACRED PLACE

	HARDWAR		VARANASI		BADRINATH	
Selected castes	Number	Percentage of caste group	Number	Percentage of caste group	Number	Percentage of caste group
Brahman	31	39	13	16	6	8
Rajput	14	48	1	3	4	14
Khatri-Arora	28	33	8	10	5	6
Other mercantile castes	22	31	4	6	10	14
Total of all castes	115		27		26	

NOTE: Total pilgrims of all castes 300*

Brahman	79
Rajput	29
Khatri-Arora	84
Other mercantile castes	71
All others	37

*See table 6-4.

[16]Henceforth in the text referred to simply as mercantile castes.

tively, the chance of a biased response would appear quite possible.

(3) At Chintpurni (table 6-6): There is not much difference in the number of pilgrims favoring Chintpurni over Hardwar. However, the Rajputs seem to be less inclined toward this place than the other castes. Apparently the Brahmans and the scheduled castes seem to favor this place more than do the Rajputs.

There is a marked difference in the caste groups regarding the selection of Hardwar. Both Brahmans and Rajputs show a much greater tendency to select Hardwar than do the scheduled castes.

(4) At Hardwar (table 6-7): The Brahmans and even more so the Rajputs tend to select Hardwar, compared with the Khatri-Arora group and the mercantile castes. In each case, however, over 30 percent of the caste group selected Hardwar as the most sacred place. Varanasi is obviously favored more by the Brahmans than

TABLE 6-8
PILGRIMS OF SELECTED CASTE GROUPS AT JWALAJI WHO CONSIDER AMRITSAR OR HARDWAR OR JWALAJI THE MOST SACRED PLACE

	AMRITSAR		HARDWAR		JWALAJI	
Selected castes	Number	Percentage of caste group	Number	Percentage of caste group	Number	Percentage of caste group
Brahman	3	6	19	39	6	12
Khatri-Arora	0	0	14	34	2	5
Other mercantile castes	3	8	7	19	2	5
Cultivating castes	3	12	3	12	5	20
Scheduled castes	9	20	8	18	5	11
Total of all castes	25		58		26	

NOTE: Total pilgrims of all castes 248*

Brahman	49
Khatri-Arora	41
Other mercantile castes	37
Cultivating castes	25
Scheduled castes	44
All others	52

*See table 6-4.

by any other caste groups. Badrinath, on the other hand, is favored more by the Rajputs and mercantile castes than by the Brahmans and the Khatri-Arora group.

(5) At Jwalaji (Jwalamukhi) (Table 6-8): Hardwar is the most favored place followed at a distance by Jwalaji and Amritsar, both of which were selected by about equal numbers of pilgrims. Clearly the Brahman and Khatri-Arora castes tend to select Hardwar more than do the cultivating castes, the scheduled castes, and the mercantile castes. On the other hand, the cultivating castes seem to favor Jwalaji rather than Hardwar as their first choice.

The appearance of Amritsar in our data as one of the most sacred places is interesting because it is of little importance from the purely Hindu religious viewpoint. The fact that this sacred place is especially mentioned by the scheduled castes is a reflection of the religion of the scheduled castes—many of whom at our place of interview were *Mazhabi* Sikhs. The Sikhs consider Amritsar the most sacred place of their religion.

TABLE 6-9
PILGRIMS OF SELECTED CASTE GROUPS AT KANGRA WHO CONSIDER HARDWAR OR KANGRA THE MOST SACRED PLACE

	HARDWAR		KANGRA	
Selected castes	Number	Percentage of caste group	Number	Percentage of caste group
Brahman	10	21	6	12
Rajput	3	10	5	16
Khatri-Arora	7	24	1	3
Other mercantile castes	7	23	7	23
Cultivating castes	6	19	6	19
Total of all castes	42		29	

NOTE: Total pilgrims of all castes 200*

Brahman	48
Rajput	31
Khatri-Arora	29
Other mercantile castes	30
Cultivating castes	32
All others	30

*See table 6-4.

(6) At Kangra (table 6-9): Hardwar once again emerges as the most sacred place according to the pilgrims at Kangra, followed by Kangra itself.

Except the Rajputs, all other caste groups seem to favor Hardwar almost equally. The mercantile castes and the cultivating castes tend to select Kangra much more frequently than is the case with the Khatri-Arora caste group.

Analysis of the Empirical Observations

At any given sacred place the perception of different caste groups of pilgrims regarding the most sacred place varies, but the differences are marked in some cases and are only minor in others. Where the sample size of caste groups is small the probability of bias is bound to be high.

The difference between the Brahmans and the Khatri-Arora group regarding their perception of Badrinath is noticeable. The difference between the Brahmans and the scheduled castes at Jwalaji regarding their perception of Amritsar and Hardwar is even more marked—the Brahmans giving more weight to Hardwar, the scheduled castes to Amritsar. Similarly at Chintpurni, the Brahmans give more importance to Hardwar than do the scheduled castes.

There are only minor differences between the Khatri-Arora group and the mercantile caste group at Hardwar, Chintpurni, and Kangra regarding their choice of Hardwar and Chintpurni. However, these differences are considerable regarding their perception of Badrinath and Kangra. The pilgrims who constitute the "other mercantile castes" at Badrinath are derived from a much wider field than this caste group as represented at Chintpurni. The Khatri-Arora caste group largely belongs to Punjab and the adjoining areas. These different origins of the pilgrims may be reflected in the differences in the perception of Badrinath as the most sacred place. The differences in the perception of Kangra by the two caste groups are almost certainly a result of the different areal origin of these castes. Most pilgrims of the mercantile castes at Kangra belonged to western Uttar Pradesh while the Khatri-Arora group (no matter where their present home is) were almost exclusively Punjabi. The goddess at Kangra is venerated more by the pilgrims from western Uttar Pradesh than from Punjab.

I feel that caste differences, where they are fortified also by regional differences, may result in a greater variation of the perception of sanctity of a given place. Different castes from the same region (excepting scheduled castes) normally do not show wide variations in the selection of the holiest place unless a particular caste also has strong sectarian bias. We have noted above the greater preference of Brahmans than of scheduled castes for Hardwar. There seem to be at least two reasons for this. First, the importance of Hardwar is based on the Brahmanic rituals and concepts. Such rituals have a limited meaning for many members of the scheduled castes. However, as some of the scheduled castes adopt higher caste Hindu values and practices, Hardwar will presumably assume greater importance to them than it hitherto has. Second, many scheduled-caste pilgrims were Sikhs, which suggests a limited significance of the purely Hindu places of pilgrimage in their life.

The overall relationship between the caste groups and their perception of sacred places is not very clear. Perhaps greater clarity could be achieved by taking appropriate samples from the fields of certain sacred places after those fields have been outlined on the basis of pilgrim interviews at the desired sacred places.

Two-Caste Comparison of Ranking Sacred Places—Examples

If caste is a significant variable in the selection of sacred places, it should be reflected in the choices made by the ritually higher castes on the one hand and the scheduled castes on the other. We shall compare the first choice of the mercantile castes with that of the scheduled castes at two places of pilgrimage. The mercantile castes, rather than Brahmans, have been selected for comparison with the scheduled castes because the former, apart from being in the category of ritually higher castes, usually seem to be more pilgrimage-oriented, hence are familiar with more sacred places. Also, they are, on the whole, economically better off than the Brahmans and are certainly so in comparison with the scheduled castes. Thus, the mercantile and the scheduled castes should be good examples of polarity of perception of the ranks of sacred places, should caste be a determining factor.

Table 6-10 compares the mercantile-caste pilgrims with the scheduled-caste pilgrims insofar as their choice of the most sacred

TABLE 6-10

TWO-CASTE COMPARISON OF THE PERCEPTION OF THE MOST SACRED PLACES (*Navarātrās* 1968)

Mercantile Castes			Scheduled Castes		
Sacred Place chosen	Number making choice	Percentage of the caste	Sacred place chosen	Number making choice	Percentage of the caste
		At Chintpurni			
Chintpurni	7	23.3	Chintpurni	7	26.9
Hardwar	7	23.3	Hardwar	3	11.5
Kangra	3	10.0	Amritsar	2	7.7
Badrinath	2	6.7	Jwalaji	2	7.7
Jwalaji	2	6.7	Vaishno Devi	2	7.7
Varanasi	2	6.7	Badrinath	1	3.9
Amarnath	1	3.3	Balmiki	1	3.9
Rajghat	1	3.3	Kartarpur	1	3.8
Rameshvaram	1	3.3	Malpur	1	3.8
Vaishno Devi	1	3.3	Prayag	1	3.8
			Varanasi	1	3.8
Total	27	(of 30 belonging to mercantile castes)	Total	22	(of 26 belonging to scheduled castes)
		At Jwalaji			
Hardwar	7	18.9	Amritsar	9	20.4
Amritsar	3	8.1	Hardwar	8	18.2
Badrinath	3	8.1	Jwalaji	5	11.4
Jagannath Puri	3	8.1	Ramtirath	3	6.8
Jwalaji	2	5.4	Beasa	2	4.5
Prayag	2	5.4	Chintpurni	2	4.5
Vaishno Devi	2	5.4	Mathura	2	4.5
Amarnath	1	2.7	Patna	2	4.5
Brindaban	1	2.7	Kartarpur	1	2.3
Keler	1	2.7	Mansa Devi	1	2.3
Kedernath	1	2.7	Prayag	1	2.3
			Rayasahib	1	2.3
Total	26	(of 37 belonging to mercantile castes)	Taran Taran	1	2.3
			Varanasi	1	2.3
			Total	39	(of 44 belonging to scheduled castes)

place is concerned. Two sacred places are selected at which the pilgrims' responses are compared. At both of these places

(Chintpurni and Jwalaji) a comparable number of the two caste groups was present. Also the occasion of pilgrimage was the same, that is, *Navarātrās* of *Caitra* (1968).

Table 6-10 shows that the mercantile castes considered Chintpurni and Hardwar at the same level—an equal number of the members of this caste group selected the two places. However, the former place was ranked clearly higher by the members of the scheduled castes. This difference in the perceived rank of Hardwar vis-a-vis Chintpurni does not seem to be a mere chance, because at Jwalaji too the mercantile-caste group ranked Hardwar at the top while the scheduled castes gave it the second position, although not very clearly. Some of the reasons for such ranking have been briefly given already. On the whole, the mercantile castes seem to have ranked such places high as reflecting more clearly their accepted sanctity in the traditional Hindu religious literature. The scheduled castes, on the other hand, do not seem to select such places with the same frequency; they seem to select several places which are of local importance, or which in fact are not primarily Hindu places of pilgrimage. Perhaps a larger sample of both of the caste groups would have given a clearer picture. It should nevertheless be pointed out that the chasm that divides the so-called higher castes from the scheduled castes because of the rules of ritual pollution is not as clearly perceptible, in regard to their comparative ranking of sacred places, as the difference of caste would have suggested. The reasons for the less noticeable differences in ranking sacred places despite sharp caste differentiation may lie in the sociology of Hinduism. The ritually "lower" castes commonly try to emulate several aspects of the religious and social practices of the so-called higher castes. This process, usually called "Sanskritization," would result in a blurring of the differences between the ritually higher and the lower castes so far as the perception of the ranks of sacred places is concerned.[17] In other words, the scheduled castes would also like to regard the same places as most holy as do the so-called higher castes. However, because of their scant knowledge of the literary religious tradition, and their limited ability to visit many distant sacred places (a

[17]For a full explanation of the concept "Sanskritization," see M. N. Srinivas, *Religion and Society Among the Coorgs of India*. Also see his *Social Change in Modern India*, chap. 1, "Sanskritization." In this essay Srinivas reexamines the scope of this concept in the light of studies done by D. F. Pocock and Milton Singer.

function of their low economic status), they may not be able to state their names as readily as can the mercantile or other Hindu castes.

In the case of the scheduled castes of the Punjab, particularly the *Mazhabi* Sikhs, "Sanskritization" may not be the best appellation for the process of emulation of higher caste practices by lower castes. The *Mazhabi* Sikhs of the Punjab seem to have been changing their customs and ideology in the direction of the religiously more orthodox Sikhs. It is not a mere coincidence, then, that many of them stated Amritsar as the most sacred place in India. In fact, at Jwalaji the scheduled-caste pilgrims (mostly *Mazhabi* Sikhs) rated Amritsar over Hardwar and also mentioned several other places sacred exclusively to the Sikhs.

CONCLUSIONS

The lack of a single clear system in Hindu religious tradition establishing the rank order of sacred places is mirrored in the varied perceptions by pilgrims about the holiest places in India today. The variety of cults and castes and the long, involved development of numerous sects militate against any single, universally accepted system of ranking. In the absence of such a religious tradition of ranks of sacred places, the familiarity with sacred places based upon their intimate role in the life of pilgrims remains the chief basis of perception of rank. The ranks are not clearly defined for the entire country, resulting in a diffuse perception of what is the holiest place. There seems to be a tendency on the part of the so-called higher castes, particularly the Brahmans and the mercantile castes, to select the more well-known sacred places because these castes as a whole are more familiar with the written tradition of Hinduism. On the other hand, the scheduled castes tend to select some rather local sacred places along with the more famous ones. Although such differences are perceptible, they are less profound than may be suggested by the deep-seated caste differences. This less-than-expected difference in the ranking of sacred places may be the result of the trend of the scheduled castes toward "Sanskritization."

Chapter VII

Determination of Levels of Sacred Places

INTRODUCTION

It has been noted already that the pilgrims' perception of the ranks of sacred places is unclear because of the lack of a single system of beliefs, the varied social structure, and a high degree of regional cultural diversity in India. There are, nevertheless, sacred places whose pilgrim field is the whole of India, while other places draw their pilgrims from more restricted areas. Thus, certain spatial levels of sacred places suggest themselves. It is tempting to call them "levels of sanctity," but we shall refrain from doing so because we have no direct means of measuring differences in sanctity. We can speak here only in terms of levels of interaction. In the following pages of this chapter we shall suggest the empirical bases for identifying certain levels of sacred places. The identification and nomenclature of levels discussed below is not to be regarded as an exercise in taxonomy. On the contrary, this ordering of sacred places is intended to be a useful preliminary step to an understanding of a partial integration of cultural elements at various levels of spatial interaction.

RANKING OF SACRED PLACES ACCORDING TO AVERAGE DISTANCE TRAVELED

As the device for ordering the sacred places, we have used distance traveled by pilgrims. This is done in two steps: first, by taking the average distance traveled per pilgrim, and second, by calculating the standard deviation of pilgrimage distances, which gives a measure of the dispersion of the pilgrimage field at each place. The fields of sacred places have been portrayed in figures 7-1 through 7-13.

Procedure

The district headquarters have been taken as the points of origin of the pilgrims. For the sample of pilgrims at each of the places studied the average distance per pilgrimage has been calculated. All distances calculated are straight-line, for reasons of simplicity. Even if the distances were calculated on the basis of actual distance traveled, the refinement achieved would not have changed the relative ranks. Furthermore, a pilgrim who comes from a long distance usually visits a number of other shrines on the way to accumulate merit. Thus, the circuitous route that a long-distance pilgrim takes poses the problem of how much distance was traveled specifically for the terminal sacred place. For the sake of uniformity, straight-line distances between the district headquarters of the pilgrims' districts of origin and the sacred places seem quite satisfactory for our purpose, except for those holy places whose field is more or less confined to the district itself. The places whose fields are confined almost exclusively to one district are Baijnath, Bhagsunag, Rewalsar (during the *Vaiśākhī* fair), and Shiv Bari. Most of the pilgrims at those places come from the nearby villages, less than fifteen miles away. However, since we are measuring the distances from the district headquarters, the distances are overstated in the case of Baijnath and Shiv Bari.[1] Bhagsunag is less than two miles straight distance from Dharmsala, the district headquarters for Kangra district. Although most pilgrims to Bhagsunag came either from Dharmsala or from villages in the immediate vicinity of this place, the average distance in this case is, nevertheless, probably slightly understated. At Rewalsar during the *Vaiśākhī* fair most pilgrims were from nearby villages. The average distance there seems to be nearly correct. The fact remains that in terms of average distance traveled by pilgrims, the four places noted above are of local importance only.[2]

Empirical Findings

On the basis of average distance traveled per pilgrim, the rank of sacred places studied is shown in table 7-1. Some comments on this table are necessary. At Ujjain and Hardwar, the pilgrims come

[1]In both cases the respective district headquarters are farther away from the sacred place than the actual places of origin of most pilgrims to these places.

[2]If large-scale (1″ : 1 mile) topographic maps had been available, it would have been possible to calculate the actual straight-line distances from the pilgrims' villages. Large-scale maps of Himachal Pradesh, however, were not obtainable because of government restrictions.

TABLE 7-1
RANKING OF SACRED PLACES ACCORDING TO AVERAGE DISTANCE PER PILGRIM
(rounded to the nearest mile)

Sacred place	Number of pilgrims in sample	Rank	Average distance
Badrinath	400	1	490
Hardwar	800	2	176
Kangra	450	3	173
Jwalaji	500	4	123
Ujjain[1]	500	5	113
Chintpurni (1st occasion)	500	6	104
Rewalsar (1st occasion)	100	7	77[2]
Naina Devi (1st occasion)	494	8	58
Mansa Devi (1st occasion)	250	9	53
Shiv Bari (1st occasion)	100	10	35
Baijnath (1st occasion)	100	11	27
Bhagsunag	85	12	2

NOTE : For the actual names of the occasions and dates, see the introduction. For a comparison of average distance at two occasions, see table 7-3.

[1]Ujjain is the only major sacred place where a number of local inhabitants of a large city were included in the sample. If, however, we exclude the local pilgrims, the average distance per pilgrim comes to 134.31 miles, which places it above Jwalaji in rank. Ujjain is more centrally located with respect to its pilgrim field compared with Badrinath or Kangra. This fact also results in a lower average distance per pilgrim.

[2]If the second occasion is used, the average distance is about 14 miles. The first occasion is used here simply for the sake of uniformity with other places. Later in the text, the variations of average distance by occasion are discussed.

throughout the year. However, during the *Kumbha* and *Ardha Kumbha* fairs at Hardwar and during the *Siṃhastha* fair at Ujjain the proportion of the regional element in the pilgrimage is greatly increased.[3] Thus, when a sample is taken at the time of these huge fairs, it is likely to show this regional effect, and suppresses the fact that both these places have all-India fields. An alternative would have been to study the fields of Hardwar and Ujjain by taking samples of pilgrims at frequent intervals throughout the year excluding the years of the *Kumbha* fair. However, this could not be done because of limitations of time. Badrinath's average pilgrim field includes that of Hardwar because almost all pilgrims going to Badrinath pass through Hardwar and bathe in the Ganga. The average distance of pilgrims in our study refers to the specific occasion rather than to the situation throughout the year.[4]

Taking average distance as the sole criterion for the ranking of sacred places, several levels seem to emerge rather clearly as shown in table 7-2. However, we have pointed out earlier that at Baijnath and Shiv Bari the distances are overestimated; therefore, levels five and six may be combined.

TABLE 7-2
LEVELS OF SACRED PLACES STUDIED ON THE BASIS OF AVERAGE DISTANCE TRAVELED BY PILGRIMS

Level	Sacred places
1. (highest)	Badrinath
2.	Hardwar, Kangra
3.	Chintpurni, Jwalaji, Ujjain
4.	Mansa Devi, Naina Devi, Rewalsar
5.	Baijnath, Shiv Bari
6. (lowest)	Bhagsunag

[3]The *Kumbha* fair falls every twelve years, and the *Ardha Kumbha* ("half" *Kumbha*) comes six years after each *Kumbha*. The *Siṃhastha* fair at Ujjain also falls every twelve years. The dates of occurrence of these fairs are published in the traditional almanacs called *Pañcāṅgs* published in regional languages. The Government of India has been publishing the *Rashtriya Panchang* (English) since 1957. Apart from other information, this annual publication gives the dates of religious festivals of different communities. See also Dilip Kumar Roy and Indra Devi, *Kumbha, India's Ageless Festival.*

[4]For the names and dates of occasions at which samples were taken, see the Introduction, table 1-1.

Some of the sacred places show marked change in their pilgrim fields depending on the occasion. For example, if the sample of pilgrims at Hardwar were taken at the same time as at Badrinath, Hardwar probably would be of the same level as Badrinath because (as was pointed out) pilgrims going to Badrinath almost invariably visit Hardwar, which is on the way to Badrinath. Kangra, Jwalaji, Chintpurni, Rewalsar, and to a lesser extent, Mansa Devi and Naina Devi show a considerable variability in their fields according to the occasions.[5] Table 7-3 shows this effect. This situation is partly

TABLE 7-3
AVERAGE PILGRIM FIELD AT TWO DIFFERENT OCCASIONS FOR SIX SACRED PLACES
(in miles)

	Number of pilgrims in sample	Average field	Mean of the average fields
BAIJNATH			
First occasion, *Śivarātri*	100	27	
Second occasion, Monday of *Śrāvaṇa*	100	26	
			26.5
CHINTPURNI			
First occasion, *Navarātrās* of *Caitra*	500	104	
Second occasion, *Śrāvaṇa Aṣṭamī*	300	72	
			88
MANSA DEVI			
First occasion, *Navarātrās* of *Caitra*	250	58	
Second occasion, *Śrāvaṇa Aṣṭamī*	175	36	
			44.5
NAINA DEVI			
First occasion, *Navarātrās* of *Caitra*	494	58	
Second occasion, *Śrāvaṇa Aṣṭamī*	400	72	
			65.0
REWALSAR			
First occasion, *Sissoo* Fair	100	53	
Second occasion, *Vaiśākhī*	100	14	
			33.5
SHIV BARI			
First occasion, *Śivarātri*	100	35	
Second occasion, *Jātrā*	100	35	
			35

[5]Although samples were not taken on two occasions at Kangra, I did visit Kangra

explained by the fact that the Mother Goddess places, like Chintpurni, Jwalaji, Kangra, Mansa Devi, and Naina Devi, have three sets of fairs each, and tradition has established which of these three occasions will be considered the more important for visits by pilgrims from different areas. For example, the *Navarātrās* of *Caitra*[6] are the most important for Chintpurni, Jwalaji, Kangra, and Mansa Devi in terms of the long-distance pilgrims. The devotees who come from outside Himachal Pradesh and Punjab make their pilgrimage during the *Navarātrās*. The place to which these pilgrims are really bound is Kangra, but on the way to Kangra are Chintpurni and Jwalaji, so they also visit these shrines. For this reason the samples at Chintpurni and at Jwalaji show a higher average pilgrim-distance.

The *Aṣṭamī* of *Śrāvaṇa*[7] is a larger fair (in terms of number of pilgrims) at Chintpurni and Naina Devi, but during this fair few pilgrims outside of Himachal and Punjab arrive there. The result is that in our sample Chintpurni and Naina Devi both have average pilgrim fields of seventy-two miles each. At Mansa Devi, on the other hand, the *Navarātrās* are of greater importance for relatively longer distance pilgrims, although few, if any, pilgrims come from outside Punjab, Haryana, and Himachal Pradesh on any occasion. So, the average pilgrim field of Mansa Devi is nearly equal to that of Naina Devi on one occasion, but is reduced considerably when Naina Devi draws the maximum pilgrimage. *Śrāvaṇa Aṣṭamī* is of little importance to pilgrims as well as priests of Jwalaji and Kangra. This was quite clear to us when we observed that the priests of both places were no longer looking for long-distance clients, who make much of the offerings at the temples and pay handsome fees to priests. Therefore, on the occasion of *Śrāvaṇa Aṣṭamī,* Jwalaji and Kangra would have shown nearly the same fields as Chintpurni. In fact, at Jwalaji and Kangra we met several of the same pilgrims we had already interviewed at Chintpurni.

---

during both the *Navarātrās* and the *Śrāvaṇa Aṣṭamī* fairs. It was quite evident through informal interviews with the pilgrims and the priests that the latter occasion is not patronized by pilgrims from Uttar Pradesh.

[6]The *Navarātrās* of *Caitra* (29 March through 6 April 1968) are of special significance to pilgrims from Uttar Pradesh who, on the way to Kangra, visit the other goddess shrines also. The dates of the *Navarātrās* vary from year to year, but they do fall twice in a year, once during March–April and again during September–October.

[7]August 2 in the year 1968; but the date varies.

The average pilgrim field of Rewalsar changes from seventy-seven miles on the occasion of *Sissoo* fair to fourteen miles on the occasion of *Vaiśākhī*. The former fair is clearly Buddhist, and the Buddhist devotees of Tibetan border areas, particularly of District Kinnaur, make pilgrimage here. Although in terms of average pilgrim field this place falls in fourth level, the fact is that for the Buddhists, particularly the Tibetan Buddhists, this is one of the most revered places of pilgrimage.[8] Throughout the year Buddhist pilgrims from Nepal, Bhutan, and Kashmir visit this place.[9] On the occasion of *Vaiśākhī,* however, the composition of pilgrims at this place is entirely different. To an observer unacquainted with the local religious complexity of this picturesque shrine, the presence of Hindu and Sikh pilgrims may seem enigmatic. The religious landscape of Rewalsar is dominated by fluttering prayer flags of Tibetan Buddhists and heaps of stones with prayers etched on them in the Tibetan language. The reason for the visits of Hindus is that they claim this place to have been the abode of Lomas *Ṛṣi*[10] while the Sikhs also claim that their tenth *Guru* (master) meditated at this place.

We have noted above that the average fields of Chintpurni, Mansa Devi, and Naina Devi show variation from one occasion to the other. The average field of Chintpurni changes by thirty-two miles, in comparison with seventeen and fourteen miles for the other two places respectively. This change of field obviously introduces the problem whether the higher or lower average value, or even the overall mean, should be used to describe the field of a sacred place. If, for example, we select the lower value of the field of Chintpurni (see table 7-3), its level falls from third to fourth (in table 7-2). Perhaps a mean of the two values is a better measure, except for Rewalsar, where a change of religion with the occasion of pilgrimage is almost complete. If a mean of the two fields is selected in case of places where samples were taken on two occasions (table 7-3), the levels of sacred places suggested in table 7-2 need not be changed.[11]

[8]See J. Hutchison, and J. Ph. Vogel, *History of the Punjab Hill States,* II, 373.

[9]On the occasion of *Sissoo* fair (1968), the Kushak Bakula of Ladakh was present and gave a long sermon to the Buddhist congregation. A number of Tibetan refugees who can no longer make pilgrimages to Lhasa visit this place. In fact, before the Chinese invasion of Tibet, pilgrims from Tibet are reported to have been visiting this venerated shrine.

[10]One of the Hindu sages of antiquity.

[11]Note, however, our remarks about Rewalsar in the foregoing.

Some Problems Arising from the Use of Average Pilgrim Distance as a Determinant of Rank of Sacred Places

The main problem arising from the use of average pilgrim distance is that places which are more centrally located with respect to their potential pilgrim field entail a shorter average travel on the part of the pilgrims. Thus, Ujjain, which has a central location, had a lower average pilgrim distance value than Kangra, even though the former, which is one of the four centers where the *Kumbha* fairs are held, is unquestionably the more venerated shrine.[12]

Similarly, there is a problem regarding Hardwar vis-à-vis Kangra. Hardwar is a renowned *tīrtha* without any sectarian bias. On the other hand, Kangra is especially sacred to the worshippers of the goddess. In other words, the sanctity of Hardwar is much more pervasive in Hinduism than that of Kangra, which has a clear sectarian bias. Nevertheless, Hardwar and Kangra, according to the criterion of average distance, fall in the same category. Thus, although the average pilgrim distance appears to be a useful criterion for determining fairly distinct levels, in some cases it creates rather divergent bedfellows in terms of accepted Hindu tradition. It is, therefore, necessary to bear in mind the deficiencies of using average distance as a determinant of rank of sacred places in the religious context.

Standard Deviation as a Determinant of Rank of Sacred Places

Instead of relying solely on the average pilgrim distance as a means for ranking the sacred places, we may now try to rank the places on the basis of a simple measure of dispersion, namely, standard deviation of the distances.[13]

From table 7-4 we can observe that Ujjain has a much more dispersed field than Jwalaji, with which it had been categorized on the basis of average distances (table 7-2). The field of Kangra is only slightly more dispersed than that of Ujjain on this basis, than was the case (in table 7-1) when average distances were

[12]The term *Siṃhastha* is used instead of *Kumbha* at Ujjain. However, as at Hardwar, Allahabad, and Nasik, this is the once-in-twelve-years fair of immense religious significance.

[13]Straight-line distances between the headquarters of the pilgrims' districts of origin and the sacred places in question.

TABLE 7-4
STANDARD DEVIATION OF PILGRIM DISTANCES

	Standard deviation
Badrinath	261.7
Hardwar	163.0
Kangra	160.5
Ujjain	151.7
Jwalaji	117.1
Chintpurni (first occasion)	111.5
Naina Devi (first occasion)	68.3
Rewalsar (second occasion)	31.8[1]
Mansa Devi (first occasion)	25.3
Bhagsunag	14.3
Baijnath (first occasion)	10.7
Shiv Bari (first occasion)	8.9

[1]If the first occasion is selected, the corresponding value is 52.8. However, it has been already noted in the text that the first occasion is of importance to the Buddhists, while from the Hindu viewpoint the second occasion is the significant one.

compared. Similarly, Mansa Devi has clearly a less dispersed field than Naina Devi, although this fact was not clear in table 7-1. Also Rewalsar (on the second occasion, i.e., *Vaiśākhī*) has a more dispersed field than Mansa Devi. The inference we can draw is that sacred places with a widely dispersed field are of higher level than those with a highly concentrated and localized field. On the basis of relative dispersion of the fields of sacred places the following levels can be suggested (table 7-5).

LEVELS OF SACRED PLACES BASED ON THE CULTURAL DIVERSITY OF THE FIELD OF PILGRIMAGE

The levels of sacred places identified in the preceding sections of this chapter can be meaningful if they suggest a corresponding

TABLE 7-5
LEVELS OF SACRED PLACES ON THE BASIS OF DISPERSION OF THEIR FIELDS

1. (highest)	Badrinath
2.	Hardwar, Kangra, Ujjain
3.	Chintpurni, Jwalaji
4.	Naina Devi
5.	Mansa Devi, Rewalsar (2nd occasion)
6. (lowest)	Baijnath, Bhagsunag, Shiv Bari

relationship between the sacred place and the Hindu population. In other words, the higher the level of a sacred place, the more diverse should its pilgrim field be. The highest-level sacred place (or places) should clearly show interconnections with the Hindu population of the entire country, despite regional cultural differences. On the other hand, the lowest-level places should reflect only local interconnections. We shall examine the field of each sacred place at which pilgrim samples were taken and try to argue their respective levels. It may be pointed out here that the levels suggested below for each place will naturally be influenced by the size of the pilgrim samples,[14] and the occasion at which samples were taken.[15] A larger sample could have possibly resulted in a more accurate map of the field of a given place.

(1) Figure 7-1 shows the origin of sampled pilgrims of Badrinath. A comparison of this map with any map depicting the major language families of India and its major languages shows that both the Indo-Aryan and the Dravidian language families are included in its field.[16] Because of the extreme northern location of Badrinath, the gross percentage of pilgrims from the Dravidian languages area is not impressive, being a little over 5 percent. A sample of a mere four hundred pilgrims shows that 148 different districts out of a total of 349 (including small union territories regarded here as "districts") are represented. The only major

[14]See Introduction, table 0-1.

[15]See table 7-3.

[16]See, for example, G. A. Grierson, *Linguistic Survey of India* (Delhi : Motilal Banarsidass, 1968 reprint), Vol. 1, map facing p. 119.

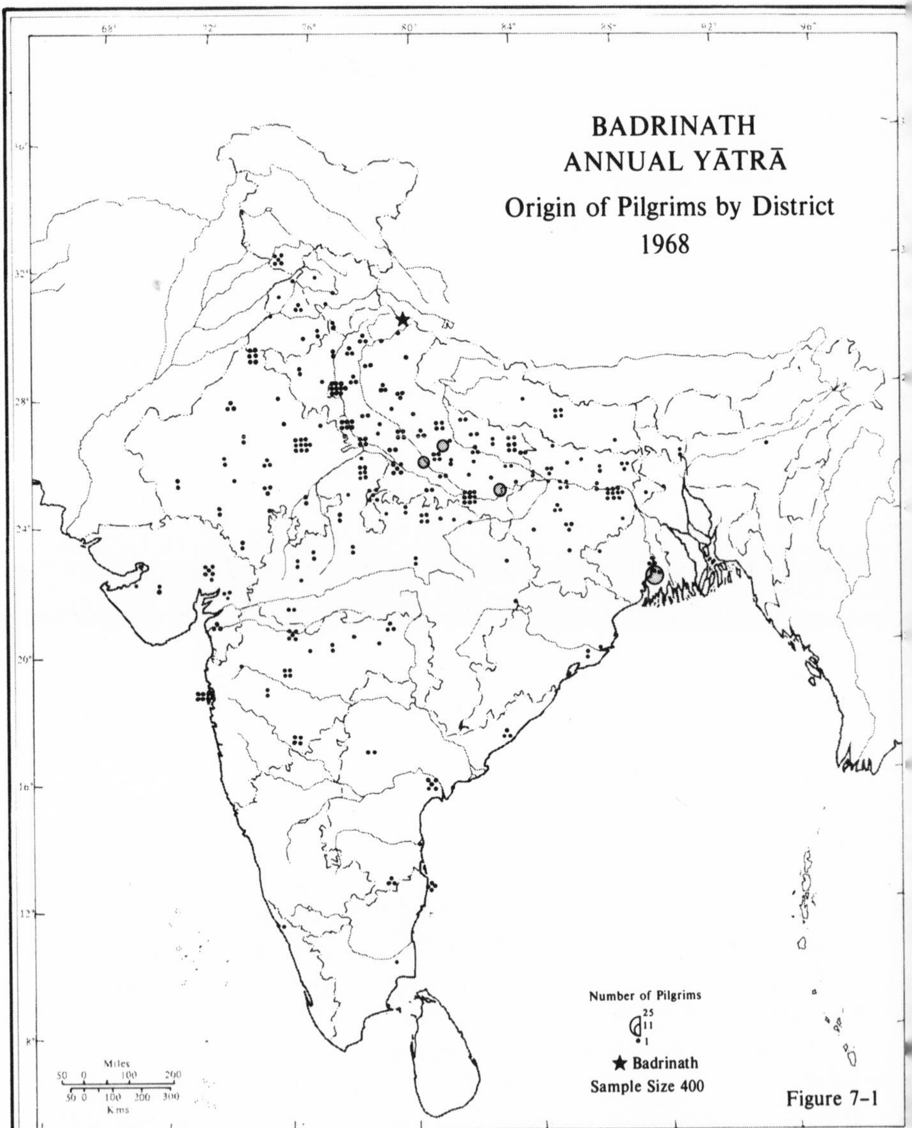
BADRINATH
ANNUAL YĀTRĀ
Origin of Pilgrims by District
1968
Number of Pilgrims
25
11
1
Badrinath
Sample Size 400
Miles
Kms

Figure 7–1

Indian language that is not represented here is Kannada of Mysore. On the basis of the pilgrim field and on the basis of the languages represented, Badrinath can be justly termed a holy place of pan-Hindu (or pan-Indian) level. The map (fig. 7-1) also shows that distance from this sacred place may not be the only factor governing the numbers of pilgrims originating from different parts of India. Districts with large cities seem to generate a somewhat disproportionate number of pilgrims. For example, Calcutta, Bombay, and Madras contributed respectively twenty-four, seven, and four pilgrims to our sample.

(2) Hardwar on the occasion of *Ardha Kumbha* (1968) attracted its pilgrims largely from the states of the Sutlej-Ganga plain, Rajasthan, Himachal Pradesh, and Jammu-Kashmir (fig. 7-2). The majority of the pilgrims, however, originated from Punjab, Haryana, western Uttar Pradesh, and Delhi. Some districts with large cities (e.g., Bombay and Calcutta) stand out in their contributions of pilgrims. The field of Hardwar was clearly more restricted than that of Badrinath in terms of linguistic diversity.[17] Only one person from the Dravidian area was present in a sample of eight hundred pilgrims. On the other hand, it definitely covered more area and more languages than Kangra. Thus, although the standard deviation of distances at Hardwar and Kangra were very close, the greater diversity of pilgrims at Hardwar must set it apart from Kangra. Hardwar may be designated as a supra-regional-level sacred place. Hardwar could be a pan-Hindu-level sacred place on other considerations, but our sample suggests that at the *Ardha Kumbha* fair its level was definitely below that of Badrinath.

(3) Ujjain drew most of its pilgrims from the Malwa region, though the dispersed nature of its field is clear from figure 7-3. Despite the central location of Ujjain in India, only two pilgrims from the Dravidian language area were encountered in our sample. There seems to be all the more reason to put Ujjain at a lower level than Hardwar. At Hardwar 92 different districts are included in the pilgrim sample (of 800), at Ujjain 76 in a sample of 500. Perhaps a larger sample would have brought the number of districts closer to those of Hardwar.

On the other hand, the number of districts represented at Ujjain is much larger than the 47 districts included in the Kangra

[17]Cf. *ibid.*

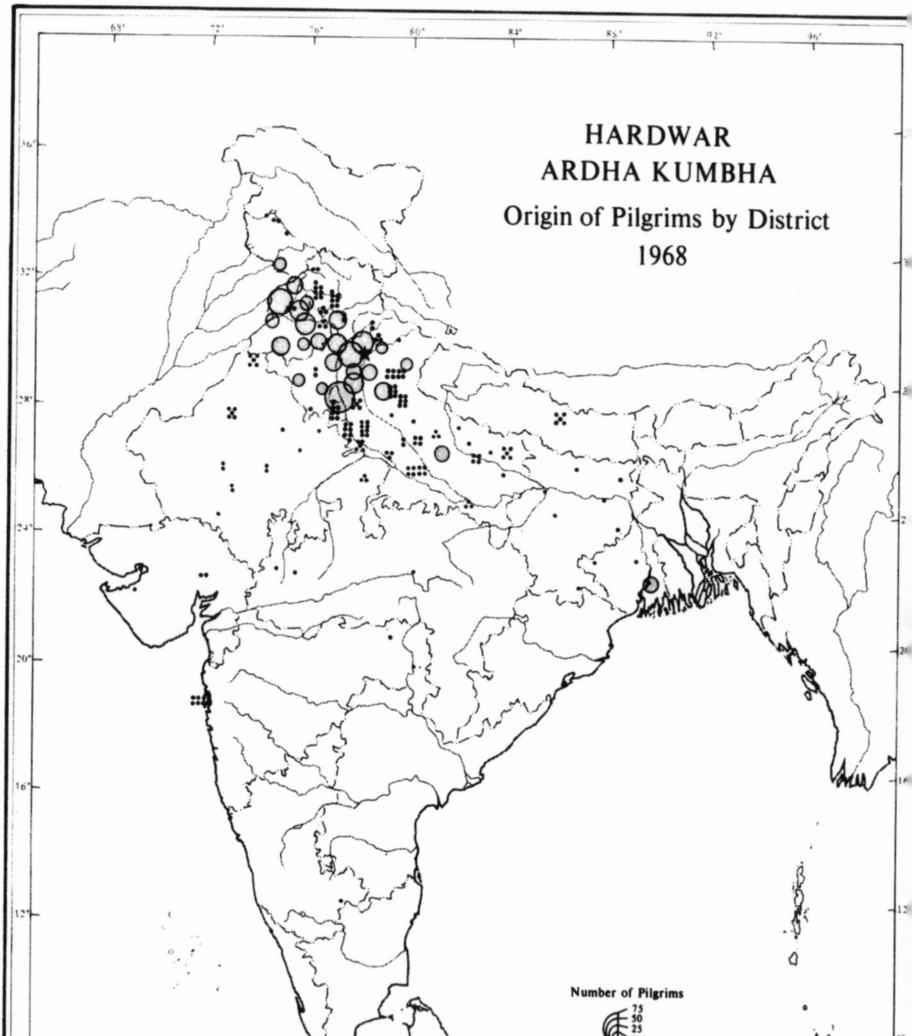
HARDWAR
ARDHA KUMBHA
Origin of Pilgrims by District
1968
Number of Pilgrims
75
50
25
11
1
★ Hardwar
Sample Size 800
Miles
50 0 100 200
50 0 100 200 300
Kms
68°
72°
76°
80°
84°
88°
92°
96°
36°
32°
28°
24°
20°
16°
12°
8°

Figure 7–2

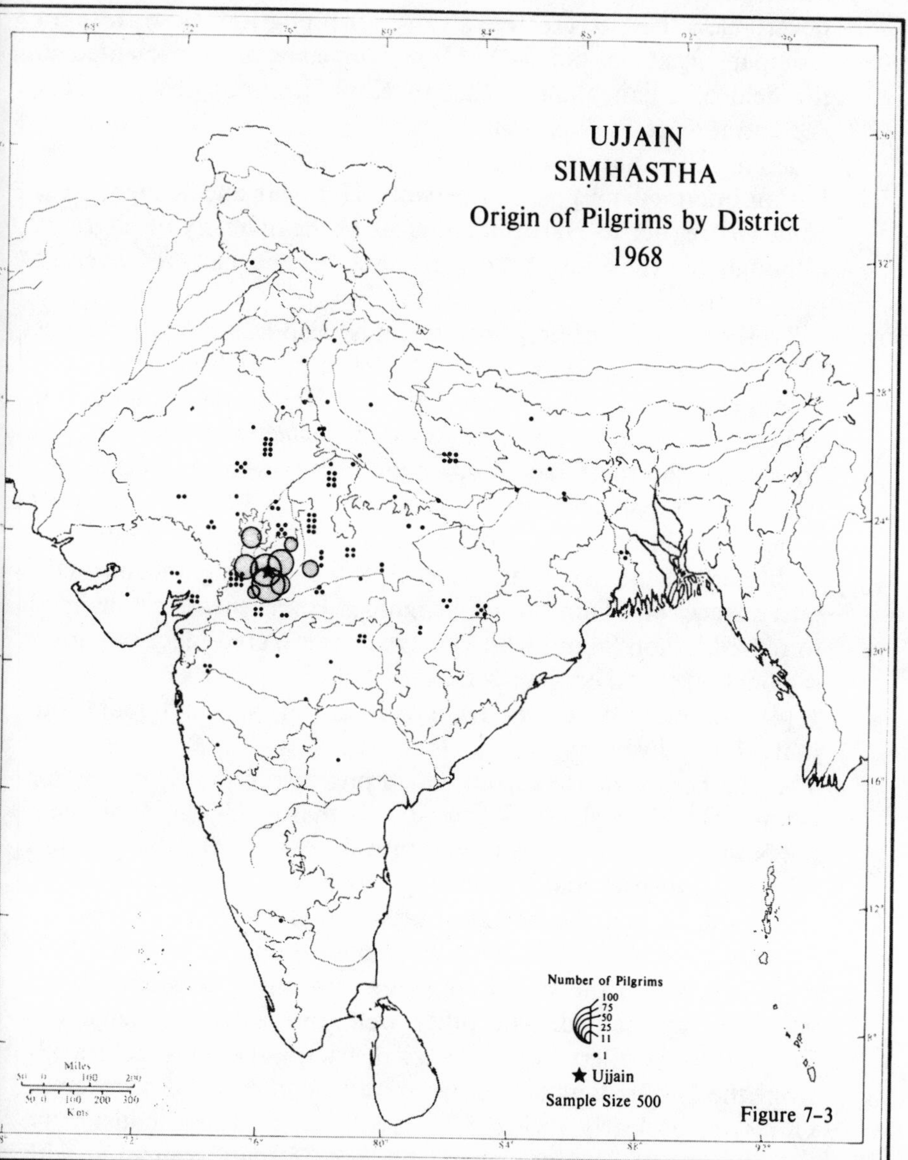
UJJAIN
SIṂHASTHA
Origin of Pilgrims by District
1968
Number of Pilgrims
100
75
50
25
11
1
★ Ujjain
Sample Size 500
Miles
Kms

Figure 7–3

sample of 450 pilgrims. Although the dispersion of the field of Kangra is somewhat larger when measured by standard deviation of distances as well as the average pilgrim distances, Ujjain nevertheless had a greater diversity of pilgrims than Kangra (compare figs. 7-3 and 7-4). More languages are represented in the field of Ujjain than in that of Kangra, although admittedly the "representation" is small.

Taking the above facts into consideration, we see that Ujjain has an intermediate position between Hardwar and Kangra. It is somewhat closer to Hardwar in terms of the diversity of pilgrims, although it ranks lower than Kangra on the basis of average pilgrim distance.

To the above considerations we must also add the significance of *Siṃhastha* fair of Ujjain for the Hindu population as a whole. Ujjain is one of the four sacred places in India where such a fair is held (at other places it is called *Kumbha* fair). Since this is considered the most sacred climactic occasion in Hinduism, this place for the particular occasion undoubtedly becomes the most sacred. Therefore, even though quantitative measurements may be important for assigning "levels," this highly significant qualitative aspect of Ujjain cannot be ignored. I am, therefore, inclined to regard Ujjain (along with Hardwar) as a sacred place of supra-regional level rather than regional level.

(4) The pilgrim field of Kangra is distinctively different from that of Hardwar and Ujjain (compare figs. 7-2, 7-3, and 7-4). The number of districts from which pilgrims in our sample came is half that of Hardwar and two-thirds that of Ujjain. Moreover, the Kangra field shows two concentrations : one of local pilgrims of Kangra district and one of pilgrims from the Doāb of Ganga and Yamuna and the neighboring areas of Delhi and Gurgaon. Linguistic diversity of pilgrims was small compared with Hardwar or Ujjain. From the Hindī language area only "Western Hindī" was well represented. The other well-represented language was Panjābī. Most pilgrims of Kangra district, although theoretically from the Pahāṛī language area, were in fact Panjābī speakers.[18] Our sample clearly shows that, areally as well as linguistically, the pilgrims of Kangra showed far less diversity compared with either Hardwar or Ujjain. The example of Kangra suggests that

[18]There was one pilgrim in the sample who came from Madras, but he was a Panjābī.

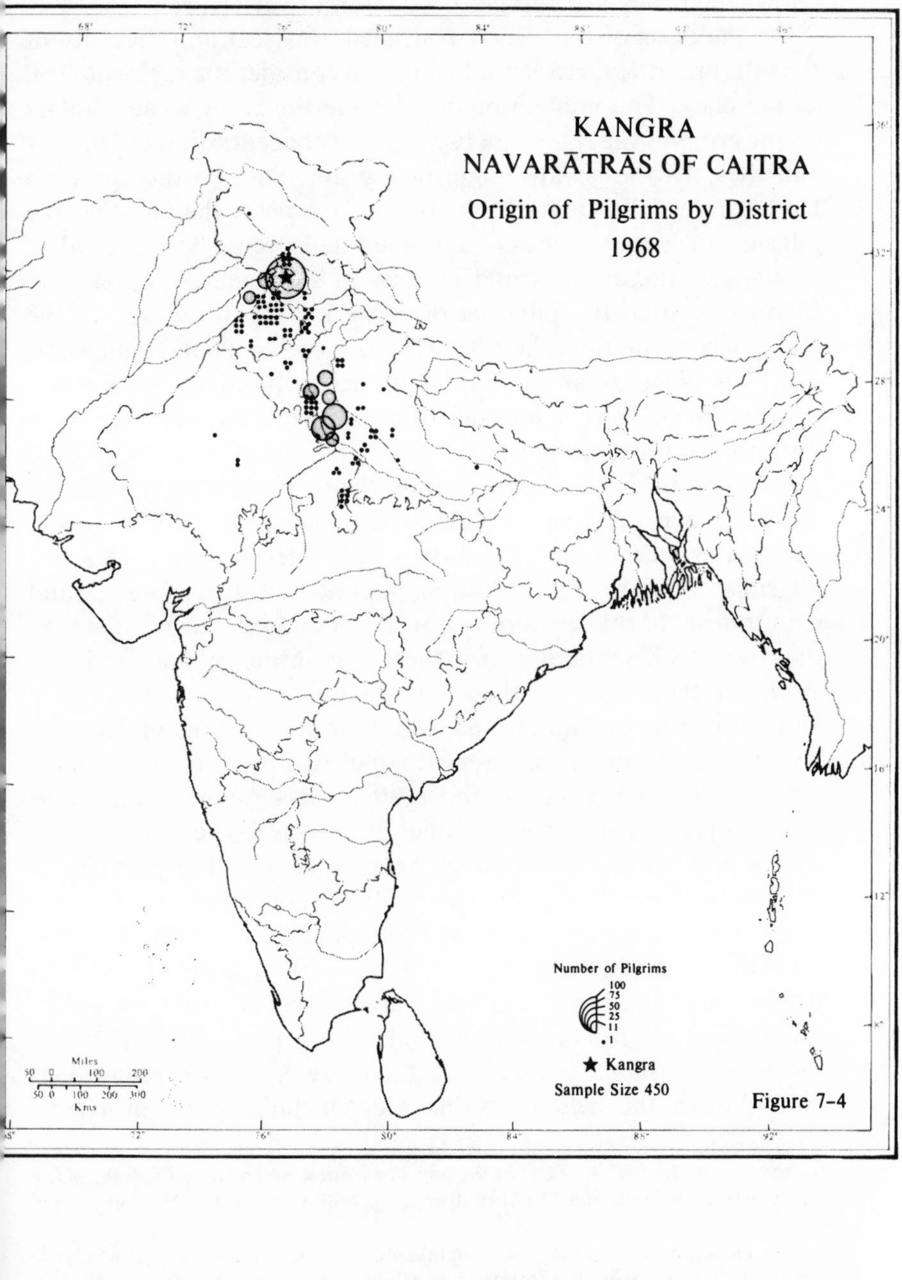
KANGRA
NAVARĀTRĀS OF CAITRA
Origin of Pilgrims by District
1968
Number of Pilgrims
100
75
50
25
11
1
Kangra
Sample Size 450
Miles
Kms

Figure 7-4

mere statistical averages of distance or standard deviations cannot by themselves define the levels of sacred places. We must also see whether they are paralleled by cultural variety.

On the basis of the clearly restricted areal cultural diversity of the pilgrims at Kangra, I am inclined to consider it a regional-level sacred place. This contention may be questioned by some scholars on the grounds that there are two areas of concentration of pilgrims and these two areas are linguistically different. To this question I submit the following answer. If it were not for the fact that the pilgrims of western Uttar Pradesh specially venerate the goddess at Kangra, this place would be only of subregional importance. In other words, the pilgrims of western Uttar Pradesh are the real pilgrims of this place.[19] Others, like the Panjābī pilgrims, visit this place as an extension of their pilgrimage from either Chintpurni or Jwalaji since all three are within a relatively short distance from each other.

(5) Jwalaji and Chintpurni draw their pilgrims from basically the same general area as Kangra (figs. 7-5, 7-6, and 7-7). But, whereas western Uttar Pradesh is the chief source of Kangra pilgrims, Punjab is the dominant contributor to Jwalaji and Chintpurni. Many western Uttar Pradesh pilgrims who are on their way to Kangra also visit these two shrines of the Goddess, although they perform their own rites specifically at Kangra. Since the field of Jwalaji and Chintpurni, like that of Kangra, is linguistically much less diverse than of Hardwar, and is basically restricted to one language and a small part of the other, these shrines may be considered regional-level sacred places. Figure 7-7 shows that on the occasion of *Śrāvaṇa Aṣṭamī* the pilgrims to Chintpurni were almost exclusively from Punjab.[20]

(6) Naina Devi derives most of its pilgrims from the Panjābī-speaking area (figs. 7-8, 7-9). A few pilgrims from the western Pahāṛī- and Hindī-speaking area were also represented, but rarely was there a pilgrim who responded to our questions in any language other than Panjābī. It is, therefore, safe to presume that even though the field of Naina Devi includes parts of Hindī-

[19]The goddess Vajreśwarī—the chief deity at Kangra—is regarded as the *Kul-Devī* (or the patron deity of the clan) of the pilgrims from western Uttar Pradesh. Many pilgrims from Aligarh and Mathura districts gave this reason for their pilgrimage here.

[20]At Jwalaji no formal samples were taken on this occasion because it was quite apparent that busloads of pilgrims from Chintpurni were proceeding to Jwalaji.

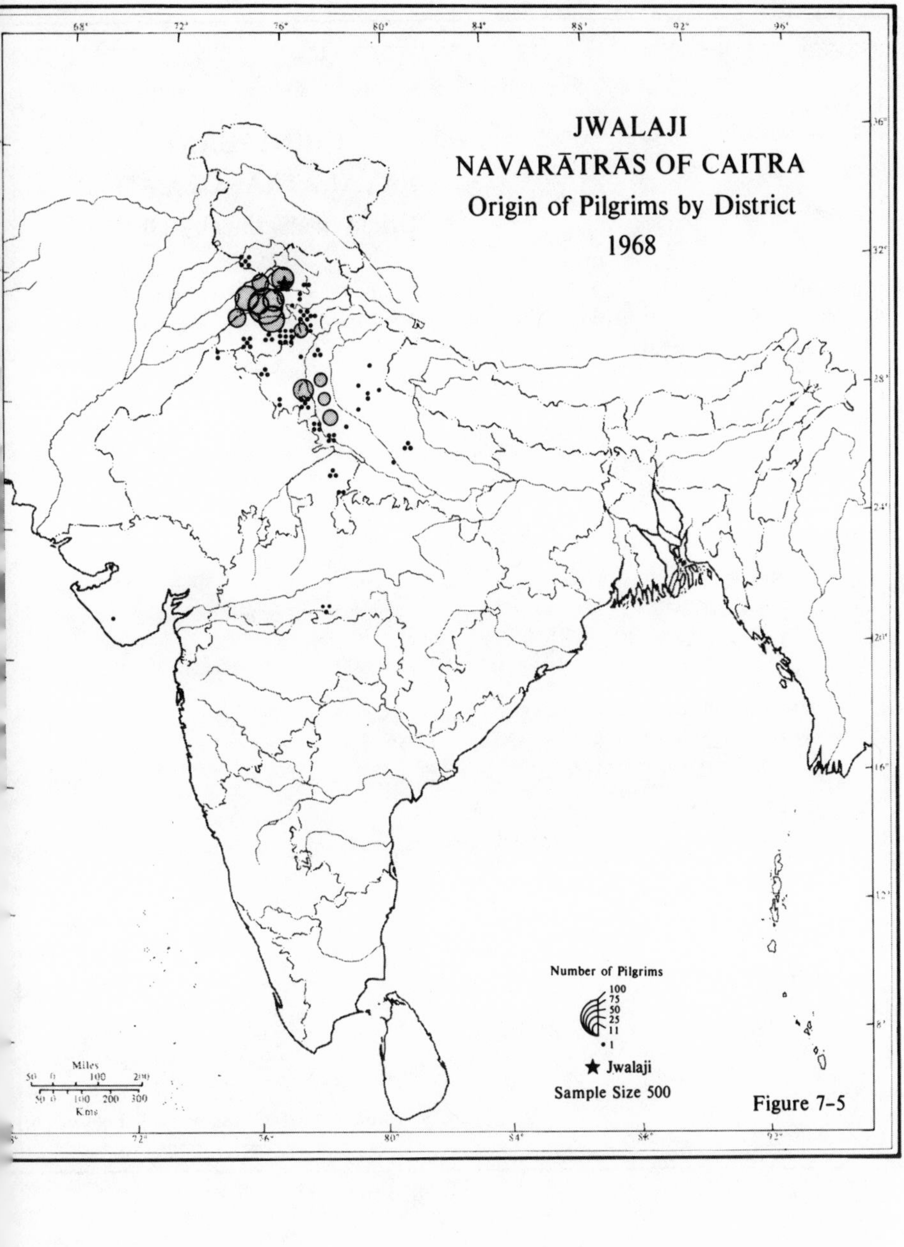
JWALAJI
NAVARĀTRĀS OF CAITRA
Origin of Pilgrims by District
1968
Number of Pilgrims
100
75
50
25
11
1
★ Jwalaji
Sample Size 500
Miles
Kms

Figure 7-5

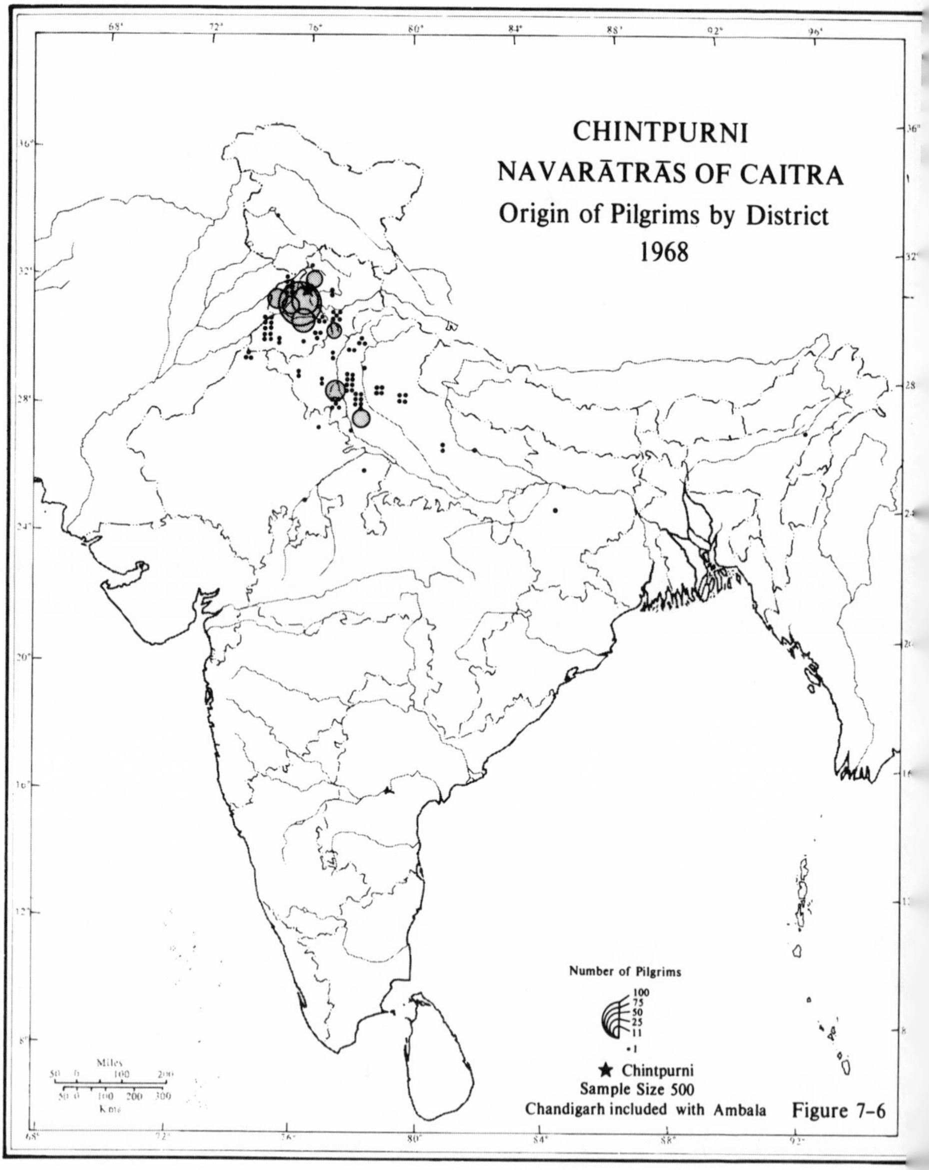

CHINTPURNI
NAVARĀTRĀS OF CAITRA
Origin of Pilgrims by District
1968
Number of Pilgrims
100
75
50
25
11
1
★ Chintpurni
Sample Size 500
Chandigarh included with Ambala
Miles
Kms

Figure 7–6

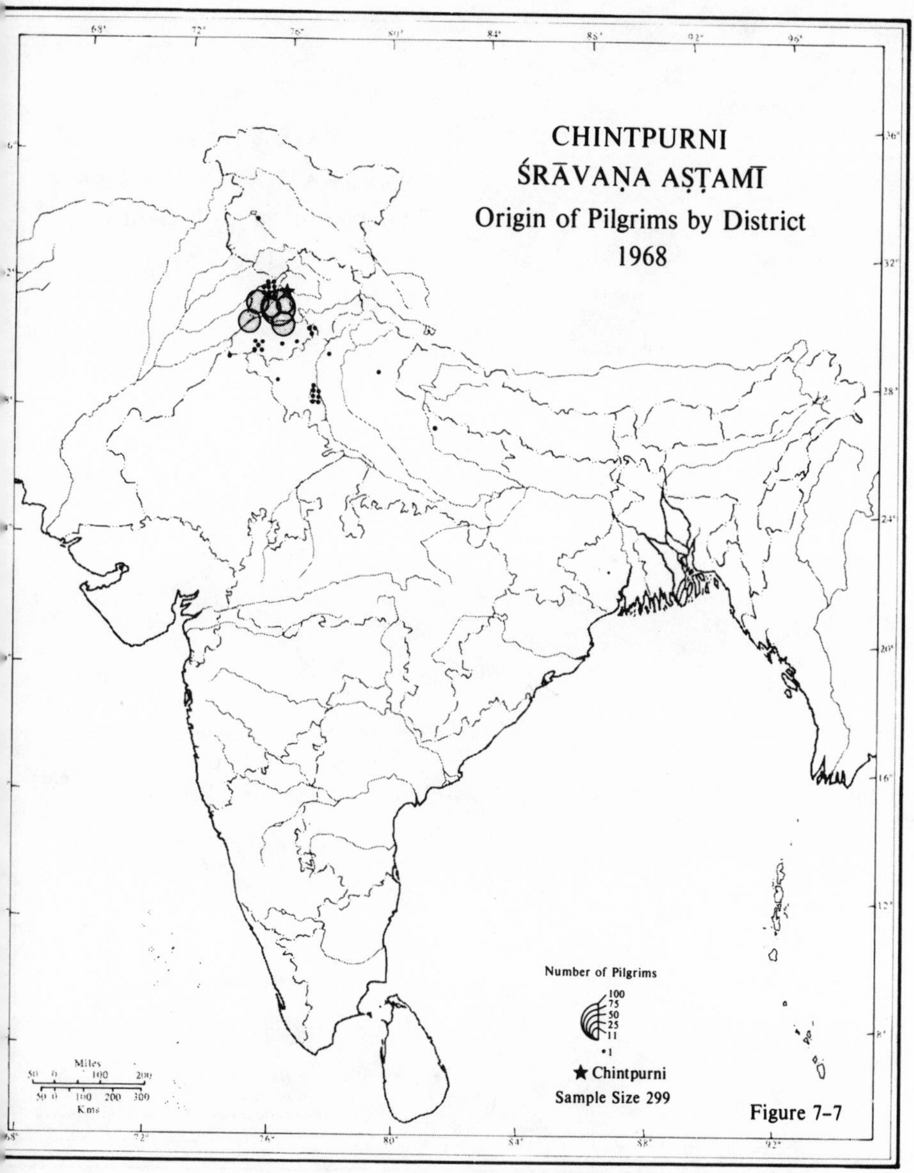
CHINTPURNI
ŚRĀVAṆA AṢṬAMĪ
Origin of Pilgrims by District
1968
Number of Pilgrims
100
75
50
25
11
1
★ Chintpurni
Sample Size 299
Miles
Kms

Figure 7–7

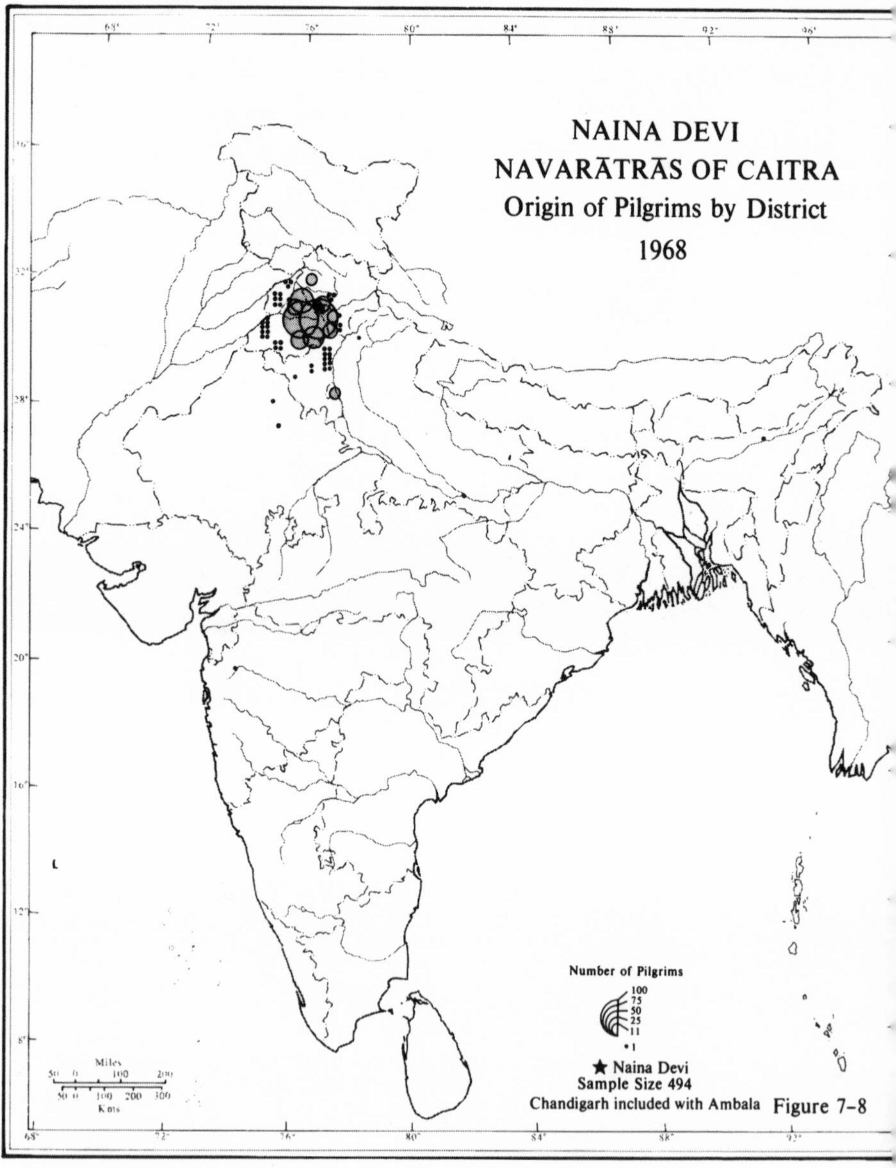
NAINA DEVI
NAVARĀTRĀS OF CAITRA
Origin of Pilgrims by District
1968
Number of Pilgrims
100
75
50
25
11
1
★ Naina Devi
Sample Size 494
Chandigarh included with Ambala
Miles
Kms
Figure 7–8

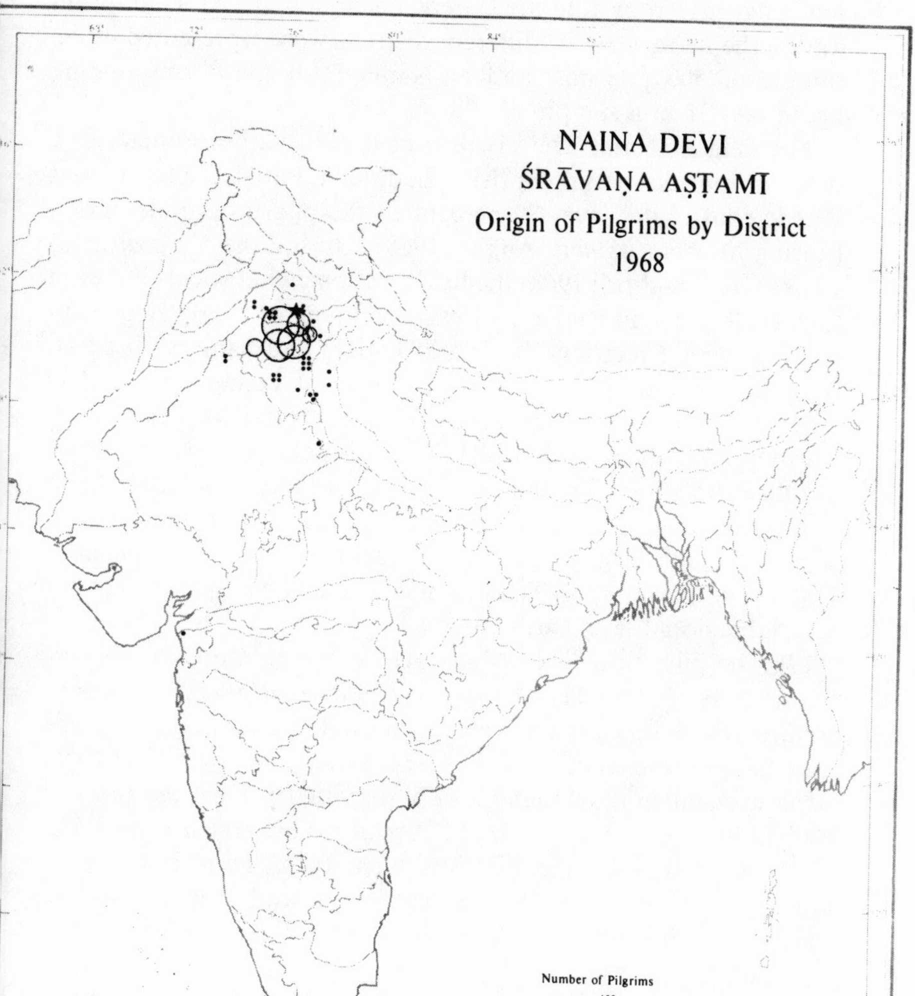
NAINA DEVI
ŚRĀVAṆA AṢṬAMĪ
Origin of Pilgrims by District
1968
Number of Pilgrims
100
75
50
25
11
1
★ Naina Devi
Sample Size 400
Chandigarh included with Ambala
Figure 7-9

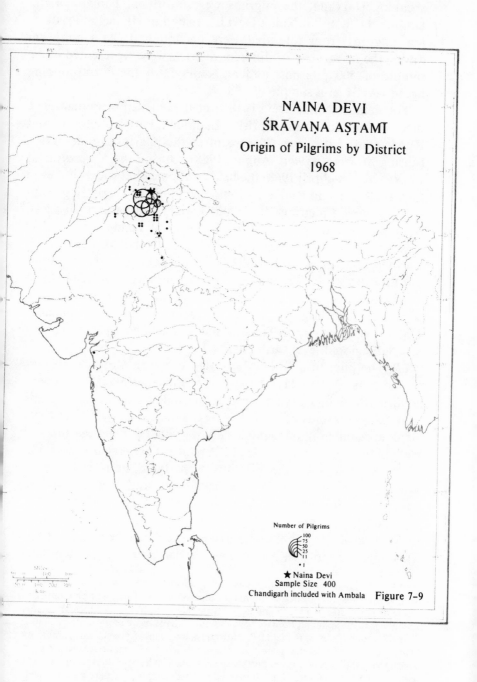

speaking Haryana, the pilgrims were mostly of Panjābī origin. Despite the fact that Naina Devi is situated in Himachal Pradesh, few pilgrims from this area were encountered. At Chintpurni during the *Navarātrās* 43 different districts were represented in the sample of 500 pilgrims, and at Naina Devi the corresponding figure was 31 in a sample of 494.

The field of Naina Devi is restricted even within Punjab. The block of four districts comprising Ludhiana, Patiala, Sangrur, and Rupar contributed over 80 percent to the pilgrim sample of 400 (during *Śrāvaṇa Aṣṭamī,* August 1968). During the *Navarātrās* of *Caitra* (March–April 1968) the field was somewhat wider, but even then Ludhiana and Rupar districts accounted for nearly 50 percent of the sampled pilgrims. If we add Patiala and Sangrur districts, the figure would be 60 percent. The field of Naina Devi is thus much more restricted than that of Kangra, Jwalaji, or Chintpurni. Furthermore, even within the Panjābī-speaking area there is, during *Navarātrās,* a remarkable preponderance of pilgrims from the Malwa tract (Ludhiana, Rupar, Patiala—not to be confused with the much larger region of the same name, which includes Ujjain) and Hoshiarpur. Thus Naina Devi can be properly regarded as a subregional-level shrine.[21]

(7) The pilgrim field of Mansa Devi is even more clearly restricted (figs. 7-10, 7-11). Although it is located on the boundary zone of Punjab, Haryana, and Himachal Pradesh, the pilgrims were almost exclusively Panjābī speakers. Only twelve districts were represented in our sample (250 pilgrims) at one occasion and eight at the other (in a sample of 175 pilgrims). On the first occasion over 88 percent of the pilgrims were from Patiala, Sangrur, Ludhiana, Chandigarh (Union Territory), and Rupar districts. More than 50 percent of the pilgrims were from Patiala district alone on the occasion of *Navarātrās* of *Caitra.* On the occasion of *Śrāvaṇa Aṣṭamī* about 48 percent were from the same district. This high proportion from one district alone is perhaps the

[21]On the occasion of *Navarātrās* eleven pilgrims from Delhi were present in our sample. This resulted from a combination of two reasons. First, a large number of Panjābīs have settled in Delhi and keep visiting their traditionally venerated places in Himachal Pradesh and Punjab. Second, and perhaps more important, by chance part of a tour group was included. Nowadays a group of people will commonly charter a bus and visit many shrines, including their traditional ones. Apart from visiting sacred places, groups in northwestern India usually visit Bhakra and Nangal dams on the Sutlej River. Thus, the sacred and secular purpose may be combined.

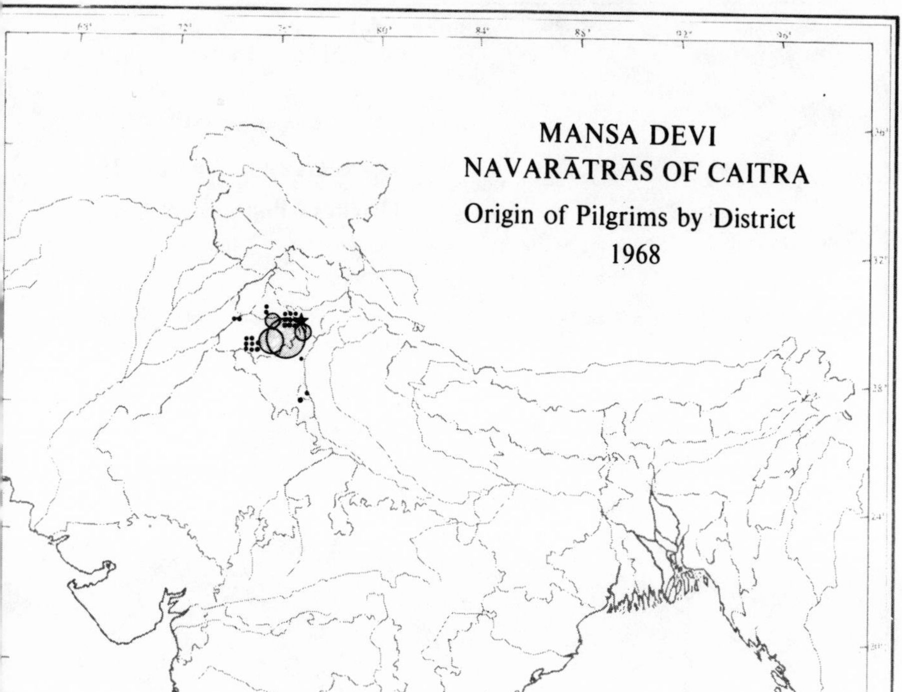
MANSA DEVI
NAVARĀTRĀS OF CAITRA
Origin of Pilgrims by District
1968
Number of Pilgrims
100
75
50
25
11
1
★ Mansa Devi
Sample Size 250
Chandigarh included with Ambala
Miles
Km

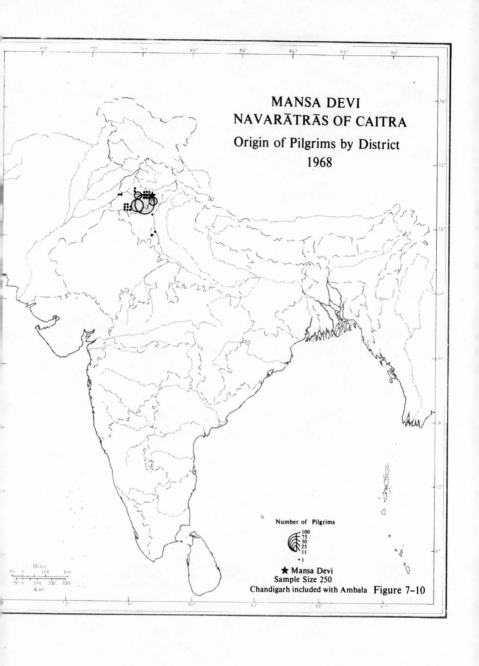

Figure 7–10

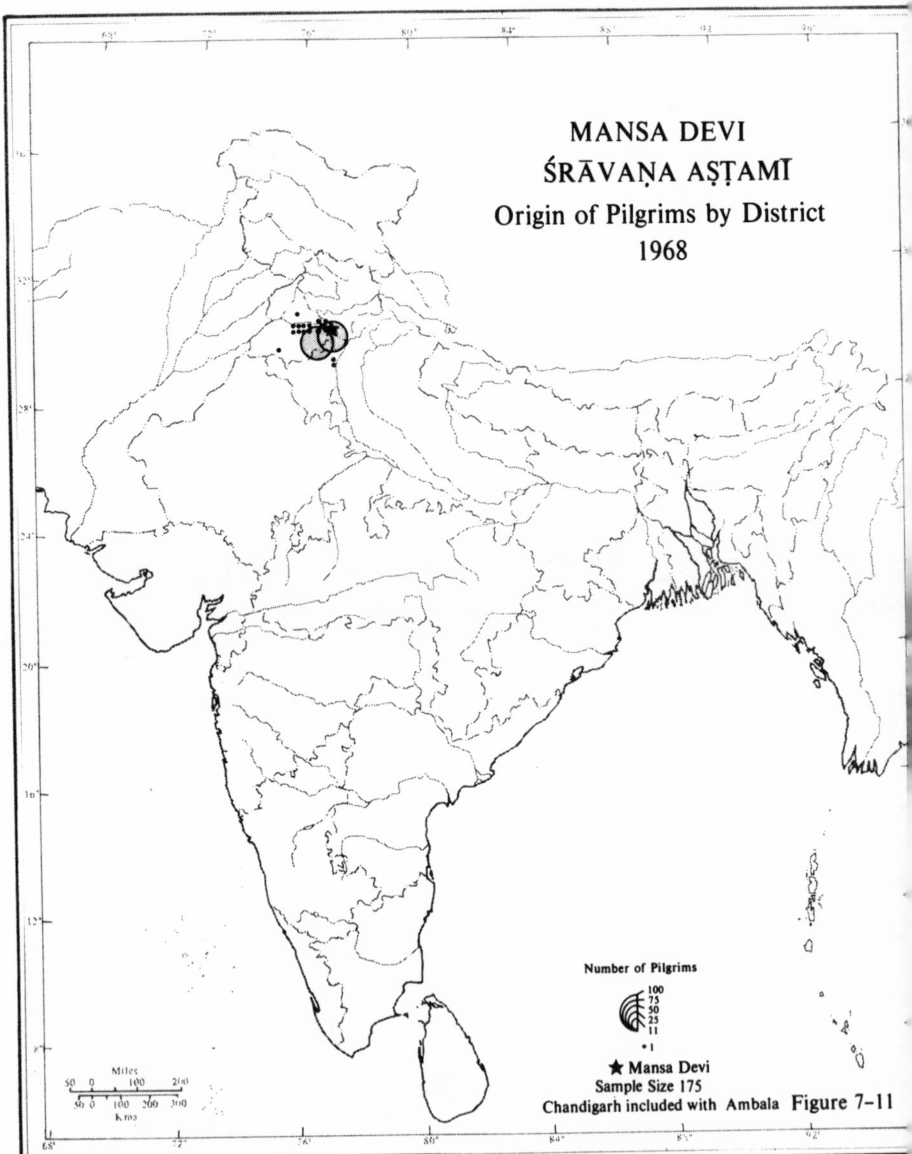
MANSA DEVI
ŚRĀVAṆA AṢṬAMĪ
Origin of Pilgrims by District
1968
Number of Pilgrims
100
75
50
25
11
1
★ Mansa Devi
Sample Size 175
Chandigarh included with Ambala
Miles
Kms
Figure 7–11

continuation of an earlier pattern of pilgrimage from the former princely states of Patiala and Nabha—particularly the latter.

Linguistically also, the pilgrim field of Mansa Devi is very restricted—almost exclusively to what Grierson calls the "Mālwī" and the "Powādhī" subdialects of the Panjābī language.[22] Because of the high degree of linguistic homogeneity of pilgrims as well as the short average distance traveled by them, this place can be considered to belong to the lower subregional level compared with Naina Devi.

(8) Rewalsar poses considerable problems when placed in the subregional level on the basis of average distance (figs. 7-12, 7-13). The main reason is that on one occasion (*Sissoo* fair) it is a place of pilgrimage for the Buddhists, while on another occasion (*Vaiśākhī*) Hindus and Sikhs visit this place. A comparison of figures 7-12 and 7-13 shows distinctly different areas of origin of the pilgrims.

The pilgrim field of Rewalsar is greatly concentrated during the *Vaiśākhī* fair,[23] one district (Mandi) accounting for 76 percent of the pilgrims. Thus the origin of pilgrims is even more strictly defined than at Mansa Devi. The total number of districts included in a sample of one hundred pilgrims is, however, about the same as at Mansa Devi. In linguistic terms also the field is very restricted, because most pilgrims came from the so-called Maṇḍiālī dialect area, which itself is confined to Mandi district (formerly the princely state of Mandi). Thus the diversity of pilgrims at Rewalsar (during the *Vaiśākhī* fair) was even less than at Mansa Devi. As at Mansa Devi, the largest proportion of pilgrims originated from the area of a former princely state. Because of the large proportion of pilgrims originating from a small district, and because of their dialectical homogeneity, Rewalsar can be categorized only with Mansa Devi as a low subregional-level sacred place as far as Hindu pilgrimage is concerned.

From the Buddhist point of view, as was noted earlier, Rewalsar

[22]Grierson, *op. cit.*, Vol. 9, part 1, map facing p. 607.

[23]Falling on the thirteenth of April each year, this fair is celebrated by both Hindus and Sikhs. The Sikhs of the Punjab attached a much greater religious importance to this fair than do the Hindus. At Rewalsar, in Himachal Pradesh, the fair is celebrated by the Hindus also, although a few Sikhs also attend because the place is associated with the visit of the tenth Guru. Strictly speaking, at Rewalsar this is hardly a religious fair, for the occasion is used, especially at night, for drinking and merrymaking.

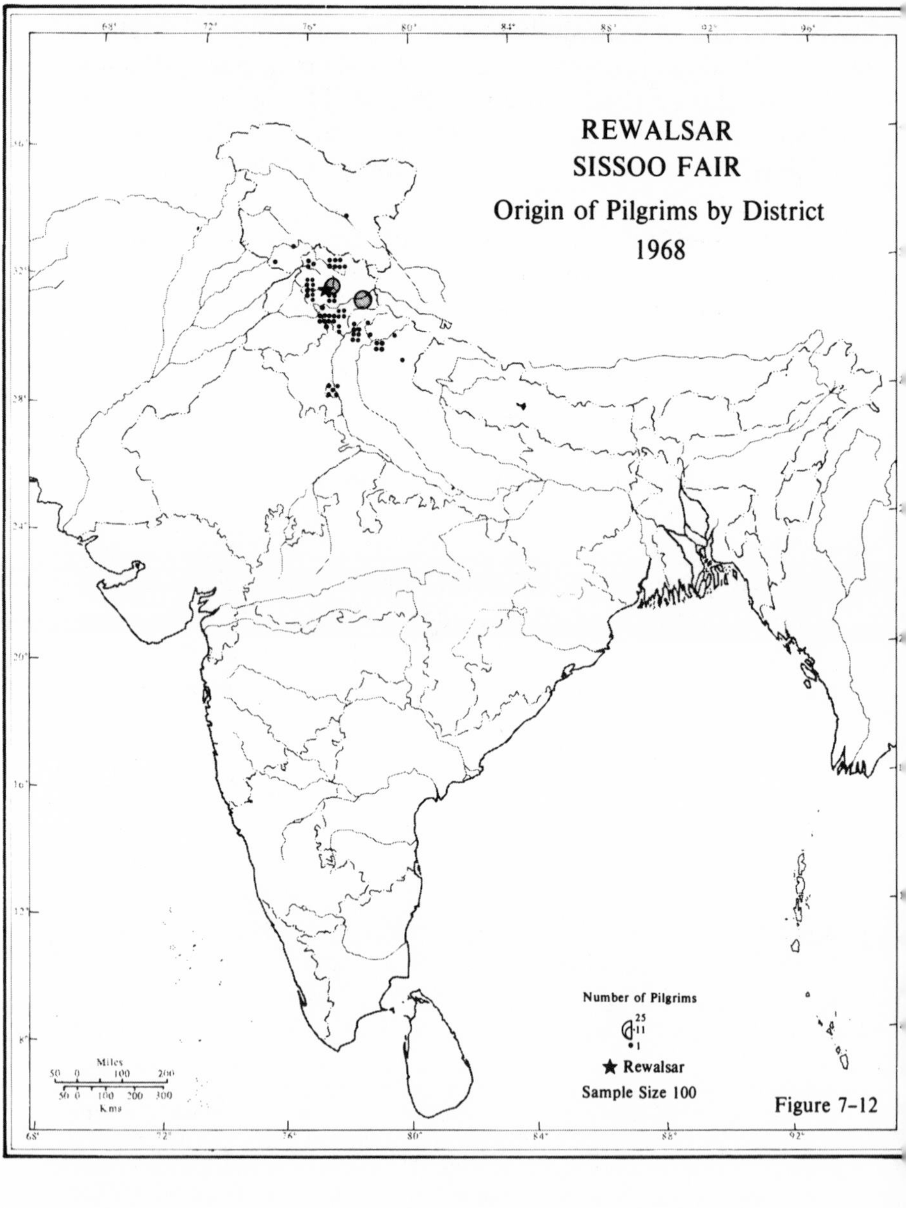
REWALSAR
SISSOO FAIR
Origin of Pilgrims by District
1968
Number of Pilgrims
25
11
1
★ Rewalsar
Sample Size 100
Miles
Kms
Figure 7–12

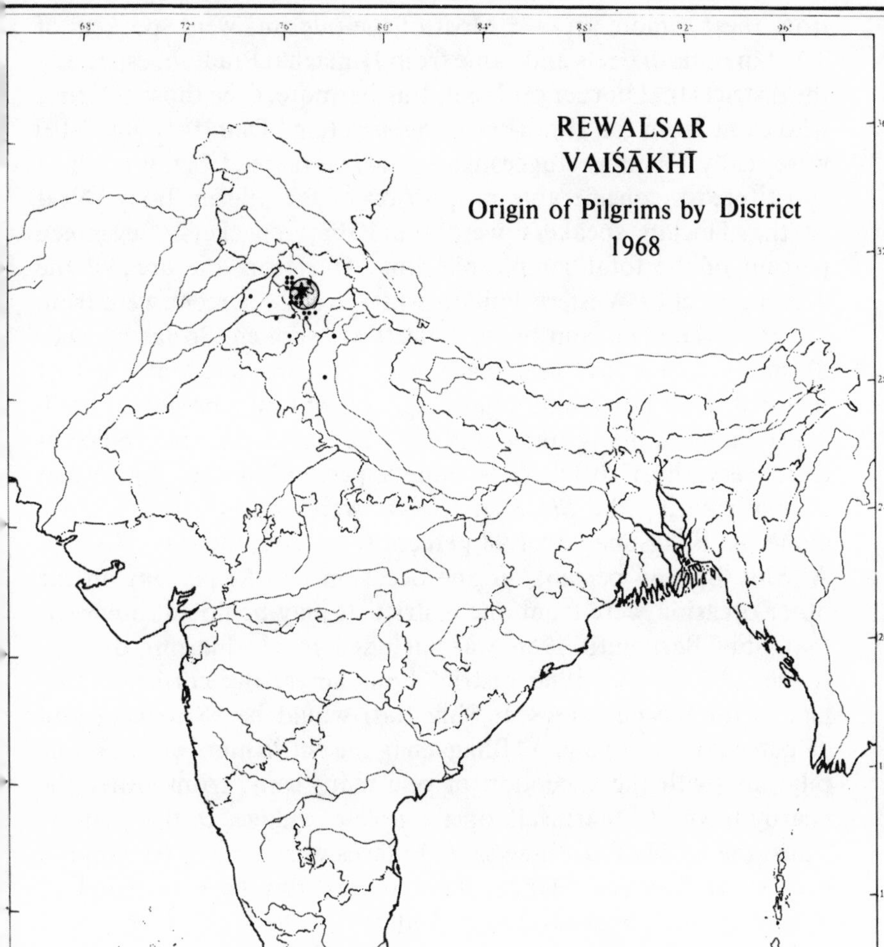
REWALSAR
VAIŚĀKHĪ
Origin of Pilgrims by District
1968
Number of Pilgrims
75
50
25
11
1
★ Rewalsar
Sample Size 100
Miles
Kms

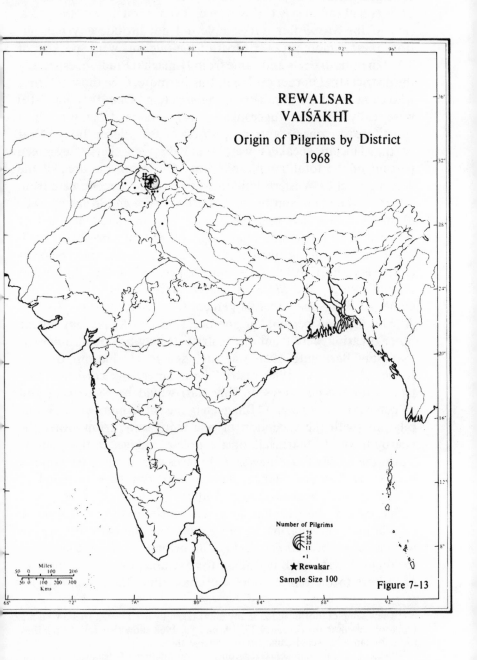

Figure 7–13

is of considerable importance, and pilgrims from Bhutan, Sikkim, and Nepal often visit this place, even though on the occasion of the *Sissoo* fair our sample did not include any pilgrims from these remote areas.[24] Most of the pilgrims were speakers of Tibetan or its dialects and came from Himachal Pradesh, especially the districts that border on Tibet. Furthermore, even those pilgrims who came from the Hindī-speaking area (e.g., Delhi; see fig. 7-12) were really Tibetan refugees who now live there. Tibetan refugees constituted a considerable proportion of the pilgrim body. Next to the Tibetan speakers were the Pahāṛī speakers. Seventeen percent of the total sample pilgrims came from the area of the Kului dialect of Western Pahāṛī, while over 28 percent were from the area where Tibetan or its dialects are spoken. So far as Buddhism is concerned, this place may be considered at least of regional level. For Hindu pilgrimage it is of low subregional level.

(9) Baijnath, Bhagsunag, and Shiv Bari all derive their pilgrims from very short distances.[25] Ninety percent of the pilgrims at Baijnath during the *Śivarātri* festival were from district Kangra alone. At Bhagsunag over 98 percent were from the same district. At Shiv Bari 84 percent on one occasion and 82 percent on the other occasion were from one district. It may be noted, however, that Shiv Bari until 1966 was included in Hoshiarpur district. If we take the pre-1966 district boundaries, the corresponding figures for the occasions at Shiv Bari would be 98 percent and 96 percent respectively. At Bhagsunag the entire number of sample pilgrims (with the exception of one man) came from either the nearby town of Dharmsala or a couple of villages in the vicinity. Thus, the fields of all three sacred places were limited to within a very short distance. Hence, these places may be considered to belong to the lowest-level sacred places or the local level.

Because of the peculiar local composition of the respective populations, the pilgrims at Bhagsunag and Baijnath (during the winter festival of *Śivarātri*) did not all belong to the same language (or dialect) area. At Bhagsunag, for example, the largest number of visitors to the temple were Gorkhas from Dharmsala canton-

[24]A few samples (not included in my data) taken by my Tibetan friend Chu-ing Lāmā of Rewalsar on February 17, 19, and 20, 1968 show that several pilgrims from Bhutan and Nepal came for pilgrimage there.

[25]Please note my comments regarding overestimating of distances for these places in the early part of this chapter.

ment,[26] followed by Panjābī people of the town of Dharmsala. Both these peoples are nonindigenous groups in Himachal Pradesh.

At Baijnath, two rather distinct cultural groups were present among the pilgrims; these were the Gaddīs and the local Pahāṛī pilgrims. The Gaddīs, a pastoral people, speak their distinctive dialect and are easily differentiated from the rest of the local pilgrims because of their markedly different dress. The Gaddīs practice transhumance and during the winter season move to the villages and towns at lower elevations. Thus, during winter the Gaddīs are also considered part of the local population although culturally they are rather different from the resident Pahāṛī groups. We have pointed this out to illustrate that at the local level one may not always find a complete linguistic homogeneity, because of peculiar circumstances of the place. At Shiv Bari, no such "distorting" factors were present, and most pilgrims actually belonged to villages within a few miles from Shiv Bari in the valley of the river Soan. There was no question about the almost complete linguistic uniformity of the pilgrims.

On the basis of the above discussion we can finally list the levels of sacred places studied as shown in table 7-6.

CONCLUSIONS

Whether we take the average distances traveled by pilgrims, or use a simple measure of the dispersion of the field of sacred places, or observe the field of each place from the viewpoint of diversity of the pilgrims present, certain levels of sacred places suggest themselves. We have tried to show that the areal and linguistic diversity is maximum at the pan-Hindu-level place and that this diversity decreases markedly at successively lower levels until at the local level certain peculiarities of the composition of local population only are reflected in the pilgrims at those places. If certain distorting factors, as was pointed out earlier, are not present in the local population, the local-level places show a minimum diversity in the pilgrims.

It may be pointed out that there would appear to be no neat hierarchy and perhaps no such place as the "most sacred" for the entire country. One would suspect that there are many places at

[26]The Gorkhas have been long stationed in the army camp at this place, and in fact they have been responsible for the local popularity of this Siva shrine.

TABLE 7-6
LEVELS OF SACRED PLACES

Level	Place
1. Pan-Hindu	Badrinath
2. Supraregional	Hardwar, Ujjain
3. Regional	Kangra, Jwalaji, Chintpurni
4. (a) Subregional (high)	Naina Devi
(b) Subregional (low)	Mansa Devi, Rewalsar[1]
5. Local	Baijnath, Bhagsunag, Shiv Bari

[1]Rewalsar from the Buddhist viewpoint should be at the regional level.

which a high degree of diversity of pilgrims can be observed. Obviously, there is need to study several sacred places before a comparative analysis of the levels can be made. Such analysis could help us to better understand the interrelationship between the levels of sacred places and the areal cultural diversity. There seems to be a promising relationship between languages and the levels of sacred places. We have merely suggested such a relationship in this study. There also seems to be a relationship between certain former political units such as princely states and the pilgrimages to those sacred places that were patronized by the rulers. There is much need to study the relationship between the fields of sacred places and the caste regions, kinship regions, distribution of specific cults, the increased mobility of pilgrims, and the processes of Sanskritization and modernization.

The implication of our study is that the sacred places may be viewed as a system of nodes at different levels. The nodes of varied levels may help us to better understand the diversity as well as the common features of Hinduism. The nodes at highest levels can throw light on those aspects of Hinduism which integrate the Hindu population of diverse cultural regions of India. The nodes at lowest level may point out the immense diversity within Hinduism and the local basis of integration. I believe that it is not possible to say whether there is uniformity or diversity within Hinduism without referring to the levels, for at one level there may be extreme diversity, at another a high degree of uniformity.

The levels of sacred places suggested in our study on the basis of empirical evidence seem to accord generally with the four different levels at which Cohn and Marriott theoretically viewed the diversity of India,[27] although our study suggests at least five such levels for the limited number of sacred places studied.

[27]Bernard S. Cohn and McKim Marriott, "Networks and Centers in the Integration of India Civilization," *Journal of Social Research,* p. 2. Cohn and Marriott suggest four levels, namely, (1) "All India, the Sub-Continent." (2) "The Region Generally Defined by a Literary Language and Distinctive Caste Patterning." (3) "The Sub-Region." (4) "The Local Level." They suggest that several other intermediate levels and scales may be distinguished. Compare these with table 7-5 in our text.

Chapter VIII

The Level of Sacred Place and the Purpose and Frequency of Pilgrimage

INTRODUCTION

In this chapter I shall explore the possibility of relationships between the levels of sacred places (as defined in chapter 7) and the purpose and frequency of pilgrimage. I shall also note the significance of location, where necessary, in terms of the frequency of pilgrimage.

Before attempting to study this relationship, certain broad categories of purposes may be suggested. A given sacred place will be visited by a pilgrim either because a purely religious desire (spontaneous or induced) arises or because a mundane need is felt to undertake the pilgrimage. Since the "desires" and "needs" for undertaking pilgrimages may vary from person to person, it is useful to discuss categories of related purposes rather than individual purposes. Moreover, "needs" may be either short term or long term and they may arise either once in a lifetime or recurrently. It is, therefore, logical to consider the purposes and frequencies in an interrelated fashion.

PURPOSES OF PILGRIMAGE IN GENERAL

The purposes of pilgrimage may be divided into the following categories.

Desire for Identification with the Sacred Order

The Hindu religious literature is replete with expressions of belief that visiting sacred places is an act of holiness. An influential Hindu religious journal tersely sums up the reason why pilgrimage to sacred places should be undertaken: "In order for achieving identity with the Cosmic Reality; the knowledge of this reality *(Bhagvān)* is acquired through lustless and greedless association with the holy men; it is at the *tīrthas* that holy men are encountered."[1] The above conclusion is based on verses taken from the *Padmapurāṇa*.[2]

The uppermost desire of a religious man is not only to live in the world of sacred order, but actually to be part and parcel of the sacred order. The sacred places are those parts of the differentiated space where the religious man believes that the sacred order exists. Hence his desire to visit sacred places. Mircea Eliade cogently describes the desire of the religious man "to live in a pure and holy cosmos."[3] The sacred place is not a mere extension of the physical profane space; it is a space of the moral order, the sacred order.

It is obviously too much to expect that all pilgrims visiting sacred places will give sophisticated and philosophically articulate answers when asked about their purpose of visit. Nevertheless, when the answers of some pilgrims are such that no specific material motive can be imputed to them, their desire to visit sacred places can only be understood on non-mundane grounds.

The ritualistic aspect of this category of pilgrimage may include worship of the deity, bathing in a sacred river or lake, the giving of alms, attending religious discourses of holy men, the singing of *bhajans* (religious songs), participating in *kīrtan* (devotional songs in chorus), and performance of other religious rituals considered appropriate for the place and occasion. Bathing in a sacred river or lake is not to be interpreted merely as a purificatory ceremony; it has much deeper significance.[4] For example, the *Kumbha* fair at Hardwar and other places means bathing in the *amrita,* or life-giving water. The life-giving water is not merely present in symbolic form. For the pilgrims a whole cosmic event is being reenacted, one in which they actually feel that they are participating. The myth is reactualized, at the specific time and at the specific place. The pilgrim is bathing in the "original" *amrita (eau de vie)*.[5]

[1] *Kalyāṇa, Tīrthāṅka,* p. 28.

[2] *Ibid.*

[3] *The Sacred and the Profane,* p. 65.

[4] For a fuller treatment, see Batuknath Bhattacharya, "Festivals and Sacred Places," in Haridas Bhattacharyya (ed.), *The Cultural Heritage of India,* IV, 487–488.

[5] An excellent conceptualization of the significance of sacred time and myths is to be found in Mircea Eliade, *The Sacred and the Profane,* pp. 68–113.

The Accumulation of Merit and the Removal of Sin

The concepts of the accumulation of religious merit and the removal of sin are among the most important purposes of pilgrimage, and yet it is very difficult to collect reliable data on these related phenomena. The problem arises largely because the pilgrims often do not overtly state that they intend to accumulate merit or shed their sin by bathing at sacred places. Nevertheless, there are usually implicit undertones of this objective. Merit accumulation and removal of sin, though not synonymous, are clearly complementary. The religious literature is quite explicit about the merit-bestowing and sin-removing qualities of *tīrthas*.[6]

Life-Cycle Purposes

In the above two categories the basic concern of the pilgrim is with the sacred order and with the life hereafter; it is the concern with the ideal and the future. However, the life-cycle purposes (and those to be discussed subsequently) belong to the mundane existence, to the life in which specific social, psychological, and economic problems exist. It is the life in which rituals, rites, obligations, and duties have to be performed in order that one may be recognized as a member of a religion, sect, caste, or class. Several of the important life-cycle rites are performed at sacred places. Among them are *muṇḍana* (tonsure), consigning the ashes of the deceased to holy waters, performance of *śrāddha* and *piṇḍa* (ceremonies for the deceased), investiture with sacred thread *(upnayana)*, purificatory bathing for the bride-to-be, and the like.

There is a certain degree of functional specialization of sacred places which is reflected in the pilgrims' responses in our questionnaire.[7] For example, the ceremony of *muṇḍana* is especially important at the Mother Goddess shrines, and several rites for the deceased are performed at Hardwar throughout the year.[8]

[6]The *tīrtha-yātrā* section of the *Mahābhārata* is replete with this idea. Also see *Agni Purāṇa*, III, 371–372.

[7]The performance of *śrāddha* at Gaya is considered especially desirable. Kurukshetra and Pehoa specialize in the performance of rites for the person whose death occurred accidentally or in bed. See also L. P. Vidyarthi, *The Sacred Complex in Hindu Gaya*.

[8]Our sample does not reflect this functional specialization of Hardwar, because it refers to a few days of the *Ardha Kumbha* fair.

Problem-Generated (or Tension-Generated) Purposes

This category of purposes is of great importance because it is intimately related with the economic and corporeal conditions of the person making a pilgrimage. There is nothing that is spiritual per se in these purposes, which may include desire for male offspring, marriage, higher profits, better crops, favorable settlement of pending court proceedings, and the like. These purposes are thoroughly mundane and personal, but may appear to belong to the realm of religion because the pilgrim shows his dependence on the supernatural power. This dependence is expressed in the form of commitments, vows, rituals, and ceremonies prescribed by the religion.

In order to better the chances of success, the pilgrim actively seeks the help of the deity. The vows that the pilgrim undertakes, and the rituals and ceremonies that he performs, are merely devices for the expectancy of the attainment of the desired result.[9] Some sacred places and deities are especially popular for these types of purposes.[10]

The "problem" as the reason for pilgrimage needs much further investigation than has been possible in our field work.[11] A potentially fruitful approach may be to study whether problems related to unpredictability of events are related to certain castes or professions.

Purposes Related to Social Motives and Desires

Pilgrimage to sacred places may be of some social value to certain castes. We feel that it may have special significance for the scheduled castes.

Within a village or any other given locality the status of the scheduled castes is low and fairly well defined vis-à-vis other castes. Several sacred places provide a religiously and socially recognized environment within which the distinction of castes melts away.

[9]For an excellent treatment of the nature of rites and rituals, see Carl Gustav Diehl, *Instrument and Purpose: Studies on Rites and Rituals in South India*, pp. 259ff.

[10]Cf. *ibid.*, p. 249.

[11]Cf. Shin-Yi Hsu, "The Cultural Ecology of the Locust Cult in Traditional China." Hsu finds a high correlation between the frequency of locust infestations and the number of cult temples established. The locust-cult rituals and temples are functionally related to the social equilibrium by helping to alleviate anxiety.

In temples at many sacred places, particularly the goddess shrines, the scheduled castes have traditionally been visiting the innermost sacred precincts of the temples. In the rush of pilgrims it is impossible for Brahmans, or other so-called higher castes, to avoid coming into physical contact with them. Furthermore the *prasāda* (food offered to the deity and later distributed among pilgrims) may not be refused by any person even if it comes from the hands of the scheduled castes. This situation may be providing the scheduled castes with a semblance of equality, in at least the limited sacred precincts, an equality which in the profane world is denied to them. At most of the goddess places in our study no distinction is made between castes in terms of accepting the *prasāda* of the goddess. This provides a clear example of integration of castes at the religious level, at least in the sacred precincts of the temples. The social order prevails *outside* the sacred precincts. The cult of the goddess thus helps to link the folk and the elite, as Ghurye rightly maintains.[12] It has not been possible in our field work to study what proportion of scheduled-caste pilgrims have this idea of social equality in the sacred precincts, but it is a subject well worth sociological inquiry.

The preceding typology of purposes does not, I believe, exhaust the manifold motivations of pilgrims, but it does provide some basis for future investigation. In his *Instrument and Purpose,* Diehl seems to approach the whole motivational aspect of pilgrimage from too pragmatic an angle. Although he concedes that "other aspects must also be taken into account to get a full understanding of the pilgrim's way," he nevertheless overemphasizes the utilitarian view.[13] Thus he claims that "often the aim of a temple visit is to make a request" and adds that "more often the temple visits are made on vows."[14] My own experience of talking, praying, and living with a large number of pilgrims at many holy places leads me to believe that Diehl's observation does not have as general a validity as, at first thought, may be imputed to it. My field data suggest that there are certain *types* of places where "request" and "vows" are significant while at others they are almost totally irrelevant.

There are other grounds for disagreement with Diehl's concep-

[12]G. S. Ghurye, *Gods and Men,* pp. 242.
[13]Diehl, p. 249.
[14]*Ibid.,* p. 256.

tualization of the motives of pilgrimage. While it is true that the expectancy of reward *(phala)* has become one of the basic ideas in pilgrimage, it is equally true that religious literature stresses a number of moral and ethical precepts without which the "fruit" of *tīrtha-yātrā* cannot be achieved. Therefore, when "vows" and "requests" are made to a deity at a shrine, they are to be understood in the much broader concept of *tīrtha-yātrā* and not simply as ad hoc contractual "relationship" between the pilgrim and the deity. Specificity of motives is a part, but only a part, of the basis of pilgrimage. For a large number of devotees pilgrimage is a religiously desirable and psychologically satisfying activity without much reference to the expectancy of a specific reward. If this were not the case, it would be impossible to explain the ordeals that pilgrims are willing to undergo on their *yātrā* to such remote places as Amarnath in Kashmir and Kailas in Tibet. It is sometimes suggested that "people tend to exert themselves more readily for a highly specified, strongly desired result than for more general, unspecified goals."[15] My experience suggests on the contrary that pilgrims who were bound for the lengthy all-India pilgrimage were least concerned about the specific goals.

PURPOSES OF PILGRIMS IN FIELD SAMPLE

In order to get a broad view of the purposes of pilgrimage, we have assembled the field data of purposes into three broad groups : general purposes, specific purposes, and miscellaneous purposes. Explanation of each category follows.

General Purposes

These include *yātrā, darśana,* and *snāna*. These terms mean, respectively, pilgrimage, visiting the deity, and sacred bath. These are all general purposes without signifying any vows or specific ceremony.[16] When a pilgrim says he has come simply for *yātrā, darśana,* or *snāna,* it means he is likely to perform certain religious observances, rites, and ceremonies appropriate to the place, including holy bath. However, rites and ceremonies are not important in themselves; they are desirable adjuncts to pilgrimage.

[15] A. Bharati, "Pilgrimage Sites and Indian Civilization," p. 87.

[16] These are such purposes as have been discussed in the first two categories above and possibly include the fifth category as well.

Specific Purposes

Muṇḍana (tonsure) is a specific ceremony related to the life cycle.[17] At places where the Mother Goddess presides, *muṇḍana* of children is an important function for which pilgrims come from considerable distances. *Muṇḍana* is an important initiatory rite marking the passage from infancy to childhood. It may also have a symbolic significance of "offering" the child to the goddess. There are several other sacred places (not associated with Mother Goddess) where *muṇḍana* is performed (e.g., Prayag, Hardwar, and Tirupati), but in these places *muṇḍana* of adults is also important, symbolizing the shedding of one's sins. At these places this ceremony is not a part of the initiatory rites as is the case at the goddess shrines of Himachal Pradesh.

Sukhnā, mannat, manauti—all these terms mean vows. This group of purposes is concerned largely with one's own person. The devotee vows to make a pilgrimage or perform certain sacrifices (animal sacrifice or monetary sacrifice) to the deity whose help he seeks for a particular problem.

Miscellaneous Purposes[18]

Because of the specific occasions at which we took samples at Hardwar and Ujjain, purposes such as *śrāddha, piṇḍa,* investiture of sacred thread, and the like did not figure significantly in our sample. Had the samples been taken over an extended period of time (excluding the bathing festivals), these ceremonies would have been well represented. On the non-festival days at Hardwar (and particularly at the downstream extension of Hardwar called Kankhal) these ceremonies are immediately noticeable. Some pilgrims who preferred to call themselves "tourists" or "visitors," as well as those who gave no response, are included in the

[17]All caste Hindus but also some Sikhs and scheduled castes perform this ceremony. It may be performed at home, but the goddess shrines of Himachal Pradesh are the most desirable places. This is why we have divided the specific purposes under two separate heads, *muṇḍana* and *sukhnā*.

[18]When the pilgrim had more than one purpose, the most important one from his viewpoint was noted. For example, a person may have said that he came for *yātrā* and his son's *muṇḍana*. In that case the specific ceremony, i.e., *muṇḍana*, was counted, rather than *yātrā*.

TABLE 8-1
LEVELS OF SACRED PLACES AND THE PURPOSES OF PILGRIMAGES

SACRED PLACE (Deity)	*Occasion*	"Level" of sacred place	Number of pilgrims	Purpose and Percentage of Pilgrims		
				Yātrā, darśana, snāna (general purpose)	*Muṇḍana* (tonsure)	*Sukhnā* (vows)
BADRINATH (Viṣṇu)	Annual *Yātrā*	Pan-Hindu	400	97.5	0.0	1.0
HARDWAR (None)	*Ardha Kumbha*	Supraregional	800	98.4	0.4	0.0
UJJAIN (Śiva)	*Siṃhastha*	Supraregional	500	99.2	0.2	0.4
KANGRA (Goddess)	*Navarātrās*	Regional	450	76.9	6.2	16.4
JWALAJI (Goddess)	*Navarātrās*	Regional	496	46.9	32.5	20.6
CHINTPURNI (Goddess)	*Navarātrās*	Regional	500	54.4	21.0	24.2
CHINTPURNI (Goddess)	*Śrāvaṇa Aṣṭamī*	Regional	298	75.2	4.0	20.5
REWALSAR (Padmasambhava)	*Sissoo*	Regional (Buddhist)	100	97.0	0.0	3.0

TABLE 8-1 (Continued)
LEVELS OF SACRED PLACES AND THE PURPOSES OF PILGRIMAGES

				Purpose and Percentage of Pilgrims		
SACRED PLACE (Deity)	*Occasion*	"Level" of sacred place	Number of pilgrims	*Yātrā, darśana, snāna* (general purpose)	*Muṇḍana* (tonsure)	*Sukhnā* (vows)
NAINA DEVI (Goddess)	*Navarātrās*	Subregional (high)	494	57.7	5.9	36.4
NAINA DEVI (Goddess)	*Śrāvaṇa*	Subregional (high)	400	56.5	0.2	42.2
REWALSAR (Lomas Rṣhi)	*Vaiśākhī*	Subregional (low)	100	100.0	0.0	0.0
MANSA DEVI (Goddess)	*Navarātrās*	Subregional (low)	250	44.0	19.2	36.8
MANSA DEVI (Goddess)	*Śrāvaṇa*	Subregional (low)	175	72.0	4.0	24.0
BAIJNATH (Śiva)	*Śivarātri*	Local	100	82.0	0.0	14.0
BAIJNATH (Śiva)	*Śrāvaṇa*	Local	100	97.0	0.0	3.0
BHAGSUNAG (Śiva)	*Śivarātri*	Local	85	80.0	0.0	15.3

TABLE 8-1 (Continued)
LEVELS OF SACRED PLACES AND THE PURPOSES OF PILGRIMAGES

				Purpose and Percentage of Pilgrims		
SACRED PLACE (Deity)	*Occasion*	"Level" of sacred place	Number of pilgrims	*Yātrā, darśana, snāna* (general purpose)	*Muṇḍana* (tonsure)	*Sukhnā* (vows)
SHIV BARI (Śiva)	*Śivarātri*	Local	100	83.0	0.0	11.0
SHIV BARI (Śiva)	*Jātrā*	Local	100	91.0	0.0	2.0

NOTE : The totals may not add up to 100 percent because the "miscellaneous purpose" category has been omitted here. "Miscellaneous" would also include "no response" and such pilgrims who call themselves "tourists."

miscellaneous category.[19] On the whole, at all the places only an insignificant number of pilgrims were included in the miscellaneous category.

RELATIONSHIP BETWEEN THE LEVEL OF SACRED PLACES AND PURPOSES OF PILGRIMAGE

Table 8-1 shows the levels of sacred places and the proportion of different groups of purposes of pilgrimage.

It is quite clear that the pan-Hindu and supraregional places were almost exclusively visited for general purposes. At Hardwar and Ujjain the religious occasions dictated that a holy dip be the chief purpose of pilgrimage. At Badrinath the main object of pilgrimage was to have a *darśana* of the deity Badrinārāiṇa. Most pilgrims to Badrinath, however, also bathe in the hot springs at that place as well as in the icy waters of the adjacent Alkananda River. An insignificant number of pilgrims at these high-level places came for vows or *muṇḍana*. Since ritual purification by bathing in sacred waters is the most universal overt expression of Hinduism, it is very evident at the high-level sacred places.

Why do the purposes of pilgrims at high-level places not include specific purposes like *sukhnā* (vows)? I feel that part of the answer may be found in the nature of their fields and their location with respect to their fields. Since the fields of high-level places are spatially wide and culturally diverse, it is not possible for the pilgrims to associate the deities of these distant places with their personal problems. For the fulfillment of material desires a deity situated closer to the sociocultural milieu of the pilgrim seems to be more desirable. Moreover, some high-level places like Hardwar may have no specific presiding deity at all. The religious importance of Hardwar (even though nominally associated with Śiva) is largely due to the periodic reactualization of a mythological sacred event. Obviously it would be irrelevant for a pilgrim to pray there for a male offspring or a good harvest.

At the regional and subregional shrines the objectives of pilgrims show a marked significance of the specific purposes—whether it is *muṇḍana* or *sukhnā*. The pilgrims were often reluctant to admit that they came for *sukhnā* for fear of offending the deity, but even

[19]It seems to be fashionable among the so-called "westernized elite" to speak of themselves as "tourists" even though such people may perform many of the same ceremonies as the more traditional pilgrims.

so, the figures in table 8-1 show that as high as 42 percent of pilgrims at Naina Devi and 36 percent at Mansa Devi came to fulfill their vows. The only glaring exception was Rewalsar. We have already explained that the *Vaiśākhī* fair at Rewalsar was an occasion for merrymaking rather than for religious observances. Even at the Buddhist fair no significant proportion of pilgrims came for *sukhnā*. Possibly the concept of *sukhnā* is not important in Buddhism.

The local-level sacred places showed a decreased importance of *sukhnā*, and the *muṇḍana* ceremony was completely absent. The smaller proportion of pilgrims who came for *sukhnā* to the local-level shrines (compared with regional and subregional ones) may be attributed to at least two reasons. First, these shrines are readily accessible at all times to the local population. Therefore, a special religious occasion need not be waited for to fulfill a vow to the deity. Second, the presence of shrines where *sukhnā* is a specialty perhaps reduces the importance of the local deity for this purpose. The study of local-level places for an extended period of time can perhaps clarify whether *sukhnā* is more significant at these places than our samples suggest.

The deities at local-level places do seem to be intimately related with the local needs, not only in the religious sphere, but also in the economic and social life. We shall give one example of such a relationship from our study.

Shiv Bari, as its name suggests, is a small Śiva temple situated near the village Ambota in the Una tehsil of Kangra district. The temple is located on the right-hand bank of the river Soan and is surrounded by a patch of dense forest whose wood can be used for no other purpose but cremation. Some devotees from Ambota visit the temple daily, but the main religious fair is *Śivarātri* (February), when people from nearby villages come to the temple. Another fair, *Jātrā Melā,* is held in April, when the grounds near the temple are used for sports competitions between different teams of the villages, and the villagers also visit the shrine. Relatives from neighboring villages may meet each other and exchange information.

When the rains show signs of failing, the local population assembles and pours water over the *liṅga* of Śiva and keeps on doing so until the water from the temple flows out and joins the Soan River. This effort is undertaken to propitiate the deity so that he may bring the needed showers on which the prosperity of the population depends. I confirmed the truth of this practice both from the local priest and from other persons of Ambota village.

DEITIES AND THE PURPOSES OF PILGRIMAGE

At the sacred places studied by the writer there is a fairly obvious relationship between the type of deity and the purposes of pilgrimage (see table 8-1). The concept of *sukhnā* is clearly associated more with the Mother Goddess than with the male gods, and *muṇḍana* even more so. The goddess is a symbol of fertility, abundance, and prosperity. This ancient idea continues to exist in the Hindu population and manifests itself at the goddess shrines in the form of *sukhnā*. The songs (locally called *bhetā*, offering) sung by the pilgrims at these shrines unmistakably narrate the wish-granting character of the goddess.

The central theme of all the *bhetā* sung by the devotees may be summarized as follows : "The *Devī* (Goddess) is the storehouse of abundance. The devotee of the *Devī* will get all his wishes fulfilled. Sing the praise of the *Devī*! Victory to the *Devī*!" One could cite numerous instances of pilgrims who came to visit the temple of one goddess or the other in order to seek her help in personal problems. In fact, it seems that the prominent *Devī* shrines of Himachal Pradesh specialize in this aspect of pilgrimage.

FREQUENCY OF VISITS TO SACRED PLACES

Our study indicates no direct relationship between the levels of sacred places and the frequency of pilgrims' visits. On the other hand, it indicates a strong tendency on the part of the pilgrims to repeat their visits (see table 8-2). The rather low proportion of pilgrims repeating their pilgrimage to remote shrines such as Badrinath is of course understandable. The difficulty of reaching Badrinath is made all the more pronounced by the long journey in the Himalayas.[20]

At the shrines of the local level it can only be expected that many a person will, during the course of his life, attend fairs and festivals

[20]A motorable road now makes Badrinath fairly accessible. The number of pilgrims is likely to increase considerably.

TABLE 8-2

PILGRIMS WHO PAID FOUR OR MORE VISITS TO THE SACRED PLACE
(including those who claim they come each year or several times during the year)

Sacred place	Number[1]	Percentage of sample	"Level" of sacred place
Badrinath	9 (400)	2.2	Pan-Hindu
Hardwar	210 (300)	70.0	Supraregional
Kangra[2]	90 (200)	45.0	Regional
Jwalaji	98 (247)	39.7	Regional
Chintpurni	104 (250)	41.6	Regional
Rewalsar (S)[3]	39 (100)	39.0	Regional (Buddhist)
Naina Devi	106 (194)	54.6	Subregional (high)
Rewalsar (V)[3]	34 (100)	34.0	Subregional (low)
Baijnath[4]	95 (100)	95.0	Local
Bhagsunag	54 (85)	63.5	Local
Shiv Bari	81 (100)	81.0	Local

[1]The figures within parentheses represent the sampled number of pilgrims from whom the question related to number of visits was asked.

[2]At Kangra, Jwalaji, Chintpurni, and Naina Devi the occasion of these samples was *Navarātrās* of *Caitra* (March-April 1968).

[3]S = *Sissoo* Fair (Buddhist); V = *Vaiśākhī* (Hindu-Sikh).

[4]At Baijnath, Bhagsunag, and Shiv Bari the occasion of the samples was *Śivarātri* (February 1968).

at the nearby sacred place. However, even at higher-level shrines many pilgrims repeat their visits. The repetition of visits to sacred places suggests that they—particularly ones to which repeated *sukhnā* visits are made—play more than an ephemeral role in the life of the pilgrims. The rather high frequency of pilgrims' visits to Hardwar is bound up with the necessity to perform rites for the dead and the occurrence of the *Kumbha, Ardha-Kumbha,* and several minor fairs on which bathing in the Ganga bestows special religious merit. *Sukhnā* visits to Hardwar, as was already noted, are rare.

The frequency of visits to the Mother Goddess shrines, it seems, is related to the specific-purpose visits more than to the general purpose, even though our data show that there were more pilgrims with a "general" purpose.

A thorough, comparative analysis of the functional aspects of similar-level places, particularly supraregional and pan-Hindu, is necessary before the lack of direct relationship between levels and frequencies of visits can be established.

CONCLUSIONS

A categorization of purposes of pilgrimage allows us to study the relationship between the levels of sacred places and the purposes of the visits of pilgrims. The high-level sacred places (pan-Hindu, supraregional) are visited largely for general purification. On the other hand, the visits of pilgrims to the regional- and subregional-level shrines seem to be specific-purpose oriented. We do not suggest that high-level shrines are not visited for specific purposes. They are, but the purposes are not related to afflictions and problems of daily life. The regional and subregional shrines, particularly those with the Mother Goddess as the presiding deity, seem to be especially favored by pilgrims with specific personal or material desires, motives, and problems. The spatially wide and culturally diverse fields of high-level shrines are not conducive to the development of pilgrims' dependency on distant deities for solution of personal problems.

The frequency of visits to sacred places is directly related neither to the level of sacred places nor to the deity. Location of a place with respect to its field and the nature of the purpose of visit may be more important considerations. In any case, comparative studies on these aspects are needed before the final word can be said.

Chapter IX

Level of Sacred Place and the Religious Travels of Pilgrims

INTRODUCTION

In the previous chapter we observed that the purposes of the pilgrims show considerable relationship to the levels of sacred places. In this chapter we shall examine the relationship, if any, between the levels of sacred places and the religious travels of the pilgrims. Intuitively, it appears that the higher-level shrines should have a greater proportion of the religiously more mobile pilgrims than the lower-level ones. Based on data of the religious travels of pilgrims, we have tried to identify two distinct patterns of religious circulation, one related to the pan-Hindu-level sacred place and the other to the subregional-level sacred place. Some implications of the role of these two patterns of religious circulation are also pointed out.

ASPECTS OF RELIGIOUS TRAVEL CONSIDERED

Three aspects of the religious travels have been briefly studied on the basis of field data.

(1) Number of sacred places visited by a pilgrim in his life. The actual question was "Which sacred places have you ever visited in your life time?"

(2) Number of "first level" sacred places visited in life. ("First level" in this case refers to place of first category as defined in chap. 5 and shown in fig. 5-1.)

(3) Location of "first level" places. Location here refers to whether the places visited are situated in the pilgrims' own language area, in the Indo-Aryan language area, or in both the Indo-Aryan and the Dravidian language areas.

TABLE 9-1
NUMBER OF SACRED PLACES VISITED BY PILGRIMS IN THEIR LIVES

Sacred place of interview	Level	Number of pilgrims responding	Percentage of pilgrims who visited the given number of sacred places				Totals of last two columns
			1–2	3–7	8–10	11+	
Badrinath	Pan-Hindu	399	1.2	27.6	29.6	41.6	71.2
Hardwar	Supraregional	293	22.2	68.5	9.9	19.4	29.3
Kangra	Regional	199	30.1	67.8	1.5	0.6	2.1
Jwalaji	Regional	251	34.2	59.0	6.4	0.4	6.8
Chintpurni	Regional	250	19.6	61.6	7.6	1.2	8.8
Rewalsar	Regional[1]	100	65.0	33.0	2.0	0.0	2.0
Naina Devi	Subregional	194	51.0	49.0	0.0	0.0	0.0
Rewalsar	Subregional	100	56.0	41.0	0.0	3.0	3.0
Baijnath	Local	100	25.0	70.0	2.0	3.0	5.0
Bhagsunag	Local	85	31.8	63.5	4.7	0.0	4.7
Shiv Bari	Local	100	21.0	77.0	1.0	1.0	2.0

[1]Regional level for the Buddhists only.

Number of Sacred Places Visited by the Pilgrims

Table 9-1 shows that the proportion of pilgrims who visited a large number of sacred places in their life (eight or more) was highest at the pan-Hindu level (Badrinath)—over 71 percent. At Hardwar, a shrine of next lower level (supraregional), the corresponding proportion was over 29 percent. Similarly, the three regional-level shrines had on an average a smaller proportion of pilgrims (about 6 percent) in this category than the supraregional shrine. The two subregional shrines had a lower proportion of pilgrims than the regional ones on the average. However, in the case of local-level shrines, the proportion of pilgrims who have visited more than eight sacred places increases. Thus, except for the local-level shrines, the relationship between the level of sacred place and the proportion of religiously more mobile pilgrims seems to be clear. In other words, the religiously more mobile pilgrims are more likely to be associated with high-level sacred places than with lower-level ones. At the local level the relationship may be distorted by certain peculiar local circumstances. For example, at Bhagsunag the proportion of pilgrims who have visited over eight places is clearly higher than at Kangra—a regional-level place.

Number of "First Level" Sacred Places Visited in Life

Table 9-2 shows the proportion of pilgrims in our samples who claimed (*a*) that they have visited more than four places of "first level,"[1] and (*b*) that they have never visited a first-level sacred place.[2]

At the pan-Hindu level over 74 percent of the pilgrims had visited four or more first-level sacred places. At the supraregional, regional, and subregional levels respectively the figures are 29.3 percent, 6.1 percent (average), and 2.5 percent (average). At the local level there is a slight rise, compared with the subregional level.

[1]"First-level" in this case refers to places of first category as defined in chap. 5 and shown in fig. 5-1.

[2]At Badrinath, Hardwar, and Jwalaji the figures of the pilgrims who had visited four or more first-level shrines do not include their current visit to these shrines, because the map in fig. 5-1 defines these places as of the first category. For example, if a person at Jwalaji made a statement that he had never visited any of the shrines of first level, it means he did not visit any *other* of the first level.

TABLE 9-2

PILGRIM VISITS TO FIRST-LEVEL SACRED PLACES

Sacred place of interview	Level[1]	Number of pilgrims responding	Percentage who have visited: four or more	Percentage who have visited: none at all
Badrinath	Pan-Hindu	399	74.3	1.5
Hardwar	Supraregional	293	29.3	26.9
Kangra	Regional	199	4.5	25.1
Jwalaji	Regional	251	4.5	49.8
Chintpurni	Regional	250	9.2	26.4
Rewalsar	Regional[2]	100	3.0	56.0
Naina Devi	Subregional	194	2.0	57.7
Rewalsar	Subregional	100	3.0	56.0
Baijnath	Local	100	5.0	24.0
Bhagsunag	Local	85	2.3	30.6
Shiv Bari	Local	100	3.0	34.0

NOTE : See fig. 5-1, chap. 5.

[1]Level of sacred places in our field sample as determined in chap. 7.

[2]Rewalsar had a regional level on the Buddhist Fair.

On the whole it can be maintained that the higher the level of sacred place at which pilgrim samples are taken, the higher is the proportion of pilgrims who have visited other first-level sacred places. In other words, the pilgrims who visited the high-level shrines in our sample are distinctively more pilgrimage oriented than those who visited the lower-level shrines (except the local ones).

Table 9-2 also shows that at the pan-Hindu level (Badrinath) only 1.5 percent of the responding pilgrims had not visited any other first-level place. At the supraregional level the corresponding figure is about 27 percent. The average figures for the regional and subregional level are 30.4 percent and 56.8 percent. If we compare the actual rather than the average figures, the relationship is obscured. At the local level there is a considerable decrease in the proportion of pilgrims who never visited a first-level sacred place. Excluding the local-level places, there seems to be an inverse relationship between the levels of sacred places and the proportion of pilgrims who never visited first-level sacred places.

A very significant proportion of pilgrims at the regional and subregional sacred places had never visited high-level places. The conclusion is compelling that there is a great difference in the *kind* of pilgrims who visit places of different levels. One might say that the elite shows a decided preference for the sacred places that are better known through the religious literature. This does not mean that the elite does not visit lower-level shrines—it does indeed—but the fact of *preference* remains in favor of high-level places. Unfortunately, in our questionnaire we did not enquire about the level of education of pilgrims, but our conversations with several thousand pilgrims suggest that the average level of literacy is high at high-level shrines and lower at regional and subregional holy places.

Location of "First Level" Sacred Places Ever Visited by Pilgrims

In order to differentiate the kinds of pilgrims at sacred places of different levels, the location of the first-level sacred places visited by pilgrims with respect to their own language area was analyzed. It appears that the kind of pilgrims at lower-level sacred places is such that their visits to places of first level are more likely to be either in their own language area (if there is a first-level place in that area) or in the immediately neighboring language area. On the contrary, the kind of pilgrims at the high-level places may exhibit a far wider contact with other high-level places in India.

Most of the sacred places I studied lie largely in transitional language zones, making such an analysis extremely difficult. Nevertheless, if we compare the proportion of pilgrims at different sacred places who have visited high-level holy places both in the Indo-Aryan language area and the Dravidian language area, some suggestive observations can be made.

Table 9-3 shows that at the pan-Hindu level (Badrinath) over 35 percent of the pilgrims had visited first-level shrines in both of the major language families of India. The corresponding figures for the supraregional (Hardwar), regional (average of Kangra,

TABLE 9-3

PILGRIM VISITS TO FIRST-LEVEL SACRED PLACES IN BOTH THE INDO-ARYAN AND THE DRAVIDIAN LANGUAGE AREAS

Sacred place of interview	Level	Number of responding pilgrims (sample)	Percentage of sample
Badrinath	Pan-Hindu	399	35.3
Hardwar	Supraregional	293	10.2
Kangra	Regional	199	2.5
Jwalaji	Regional	251	1.2
Chintpurni	Regional	250	2.0
Rewalsar	Regional[1]	100	0.0
Naina Devi	Subregional	194	1.0
Rewalsar	Subregional	100	3.0
Baijnath	Local	100	2.0
Bhagsunag	Local	85	0.0
Shiv Bari	Local	100	1.0

NOTE : "First level" is the first category in fig. 5-1, chap. 5.
[1]Rewalsar had a regional level on the Buddhist fair.

Jwalaji, and Chintpurni), and subregional (average of Naina Devi and Rewalsar) are 10.2 percent, 1.9 percent, and 2.0 percent. The distinction between the pilgrims of pan-Hindu-level shrines on the one hand and those of supraregional and regional ones on the other is clear. From the regional downward to the local levels there seems to be no clear basis for differentiation. Table 9-3 also brings out the fact that religious circulation between the two major language areas is significant in reference to high-level sacred places.

TWO BASIC PATTERNS OF PILGRIM CIRCULATION

In the preceding discussion we have pointed out that pilgrimage-oriented people are more likely to be encountered at a high-level shrine than at one of a lower level. In the previous chapter we noted that the purposes for which pilgrims travel also seem to bear significant relationships to the levels of sacred places that they visit. From the interrelationship between the levels of sacred places and the purposes of pilgrimage, and from the rather obvious differences in the extent of religious travels of pilgrims at different levels of sacred places, two distinct patterns of religious circulation seem to emerge. These may be called (*a*) the merit (or general) pattern, and (*b*) the specific pattern. We shall discuss below the nature of these two patterns, with selected examples of the sacred places of distinctively different levels.

The Merit Pattern

This pattern usually consists of pilgrimages to high-level sacred places—places of ancient origin, which are eulogized in the Puranic Sanskrit literature. These places may or may not be associated with a specific presiding deity; that is, the deity per se may not necessarily be the object of attraction to the pilgrim. Instead of the deity there may be the attraction of a particular reactualized mythological event with a widely recognized sacred quality. The purpose of pilgrimage is least likely to originate from a desire for material benefit. Such a pilgrimage is likely to be combined with a visit to other sacred places, depending on the total time that the pilgrim has decided to devote to this undertaking. Since such a pilgrimage is likely to take considerable time—several weeks or more—relatively affluent pilgrims are likely to constitute significant, even predominant, proportions of the pilgrim body at any given sacred place of high-level.

The chief object of such a pilgrimage is the gaining of religious merit, howsoever difficult the definition of "religious merit" may be. This object seems to be best fulfilled in two ways. First, the pilgrim may visit as many shrines as possible given the monetary resources at his disposal. Second, he may visit a place where an event of supreme religious significance may be happening. Thus, this pattern of circulation is likely to transcend spatial linguistic differentiations because it has little to do with such intervening non-religious aspects of space.

The merit pattern of religious circulation is best illustrated by the pilgrims of Badrinath—one of the four *dhāms* of Hindu religion.[3] We have already dealt with the field of Badrinath and pointed out that both of the major language families of India are represented (see chap. 7).

A high proportion (86 percent) of the Badrinath pilgrims were expecting to spend over two weeks on their entire pilgrimage, including about 43 percent who intended to spend over thirty days. Obviously, a large part of the pilgrim body had committed themselves to the pilgrimage for an extended period of time. The length of time (from home, back to home) was determined by three chief reasons. First, transportation was difficult despite the new bus service.[4] Second, many pilgrims consider the *yātrā* (pilgrimage) incomplete unless they also visit Yamnotri, Gangotri, and Kedarnath.[5] Third, wealthy businessmen, well-to-do farmers, and salaried government employees may take a vacation and spend time on pilgrimage combined with "tourism" away from the cares and worries of home, business, or office.

Most pilgrims to Badrinath had already visited a number of prominent holy places en route to this place. Ninety-three percent of the Badrinath pilgrims had either visited or intended to visit more than two other sacred places. About half the number of pilgrims interviewed (47 percent) had visited more than four sacred places on the way to Badrinath, almost always including Hardwar. Many pilgrims went to Yamnotri first, then to Gangotri and Kedarnath before reaching Badrinath. The pilgrims from Andhra and Tamilnadu usually visited Varanasi and Prayag on their way.

The purpose of almost all the pilgrims to Badrinath was to have *darśana* (sight) of the deity and to have holy baths in the Alkananda River as well as in the several confluences called "*prayāgas*" (e.g., Viṣṇu Prayāga, Karṇa Prayāga, Rudra Prayāga). Thus,

[3]*Dhām* refers to one of the four abodes of sanctity in the cardinal directions, for the Hindus of the entire subcontinent. These are Badrinath (or Badrinarain) in the north, Jagannath Puri in the east, Rameshwaram (Ramesvaram) in the south, and Dwarka in the west. Badrinath is not specifically mentioned in the critical edition of the *Mahābhārata*; however the Puranic eulogies are abundant. See also *Kalyāṇa, Tīrthāṅka*, p. 47.

[4]Several pilgrims had to wait for as many as six days before their turn came to board the bus from Rishikesh to Badrinath during the 1968 annual *yātrā*.

[5]These three places are more and more being referred to these days as the *Dhāms* of Uttrākhaṇḍa (the northern sacred quarter). Precise definition of Uttrākhaṇḍa is not known, but in common usage it comprises the Himalayan districts of Uttar Pradesh.

the purpose in reality was to purify the soul and earn religious merit rather than to pray for wealth or success in business. At Hardwar, similarly, over 96 percent of the pilgrims interviewed came for the *Ardha Kumbha* bath. No deity was to be propitiated, and rare was the pilgrim who came for *sukhnā*.

The Specific Pattern

In its ideal form this may lead the pilgrim to the place of a specific deity, at a climactic religious occasion, and with a tangible purpose. The place of the deity is usually subregional or local. A high-level shrine is unlikely to be involved in this pattern of pilgrim circulation. The deity at such a place may be male or female. The place itself is likely to be connected with an ancient legend, but it is more likely to be eulogized only in sectarian literature. Since the purpose of the visitors is specific and the level of place relatively low, distance from the devotee's area of origin is likely to be short, and therefore the *yātrā* (pilgrimage) may take a short time, usually a few days.

Probably the best example of this pattern of religious circulation in our study is provided by the pilgrims of Naina Devi. As the name suggests, the place is sacred to the Mother Goddess. Although there are several laudatory local legends about the place, there is no mention of this particular deity even in the recognized list of places sacred to the Mother Goddess.[6] The temple is situated on the pinnacle of a hill in the Siwalik Range called the Naina Devi *Dhār*. Although politically it is included in district Bilaspur (a former princely state), most pilgrims are from the plains (see figs. 7-8 and 7-9 in chap. 7). The field of this place is restricted largely to a few districts, particularly Rupar, Ludhiana, Chandigarh (Union territory), and Patiala. Samples of pilgrims were taken on two occasions—the *Navarātrās* of *Caitra* (March–April 1968) and *Śrāvaṇa Aṣṭamī* (August 1968)—referred to in this discussion as the first and the second occasion respectively. Both of these occasions are specifically significant for this pilgrimage.

On the first occasion from a sample of 494 responding pilgrims over 36 percent had come for *sukhnā* (vows). The corresponding figure for the second occasion was over 42 percent in a sample of 400 pilgrims. On the first occasion about 6 percent of the pilgrims

[6]See D. C. Sircar, "The *Śākta Pithas.*"

sampled had come for *muṇḍana* (tonsure), but on the second occasion only one person with this motive was encountered. I suspect, though, that many of the persons who did not specifically state *sukhnā* as their motive had indeed come for *sukhnā* although they would not admit it to an unfamiliar observer. A large number of pilgrims came to the temple as *dandotis* on the second occasion.[7] It was no mean task to cover a distance of about five miles from the foot of the hill to the top in the manner prescribed for such a pilgrim.

Most pilgrims to Naina Devi came directly from their home without visiting any other sacred place on their way; that is, they came specifically to this particular deity. A sample of 194 pilgrims on the first occasion was asked "Which sacred place did you visit while coming to this place, and which sacred place are you going to visit on the return journey?" It was found that over 95 percent of the pilgrims came directly to the place from their home and over 88 percent intended to go directly home after visiting this sacred shrine of the Goddess. Of those few who did visit another sacred place en route to Naina Devi or intended to visit one en route home, virtually all were Sikhs by religion (including Jats and scheduled castes). The shrine they visited or intended to visit in almost all cases was Anandpur Sahib. The latter is one of the chief sacred places of the Sikhs. Almost all pilgrims intended to spend only a day or two on the pilgrimage.

A substantial percentage of pilgrims on both occasions belonged to the cultivating castes and the scheduled castes. On the first occasion the cultivating castes and the scheduled castes made up respectively 25.1 percent and 10.5 percent of a sample of 494 pilgrims. The corresponding figures for the second occasion (sample of 400) were 16.7 percent and 11.7 percent. This was in very marked contrast to the pilgrims at Badrinath, where the cultivating castes made up only 4.5 percent while only two persons of the scheduled castes were encountered in a sample of 400 pilgrims.

[7]A *dandoti* pilgrim is one who covers a certain precommitted distance to the temple by prostrating at each body-length. This arduous task is undertaken to fulfill a vow that a pilgrim may have decided upon. Usually the vows are taken by devotees who wish the deity to help solve a specific problem or remove an affliction. As many as thirty *dandotis* were interviewed, and in each case an intimate personal problem was found to be the reason for pilgrimage.

Suggestions for Further Research

We have found that Badrinath and Naina Devi present a contrasting picture of pilgrim circulation in almost all respects. This contrast is clear whether we study the respective fields, the nature of the deity, the kinds of pilgrims, the time spent on pilgrimage, or the purposes for which pilgrimages are undertaken. It is possible to compare several other aspects of the two sacred places. A particularly rewarding inquiry could be a comparative analysis of the ritual complex of sacred places of different levels. We can only hint at such a contrast. At Badrinath the rituals of the temple are based on ancient Vedic tradition, while at Naina Devi they are based on the Śākta tradition. A considerable folk element has entered into the latter mode of worship. The priests while performing the *ardāsa*[8] (supplication on behalf of the pilgrim) use a mixture of Hindī and Panjābī at Naina Devi. On the contrary, at Badrinath there is no such institution. Instead, the *pūjā* (worship) is highly Sanskritic. This contrast alone brings out the dominance of the folk element in the lower-level shrines and of the literary Sanskritic Hinduism at the high-level ones.

IMPLICATION OF RELIGIOUS CIRCULATION AT DIFFERENT LEVELS

Pilgrims at sacred places of different levels participate in recognizably different patterns of religious circulation. At the highest level the religiously oriented elite, by making pilgrimages to famous shrines eulogized in the traditional Sanskrit literature, maintains the vitality of a pan-Indian Hindu holy space. Such pilgrimages, arising from the philosophical-religious ideals of Hinduism, encompass sacred places irrespective of their regional location, thus fostering a high level of spatial integration within the religion. These pilgrimages, moreover, continually define the limits of Hindu religious space and of Hinduism in the secular sense. They provide a perpetual link with the past—as far back as the epic period. We regard high-level pilgrim circulation as having a significant Indianizing influence on the pilgrims. Long-distance religious pilgrimage provides a mechanism whereby the

[8]A priest usually acts as the intermediary (between the pilgrim and the goddess) and "conveys" to the goddess the desire of the pilgrim after the latter has paid certain fees to him.

pilgrims transcend the political and cultural boundaries within India. It is this aspect of pilgrimage which, we believe, commonly helps in an identification with a wider religious space than a subregion or a region.

At the lower levels of religious circulation both the materialistic aspects of Hinduism and its regional or subregional folk elements find expression.[9] The gods and goddesses no longer remain philosophical abstractions; instead man begins to "use" them as instruments for tangible purposes. It is also within the framework of this religious circulation that elements of the "little tradition" may become parts of the "great tradition"—a local goddess may be transformed to Durgā, or a local male deity may eventually become Śiva. The goddess at Chintpurni, for example, is considered by the priests and the devotees to be one of seven Mother Goddesses of ancient tradition. The priests and devotees alike will enumerate seven goddesses within Himachal Pradesh, although they do not agree on the exact places. On the other hand the concept of seven Mother Goddesses is far from restricted to Himachal Pradesh.[10] Nevertheless, the priests and pilgrims consider this goddess to be a form of Durgā—the consort of Śiva, hence as ancient as Śiva himself. In other words, the goddess at Chintpurni, who at one time must have been a local deity, has now been accorded a high status although she remains a regional deity in terms of the field of her devotees.[11]

The two broad levels of religious circulation thus reflect the philosophical and the mundane aspects of Hinduism. The Sanskritic universal aspects of Hinduism continue to be circulated through one pattern while the regional cultural elements circulate through the other. The two complementary patterns of religious circulation, when studied in greater detail, may provide us with a better insight into the diversity as well as the uniformity within Hinduism.

[9]The materialist aspects of Hinduism have been much neglected by scholars. One of the few examples of these aspects of Hinduism is Debiprasad Chattopadhyaya, *Lokāyata: A Study in Ancient Indian Materialism.*

[10]For a scholarly discussion on the subject of Mother Goddess, see G. S. Ghurye, *Gods and men*, pp. 238–263.

[11]For a detailed analysis of the absorption of local goddess traditions into the universal tradition of Hinduism, see, P. K. Maity, *Historical Studies in the Cult of the Goddess Mansa.*

Chapter X

Sacred Places and the Caste Composition of Pilgrims

INTRODUCTION

Caste (*jāti*) is one of the most fundamental aspects of the sociology of Hinduism.[1] When, therefore, we view the mass of pilgrims at any sacred place, we are looking at a socially differentiated congregation. Depending on the nature of the sacred place, its level, and the religious occasion, we may expect to find wide variations in the caste composition of pilgrims present.[2] The study of the caste composition of pilgrims is not an end in itself for us. I am interested in the panorama of castes of the pilgrims because it throws light on the areal interconnections of sacred places through social strands of Hinduism. These interconnections are significant from the viewpoint of cultural geography.

The caste composition at each sacred place studied is shown in the figures at the end of this chapter.[3] It may be observed immediately that this composition varies from place to place and also, at a single place, from one occasion to the other. We shall first make some observations regarding the prominent aspects of caste composition at each place and then discuss the probable relationship of caste to the levels of sacred places. Following this

[1]A very large number of studies on Hindu caste system exist. For one of the best, and a most concise analysis, see M. N. Srinivas, *Caste in Modern India*. Interested readers who wish to understand the concept of caste ranking may pursue McKim Marriott, *Caste Ranking and Community Structure in Five Regions of India and Pakistan* (Poona : Deccan College Post-Graduate and Research Institute, 1965). For traditional Western sociological analysis of caste system, see Max Weber, *The Religion of India*.

[2]See the appendix for the bases of caste groupings and the nature of each group.

[3]In the figures Sikhs have been considered a separate group when they did not mention their caste. When they did tell their caste, they were included in the appropriate caste group. For example, an Arora by caste may be Sikh by religion. If he replied "Arora," he was grouped with Khatri-Arora. If, however, he stated "Sikh," he was categorized separately as "Sikh." If he replied "Arora-Sikh," he was included in Khatri-Arora. Where it is appropriate in the following text, the effect of this classificatory decision on our analysis of the data will be noted.

we shall study the possible relation between castes of pilgrims and distance traveled to the sacred places.

GENERAL FINDINGS ON CASTE COMPOSITION

Place-by-Place Descriptions

BADRINATH. Mercantile castes,[4] Brahmans, and Khatri-Arora castes dominated the total mass of pilgrims at this place (see fig. 10-1). Despite the fact that Rajputs are numerically the most predominant caste in the region in which Badrinath is situated,[5] they were negligible in our sample. The Rajputs formed only about 4.5 percent of the pilgrims interviewed and came from different parts of the country. Scheduled-caste pilgrims were also negligible numerically—even more so than the Rajputs. In the unclassified category are several Nepali pilgrims who had specifically come for this pilgrimage.

The caste composition of the Badrinath pilgrims reflects neither the regional proportion of caste nor the overall proportion of castes in India. Most pilgrims here belong to "higher" castes, which is in part a reflection of their relatively higher economic level. Since Badri *yātrā* is often combined with *yātrā* to one or more places in the Uttrākhaṇḍa, it is expensive and takes a minimum of two weeks. Usually, therefore, only those who can arrange for someone else to manage their business, and those who take vacations, can afford to come on this long pilgrimage. Some poorer, but ardent, devotees may, of course, come with their savings of a considerable period of time for this once-in-a-lifetime type of *yātrā*. Also, cultivating castes may increase in proportion following a period of good harvest, as in fact was the case in the year 1968.

BAIJNATH. The caste composition at Baijnath on the two occasions studied was different, although both reflected the narrowly circumscribed field of this sacred place. Brahmans and Rajputs clearly predominated on the occasion of *Śivarātri* (fig. 10-2a). The Gaddī tribesmen who visit this place during this

[4]"Mercantile castes" referred to in the text are the same as "other mercantile castes." The prefix "other" has been omitted simply to avoid repeating the otherwise cumbrous tile.

[5]See Joseph E. Schwartzberg, "Caste Regions of the North Indian Plain," in Milton Singer and Bernard S. Cohn, *Structure and Change in Indian Society*, figs. 5 and 6, facing pp. 90–91.

occasion have a caste system of a type similar to that of the Hindus of this area. Most of the Gaddīs belong to Rajput and Brahman castes. This fact results in the increased proportion of these two castes on *Śivarātri*. On the second occasion the Gaddīs are absent because the fair comes in the summer season when these tribesmen are busy grazing their flocks on the higher slopes of mountains. Thus the second occasion more clearly reflects the local caste composition in the assembled pilgrims. On the second occasion (fig. 10-2b) the proportion of Khatri-Arora, mercantile castes, and local cultivating castes increased. Both occasions were attended largely by women folk with whom the worship of Śiva is very popular. The cultivating castes here are represented largely by the Bahtis and Chaudharies, typical of this hill region.

BHAGSUNAG. Like Baijnath, this is a local pilgrimage place. The caste composition reflects the local composition of castes (fig. 10-3). However, there is a large proportion of "unclassified" castes here. The predominant group in this category was the Gorkha, whose association with the chief deity, Śiva, is clear. Gorkhas, however, do not belong to the local social structure. Dharmsala, the nearby town, has a large number of Gorkha soldiers stationed, who have built this temple as a place for their worship. Some scheduled tribes of the hills also visit this place.

CHINTPURNI. Punjab and Uttar Pradesh contributed most of the pilgrims to Chintpurni. The caste composition, therefore, does not reflect the local mix of castes in Himachal Pradesh. Rajputs are numerically the most predominant caste in the region, but their small proportion in our sample is conspicuous (see figs. 10-4a and 10-4b). Their small proportion should not be taken to mean that they do not visit Chintpurni as much as other castes do. Local inquiries from the priests suggested that the castes of the neighboring area make pilgrimage following the major festival celebrated here by pilgrims coming from distant areas. Thus, had the samples been taken after that festival, the local castes would have become dominant. The scheduled castes make up a considerable proportion of the pilgrims. It is to be noted that some of the pilgrims who mention their "caste" as Sikh also belong to the scheduled castes but do not wish to be so classified. The Khatri-Arora caste group was numerically dominant during the *Śrāvaṇa Aṣṭamī* fair. During the *Navarātrās,* however, the pilgrims from Uttar Pradesh visit in large numbers, and this is reflected in the reduced proportion of Khatri-Arora castes, which are mostly Panjabi.

The caste composition at Chintpurni does not reflect the caste composition of the respective regions from which the pilgrims come, but rather indicates the high propensity of certain castes to make pilgrimages. Compared with the mercantile castes and Brahmans, the scheduled castes seem to travel relatively shorter distances and thus patronize a nearby place more than a distant one. If a measure could be evolved to weight the castes according to their income, then perhaps scheduled-caste pilgrims would show a greater total effort to reach a given place of pilgrimage than the more well-to-do castes.

HARDWAR. From among the sacred places studied, Hardwar is perhaps the most complex. For a proper study of its pilgrimage pattern no less than one full year is needed, because different seasons of the year are associated with a different regional representation of pilgrims. Interviews with several *purohits* (priests) of Hardwar, and particularly with the president and the secretary of the *Gaṅgā Sabhā,*[6] confirmed the varying regional predominance of pilgrims during different parts of the year. Inevitably our sample cannot represent this situation, since it was taken on one specific occasion, namely *Ardha Kumbha.*

Figure 10-5 shows the caste composition of the Hardwar pilgrims. Numerically the predominant caste group was Khatri-Arora. Since Punjab and Delhi accounted for over 37 percent of the pilgrim sample (800 persons) and because Khatri-Aroras are surely among the most numerous Hindu caste groups in these areas, the predominance of this group was quite expected at Hardwar.[7] Compared with Hardwar, Badrinath—whose field is much wider—shows a much larger proportion of the mercantile castes, which are far more widespread than the Khatri-Arora group. Like Badrinath, Hardwar had a small number of scheduled-caste pilgrims.

[6]Information based on interviews with Shri Ram Murti, president, and Shri Raj Kumar Sharma, secretary, of the Gaṅgā Sabhā, Hardwar. Gaṅgā Sabhā is a local organization of the *purohits* (priests), which helps in the management of the sacred precincts and plays a prominent role in the arrangement of large and small bathing festivals held at Hardwar.

[7]The proportion of this caste group has considerably increased in Punjab, Delhi, Haryana, and parts of western Uttar Pradesh since the partition of India in 1947 when the Hindus from West Pakistan migrated to these areas. Post-partition data of caste composition are not available. See, however, Schwartzberg, "Caste Regions."

JWALAJI. While at Chintpurni the fair on *Śrāvaṇa Aṣṭamī* is better attended, at Jwalaji the fair of *Navarātrās* is more important. The most noteworthy fact about the caste composition of pilgrims at this place was that scheduled-caste pilgrims outnumbered any other single caste group in a sample of five hundred pilgrims (fig. 10-6).

The proportion of the scheduled castes at Jwalaji does not reflect their relative numerical strength either in the Punjab or in Uttar Pradesh, from where most of them came. I believe that their predominance at Jwalaji is related to the ritual complex of this shrine.[8] This is the only major sacred place in the region where animal sacrifice is allowed within the temple precincts. High-caste Hindus of the plains rarely perform this sacrifice, but the practice is still common among the scheduled castes, although it is decreasing. This place, therefore, may have a special attraction for the scheduled castes. Since animal sacrifice is on the decline here, probably because of the inroads of the orthodox Hinduism, this place can provide an excellent laboratory for the study of the process of Sanskritization with respect to both the sacred place and the scheduled castes.

In the area where Jwalaji is situated, Rajputs and Brahmans are among the major castes numerically, yet neither of the two dominated the pilgrim body. The Khatri-Arora and the other mercantile castes together consider this place highly sacred. The *muṇḍana* ceremony of many Khatri families is performed here.[9] The local influences of caste composition are thus limited. About 9 percent of the pilgrims belonged to cultivating castes, most of whom came from outside the state in which the sacred place is situated.

The composition of the pilgrims may have changed considerably, owing to the partition of India and the resulting changes in the relative proportion of castes in the Punjab. The construction of a bridge over the Beas River near Dehra Gopipur has linked the central and the eastern districts of the Punjab directly with Jwalaji. Formerly the western districts of Punjab contributed most pilgrims to this place.

[8] I have developed this idea further in "Some Spatial and Social Aspects of the Mother Goddess Cult in North India," a paper presented for discussion at the Third Punjab Studies Conference held at the University of Pennsylvania, May 1971.

[9] In a personal communication to the writer, Professor Kenneth Jones (Kansas

KANGRA. At Kangra the largest single caste was Brahman, followed by Rajput (fig. 10-7), despite the fact that the Rajputs have a majority in the region. Two areas influenced the caste composition heavily : Kangra district itself and a few districts of western Uttar Pradesh. Kangra district contributed about 39 percent of all the Brahmans, while Mathura district of Uttar Pradesh accounted for another 17 percent. The Rajputs of Kangra district made up only 23 percent of all the Rajputs; the rest came in small numbers from various districts. Over half the members in the artisan caste group came from Kangra district itself.

The scheduled-caste pilgrims at Kangra were largely from Uttar Pradesh and Haryana. Punjab contributed only two in a total of thirty-two. At Jwalaji over 83 percent of these castes were from Punjab. The distance between Jwalaji and Kangra is hardly twenty-five miles, but the origin of the scheduled-caste pilgrims shows a marked contrast at the two places.

Kangra and Jwalaji present a contrasting picture also, regarding the origin of their respective pilgrims of the mercantile castes. Fifty-eight percent of the pilgrims of this caste group at Kangra came from Uttar Pradesh, the corresponding figure for Jwalaji being 27 percent, while the mercantile castes of the Punjab had a decided preference for Jwalaji, compared with Kangra.

NAINA DEVI. Figures 10-8a and 10-8b show the caste composition at Naina Devi on the occasion of *Navarātrās* of *Caitra* (March–April 1968) and *Śrāvaṇa Aṣṭamī* (August 1968) respectively. Predominance of cultivating castes on the first occasion and that of mercantile castes (including Khatri-Arora) on the second is noteworthy.

Most of the cultivating-caste pilgrims were Sikh by religion, though Jat by caste.[10] If we add to this those pilgrims who mentioned no caste except "Sikh," the preponderance of Sikh pilgrims at this shrine on the first occasion becomes evident. Moreover, most pilgrims who returned their caste as scheduled, Mazhabi,

---

State University) pointed out that the Sood caste, a mercantile caste of neighboring Hoshiarpur district, may have contributed to the growth of this place.

[10]Any pilgrim who mentioned his caste as Jat was classified in the "cultivating castes" category even though from his appearance he was a Sikh. There were some pilgrims (28 in a sample of 494 pilgrims) who did not state their caste per se but returned themselves as Sikhs. Only such pilgrims are classified as "Sikhs." This point should be borne in mind while interpreting the diagrams of caste composition at sacred places. I suspect that most such pilgrims belonged to the scheduled castes.

and Camār were Sikhs by religion. Thus, on both occasions Sikhs dominated numerically. This situation is quite different from all the places we have described so far. The numerical majority of Sikhs (whatever their caste) at a Hindu shrine needs explanation because the worship of idols is expressly forbidden by Sikhism, which in theory is strictly monotheistic. The explanation seems to lie in the functional aspects of the religion, as opposed to the ideal. In the ideal sense the goddess Naina Devi may be considered a purely Hindu deity, but this is certainly not true with respect to her role in the folk society. The goddess plays an intimate role in the belief pattern of folk Hinduism as well as Sikhism, as a problem-solving device. Although the orthodox forms of Sikhism discourage belief in Hindu deities, yet the traditional pattern of beliefs at the folk level continues. The mere change of religion apparently has not changed the traditional beliefs, particularly at the folk level. Naina Devi provides an excellent example of the convergence of the beliefs of two religions at one level despite divergence at another. The significance of a deity at the subregional level, it seems, may be better understood in the framework of the social groups rather than in the ideal forms of religion of these groups.

About 41 percent of the cultivating-caste group originated in Rupar district alone. Rupar adjoins Bilaspur district wherein Naina Devi is situated. A quarter of the Brahman and about a third of the scheduled castes also came from the same district. The largest proportion of the mercantile castes came from Ludhiana district, which not only is much larger in population and area, but also has the largest city in the field of Naina Devi. About a third of both the scheduled castes and the Khatri-Arora caste group also originated from this district. Since 50 percent of all the sample pilgrims (494) came from two districts (Ludhiana and Rupar) in the *Navarātrās,* the caste composition of these areas had a profound influence on the relative proportion of castes at Naina Devi.

On the second occasion *(Śrāvaṇa Aṣṭamī)* Ludhiana district contributed more pilgrims than Rupar district despite the latter's being nearer to this sacred place. Although Ludhiana district has a numerical plurality, if not majority, of cultivating castes (predominantly Jats) there were more Brahman pilgrims from that district than Jats.[11] The scheduled castes from Ludhiana district

[11]The Jat caste of Ludhiana district is almost exclusively Sikh by religion. The Sikh Jats are likely to follow the precepts of Sikhism far more than the scheduled-caste Sikhs.

constituted 18 percent of the pilgrims from that district—a figure only slightly short of their proportion of total population in that district.[12] In a more detailed analysis it may be possible to calculate the under-representation and over-representation of certain castes at a particular shrine vis-à-vis the caste composition of its field. It is, however, quite clear, even from our rather crude data, that certain castes (for example the scheduled castes and mercantile castes), because of their preference for a particular shrine, may travel farther than others for their pilgrimage.

REWALSAR. The caste composition of pilgrims at Rewalsar undergoes dramatic change from one festival to the other (see figs. 10-9a and 10-9b). The main reason for this shift is that while the *Sissoo* fair is essentially a Buddhist festival attended by pilgrims from the districts bordering Tibet, the *Vaiśākhī* is a local Hindu fair. Most of the pilgrims coming from the districts bordering Tibet claim to be Rajputs, though many of these belong to "scheduled tribes." Most of the "unclassified" pilgrims are those Tibetans who have settled in India after the Chinese occupation of Tibet. The virtual absence of Brahmans demonstrates the non-Hindu nature of the *Sissoo* fair.

At the *Vaiśākhī* fair the caste composition largely reflected local caste composition. While Rajputs still constituted the largest number, they were no longer from the bordering districts of Tibet. Brahmans constituted the second largest caste. A considerable proportion of those present were scheduled castes, who constituted the third most numerous caste group. The mercantile castes were almost absent except for some who came here for the dual purpose of trade and pilgrimage. The Khatri-Arora castes, though few in Himachal, were nonetheless present—an indication of their mobile character.

SHIV BARI. The two occasions at Shiv Bari differed from each other mainly in the proportion of the cultivating castes (see figs. 10-10a and 10-10b). The *Jātrā* fair—the name itself connotes pilgrimage—is the more important of the two occasions. The cultivating castes outnumbered other castes on this occasion. They were almost exclusively Hindu farmers as opposed to the farmer-pilgrims at Naina Devi, most of whom were Sikhs by religion.

[12]See *Census of India*, 1961, *Union Primary Census Abstract*, 1961, table III. The scheduled castes in Ludhiana district made up about 22 percent of the total population.

Since the fair comes soon after the local harvest season (mid-April), a large number of cultivating castes visit the place for thanksgiving. The local Rajputs attend the fair outside the temple, but the actual visiting of the temple is largely done by the cultivating castes, Brahmans, and others. Rajputs come largely for enjoying themselves at the fair and may use the occasion to assert their social dominance within the local caste hierarchy.[13]

MANSA DEVI. Scheduled castes were numerically predominant on the occasion of *Navarātrās,* while the mercantile castes (including Bania, Aggarwal, Mahajan, and various groups of Jains) were most numerous on *Śrāvaṇa Aṣṭamī* (figs. 10-11a and 10-11b). Both of these caste groups originated largely from Patiala district. The proportion of the scheduled-caste pilgrims considerably exceeded their relative numerical position in Patiala district.[14] As at Jwalaji, the high proportion of the scheduled castes at Mansa Devi too seems to be related to the practice of blood sacrifice. At Mansa Devi, however, blood sacrifice is not allowed in the temple precincts, in contrast to Jwalaji, although the sacrificial goats or rams are killed here outside the temple after they have been symbolically offered to the Goddess.[15]

Many mercantile-caste pilgrims perform their *gaṭh-joṛ* ceremony at this place.[16] The newlyweds of these castes symbolically reenact their marriage at this shrine to seek the blessings of the deity.

UJJAIN. Brahmans and mercantile castes were the most prominent caste groups at Ujjain on the occasion of *Siṃhastha Mela* (see fig. 10-12). This was despite the fact that these castes constitute a small proportion of the total population in the area from which most pilgrims came.[17] There were some scheduled-tribe pilgrims

[13]The dominance may find its overt expression in generating a local brawl in which the Rajputs may beat up a Brahman or abuse a member of another caste. Cf. Alan R. Beals, "Conflict and Interlocal Festivals in South Indian Region."

[14]In 1961, the scheduled castes made up about 19 percent of the population of Patiala district; see *Census of India, op. cit.* The scheduled-caste pilgrims from Patiala district, however, accounted for 30 percent of all the pilgrims from that district (41 scheduled-caste persons in a total of 135).

[15]The latter practice is also followed by some scheduled-caste pilgrims at Jwalaji.

[16]*Gaṭh-joṛ* literally means "the act of tying together."

[17]Recent data of caste distribution are not available. This statement is made on the basis of 1931 caste data of Central India Agency, which now includes much of the area from which pilgrims to Ujjain came. The population of Brahmans in the above area was 573,454 in a total population of 5,852,204; *Census of India,* 1931, Vol. I, part 2, table 17, p. 534. The population of mercantile castes is not given; nevertheless it would be far less than that of the cultivating castes.

at Ujjain even though in Ujjain district and other districts of Malwa their proportion in total population is negligible. Most of the pilgrims classified in the Khatri-Arora group were actually Kayasthas. The caste composition of the pilgrims of Ujjain does not reflect their proportion in the population of Malwa region; instead it confirms our view that certain specific castes (particularly Brahmans and trading castes) tend to undertake pilgrimages more than others.

Some Generalizations

The above description of the caste composition at various sacred places allows the following generalizations. (1) The trading castes (Khatri-Arora and the other mercantile castes) and Brahmans usually form a high proportion of the pilgrims. (2) Scheduled castes are virtually absent at the famous Hindu places like Badrinath. In contrast, they show a marked preference for the Mother Goddess shrines, particularly where blood sacrifice can be performed. (3) The caste composition at the same place may vary from one occasion to the other. The reasons are diverse and need to be more fully explored. (4) The caste composition of the pilgrims does not seem to reflect the relative proportion of these castes in the field of a given sacred place. The reasons for this situation deserve further inquiry. (5) The deities at certain sacred places seem to be related more to the social strata than to a specific religion. It appears that there may be a convergence of beliefs of two different religions within the context of a specific social stratum. This is true with respect to Hinduism and Sikhism at the folk level.

RELATIONSHIP OF CASTES OF PILGRIMS TO THE LEVEL OF SACRED PLACES

The question whether there is any relationship between the caste composition of the pilgrims and the levels of sacred places deserves exploration. Leaving aside the local shrines, we may test the hypothesis that the higher the rank of a sacred place, the lower the proportion of scheduled castes. Table 10-1 shows the ranks of sacred places (excluding local shrines) and the proportion of scheduled castes at each.

Table 10-1 shows that for all the nine places a perfect inverse

TABLE 10-1
LEVEL OF SACRED PLACES AND THE PROPORTION OF SCHEDULED-CASTE PILGRIMS THERETO

Sacred place	Deity	Level	Percentage of scheduled caste pilgrims	Average for the level (%)
Badrinath	Viṣṇu	Pan-Hindu	0.5	0.5
Hardwar	none	Supraregional	3.87	5.93
Ujjain	Śiva	Supraregional	8.00	
Kangra	Goddess	Regional	7.10	14.03
Jwalaji	Goddess	Regional	23.40	
Chintpurni[1]	Goddess	Regional	11.60	
Naina Devi[1]	Goddess	Subregional	10.50	16.63
Mansa Devi[1]	Goddess	Subregional	28.40	
Rewalsar[2]	(Lomas Ṛṣi)[3]	Subregional	11.00	

[1]Refers to occasion of *Navarātrās* of *Caitra* (March-April 1968).
[2]*Vaiśākhī.*
[3]One of the ancient Hindu sages.

relationship between the ranks and proportion of scheduled castes does not exist. However, it is clear that the highest-level shrine does have the lowest proportion of scheduled castes. It is also true that the highest proportion of scheduled castes is to be found in the subregional level. The Spearman rank-order correlation coefficient was calculated. It gives a negative value of 0.64, indicating an inverse correlation between the ranks of sacred places and the proportion of scheduled castes. The hypothesis is, thus, partially valid. At the high-level Hindu places the idea of ritual purity is important, and despite current legislation, the old established practice of touch pollution may be still reflected in the exclusion of former untouchable castes from the most sacred Hindu shrines.[18] Moreover, the *purohits* who accept gifts from

[18]The sample of pilgrims at Ujjain were taken mostly close to the bathing *ghāṭs* of the Sipra River because the *Siṃhastha* was essentially a bathing festival. Had all the samples been taken within the precincts of the Mahakal (Śiva) temple, the proportion of the scheduled castes might have been lower than our data show.

the low castes are despised by other *purohits*. At high-level places it must have been extremely difficult for the untouchables to establish a relationship with the *purohits*. This social discrimination must discourage scheduled castes from making a pilgrimage to a high-level shrine.

In contrast, at regional and subregional shrines the *purohits* accept gifts from all castes. This is particularly true of the *purohits* at the goddess shrines of Himachal Pradesh. The priests at most of the shrines of the goddess that were studied in Himachal Pradesh claim to be of Bhojki Brahman caste, which is not considered Brahman by the orthodox Brahmans, and intermarriage between Bhojki Brahmans and other Brahmans is rare. The untouchable castes traditionally have been making pilgrimages to these lower-level shrines, where there has been relatively little discrimination against them, where their gifts have been accepted by Brahmans (whatever the nature of their Brahmanhood), and where they have had access to the inner precincts of the temples. Thus, there is some justification for the hypothesis that the levels of shrines are inversely related to the proportion of pilgrims of the scheduled castes.

Let us now examine a second hypothesis that the level of sacred places is directly correlated with the proportion of "high" castes. Table 10-2 gives the percentage for Brahmans and for the four high castes (including Brahman, Rajput, Khatri-Arora, and mercantile castes) in the pilgrim sample.

The Spearman rank-order correlation coefficient for the Brahmans gives a value of 0.87, and for the four high castes (Brahman, Rajput, Khatri-Arora, and other mercantile castes) a value of 0.64. It shows that the Brahmans are correlated with the levels of the sacred places more strongly than the four high castes combined together, although both are positively correlated. Thus, there is some justification for the hypothesis that the higher the level of the sacred place the greater is the tendency of high castes to make pilgrimage to it. The pan-Hindu place and the supraregional places have consistently high proportions of Brahmans, while low proportions of Brahmans tend to occur at lower-level places. The above observations may be summed up by stating that as the Brahmanic element in the shrines increases and as the place assumes a more Sanskritic character, the ritually higher castes also increase in proportion while the reverse is true for the ritually

TABLE 10-2
LEVEL OF SACRED PLACES AND THE PROPORTION OF BRAHMANS AND OF PILGRIMS OF THE FOUR HIGH CASTES THERETO

Sacred place	Level	Percentage of Brahmans	Average for the level (%)	Percentage of four high castes[3]	Average for the level (%)
Badrinath	Pan-Hindu	30.0	30.0	84.0	84.0
Hardwar	Supraregional	26.5	27.6	85.4	76.3
Ujjain	Supraregional	28.8		67.2	
Kangra	Regional	27.6	24.1	68.9	65.0
Jwalaji	Regional	18.4		58.6	
Chintpurni[1]	Regional	26.2		70.4	
Naina Devi[1]	Subregional	16.2	15.8	49.9	54.4
Mansa Devi[1]	Subregional	7.2		40.4	
Rewalsar[2]	Subregional	24.0		73.0	

[1]Refers to the first occasion, *Navarātrās* of *Caitra*.
[2]*Vaiśākhī* Fair.
[3]Includes Brahman, Rajput, Khatri-Arora, and mercantile castes.

lower castes. The level of sacred places is, thus, not merely an imaginary derivation but has significance on the basis of the all-pervasive social structure of caste hierarchy in Hinduism.

RELATIONSHIP BETWEEN THE PILGRIMS' CASTES AND THE DISTANCE TRAVELED TO THE SACRED PLACE IN THE SAMPLE

At any given sacred place (excluding local-level places), some caste groups show a greater average distance traveled to the sacred place than other caste groups (see table 10-3). This suggests the possibility that certain aspects of caste may be responsible for this situation. The aspects of caste which are most likely to be significant in this context are : (*a*) the higher or lower ritual rank of the caste; (*b*) the average relative affluence of a caste group; (*c*) relative location or concentration of a particular caste group with respect to the sacred place; and (*d*) a combination of some or all of these factors. Our data are not refined enough to assess fully the significance of all these intertwined variables. Some observations may, however, be made from a comparison of the average distance traveled by different castes to sacred places. This caste-specific average distance may be called the mean range of the given caste with respect to the sacred place.

(1) The mean range of Brahmans at four sacred places was more than for all castes combined, and at five places less (see table 10-3). The positive departure from the average was most marked at Ujjain, and the negative one, at Badrinath. In comparison to the other castes the Brahmans show no consistent departure. At Kangra, for example, their mean range was considerably smaller than that of the scheduled castes, while at Mansa Devi it was almost equal to the latter (see fig. 10-13).

(2) The Rajputs (next in rank to the Brahmans) had a mean range consistently smaller than for all pilgrims combined. The artisan castes on the whole had a broader range than the Rajputs. These facts suggest that the ritual rank of a caste is not directly related to the mean range of that caste.

(3) The mean range of Khatri-Arora (and Kayastha) caste group was wider than that of Brahmans at some places and narrower at other places, as is clear from table 10-3. Thus, there is little evidence for a direct relationship between caste hierarchy and the distances they travel to sacred places.

TABLE 10-3
PILGRIMS OF SELECTED CASTES AT SELECTED SACRED PLACES AND THEIR MEAN RANGE (in parentheses)

Sacred place	Number of pilgrims interviewed	Brahman	Rajput	Khatri-Arora	Other mercantile castes	Cultivating castes	Artisan castes	Scheduled castes	Sikh
Badrinath	400 (490)	120 (439)	—	63 (450)	135 (562)	— —	— —	— —	— —
Hardwar	800 (176)	212 (172)	66 (138)	245 (177)	160 (197)	— —	— —	— —	— —
Kangra	450 (173)	124 (166)	82 (168)	51 (150)	53 (204)	49 (201)	47 (138)	32 (241)	—
Jwalaji	500 (123)	92 (139)	57 (110)	74 (122)	70 (181)	47 (99)	— —	117 (102)	—
Ujjain	500 (113)	144 (136)	47 (70)	49 (145)	95 (117)	46 (84)	56 (92)	40 (104)	— —
Chintpurni	500 (104)	131 (113)	55 (92)	101 (82)	65 (165)	40 (88)	38 (106)	58 (83)	— —
Naina Devi	494 (59)	80 (66)	46 (49)	68 (79)	53 (80)	124 (45)	39 (56)	52 (46)	28 (49)
Mansa Devi	250 (53)	18 (50)	— —	21 (48)	51 (70)	39 (47)	22 (48)	71 (54)	16 (50)

TABLE 10-3 (Continued)
PILGRIMS OF SELECTED CASTES AT SELECTED SACRED PLACES AND THEIR MEAN RANGE
(in parentheses)

Sacred place	Number of pilgrims interviewed	Brahman	Rajput	Khatri-Arora	Other mercantile castes	Cultivating castes	Artisan castes	Scheduled castes	Sikh
Rewalsar	100	24	40	8	—	8	—	11	—
	(14)	(11)	(7)	(28)	—	(32)	—	(7)	—

NOTE : Caste groups which made up less than 5 percent of the sample are not included in this table. For notes on inclusiveness of each caste group, see the appendix. Local-level sacred places have been omitted in this table. Caste-specific average distance traveled by pilgrims to each place is given in parentheses. In the text this is referred to as the "mean range."

(4) The other mercantile castes consistently traveled more than the average distance to any given sacred place in our sample. These castes are relatively more wealthy than other castes and because of the nature of their occupation are more mobile. These attributes of the caste group seem to result in their above-average fields.

(5) The cultivating castes on the whole have a below-average mean range (see table 10-3). Except at Naina Devi, this caste group is also poorly represented in proportion to their total population. Thus, this caste group is one of the least pilgrimage-oriented.

(6) The artisan caste group had a nearly average mean range except at Kangra. On the whole they traveled longer distances than the ritually higher Rajputs.

(7) The scheduled castes traveled shorter than average distances to most sacred places in our sample. However, at Hardwar their mean range was about the average and almost equal to that of the Brahmans and exceeded that of Khatri-Arora caste group.[19] At Kangra their mean range exceeded that of all other caste groups because the deity at Kangra is considered the family goddess (Kul-devi) by these pilgrims, and many scheduled-caste members in western Uttar Pradesh visit this place despite its remoteness from their home area.

The above observations point out that the caste status may not be directly related to the mean range of respective castes for the purpose of pilgrimage. However, it is also clear that the traditionally mobile castes, namely, the mercantile castes, have the widest range. In general it appears that those caste groups which are tied to the soil, including such castes as Jats, as well as Rajputs of Himachal Pradesh, have a tendency to travel relatively shorter distances for pilgrimage. Perhaps this is partly because their livelihood depends less on cash income, which is needed for undertaking pilgrimage.[20] We must also observe, however, that the practice of touch pollution may have been responsible for making certain sacred places unappealing to the untouchable castes, no matter how near these may have been to their homes. On the other hand, reverence of a particular deity of a specific place may draw its devotees even though the chief source region

[19]Hardwar pilgrim sample of 800 included 31 members of the scheduled castes.
[20]Cf. David E. Sopher, "Pilgrim Circulation in Gujarat," p. 405.

of the devotees may be at a considerable distance from the sacred place in question. A much more thorough study of these relationships is called for.

KEY to Figures 10–1 through 10–12

Caste Composition of Pilgrims

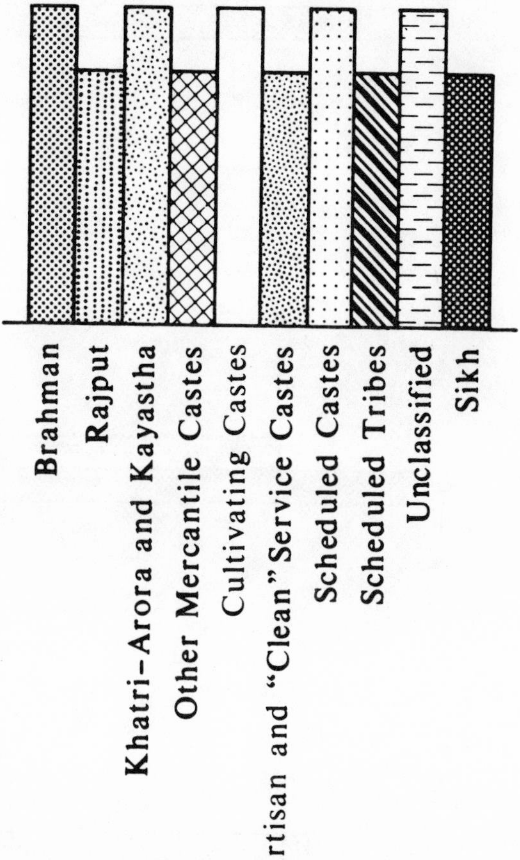

For explanations see appendix

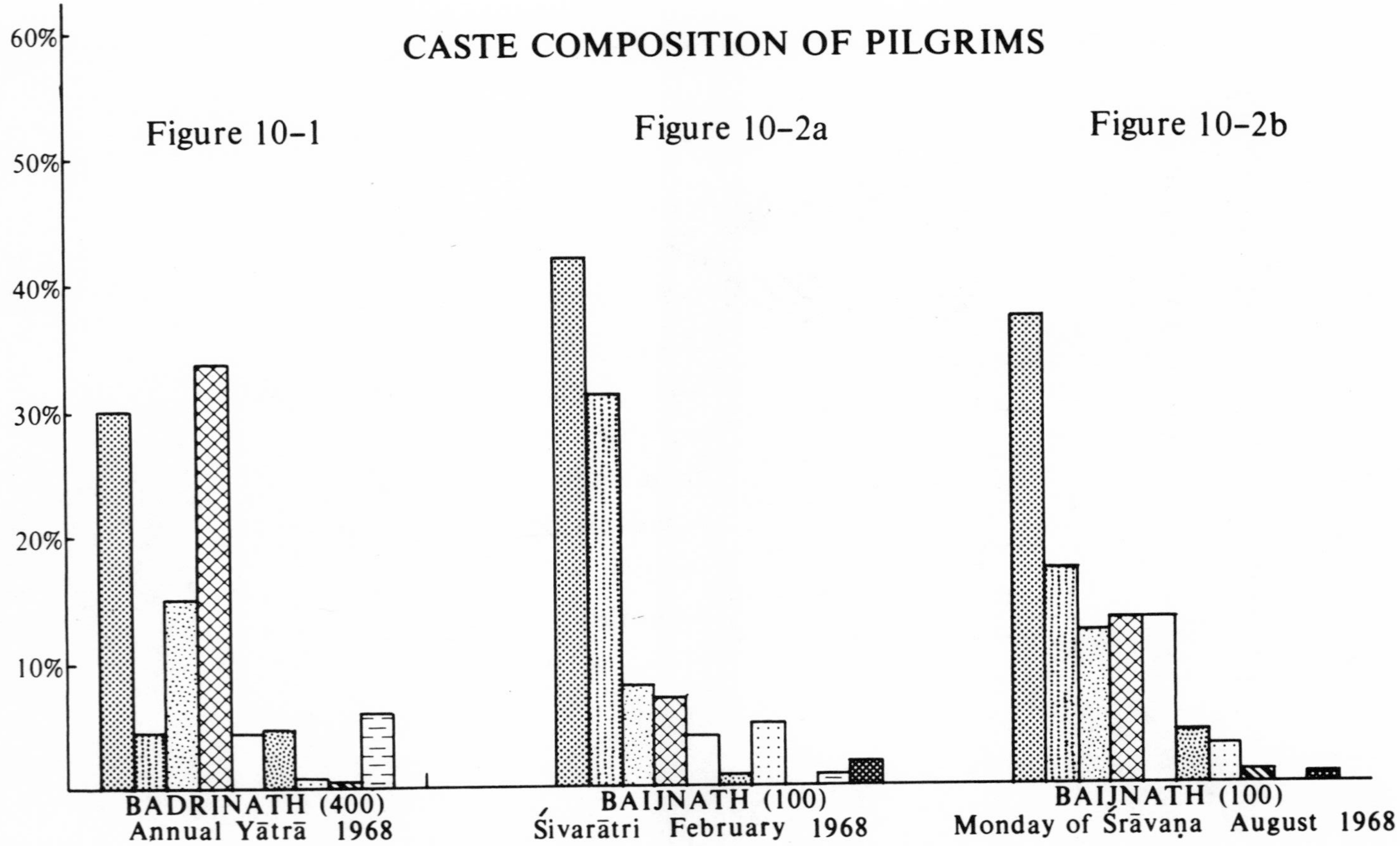
60%
50%
40%
30%
20%
10%
CASTE COMPOSITION OF PILGRIMS
Figure 10–1
Figure 10–2a
Figure 10–2b
BADRINATH (400)
Annual Yātrā 1968
BAIJNATH (100)
Śivarātri February 1968
BAIJNATH (100)
Monday of Śrāvaṇa August 1968

CASTE COMPOSITION OF PILGRIMS

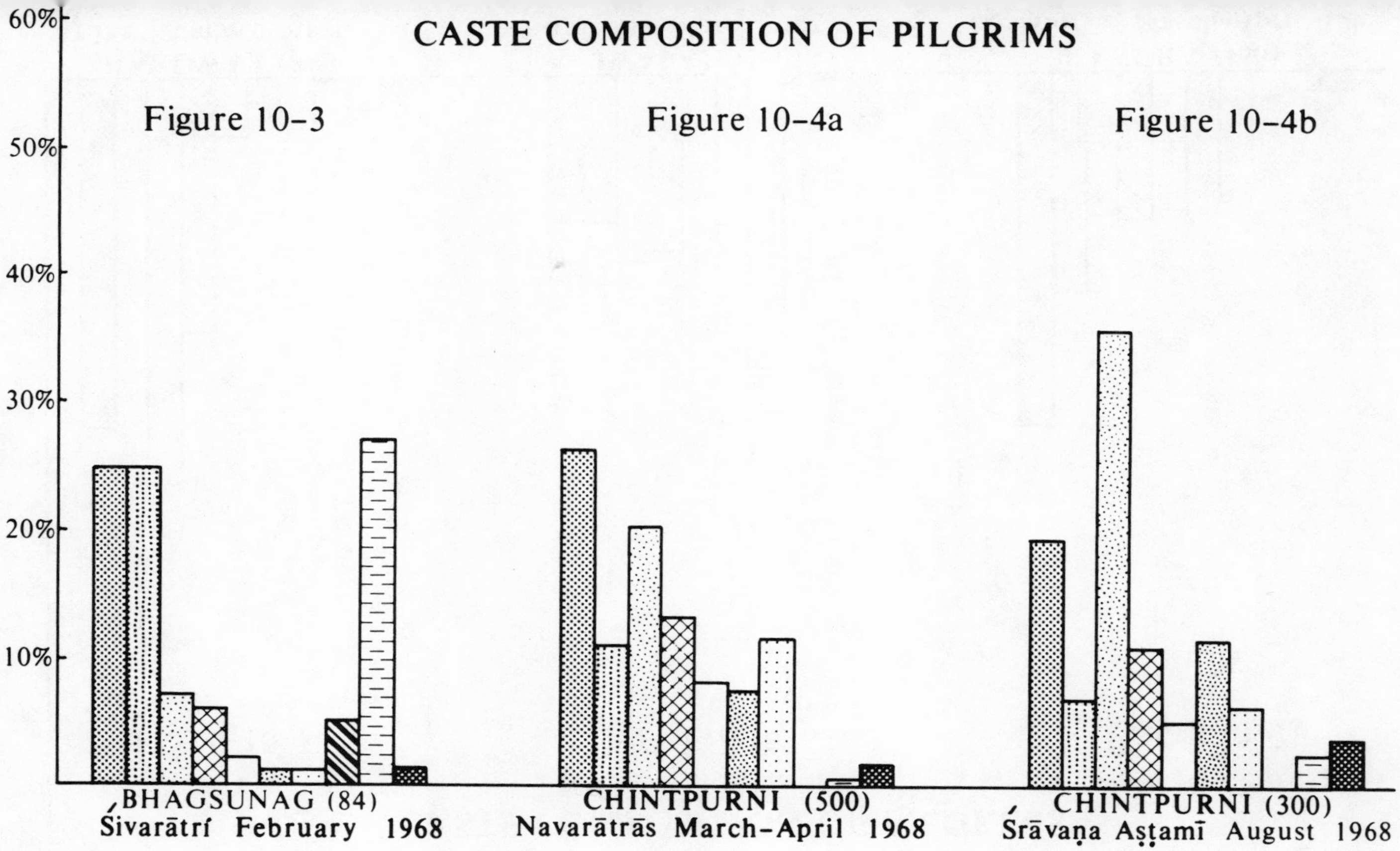

CASTE COMPOSITION OF PILGRIMS

Figure 10–5 Figure 10–6 Figure 10–7

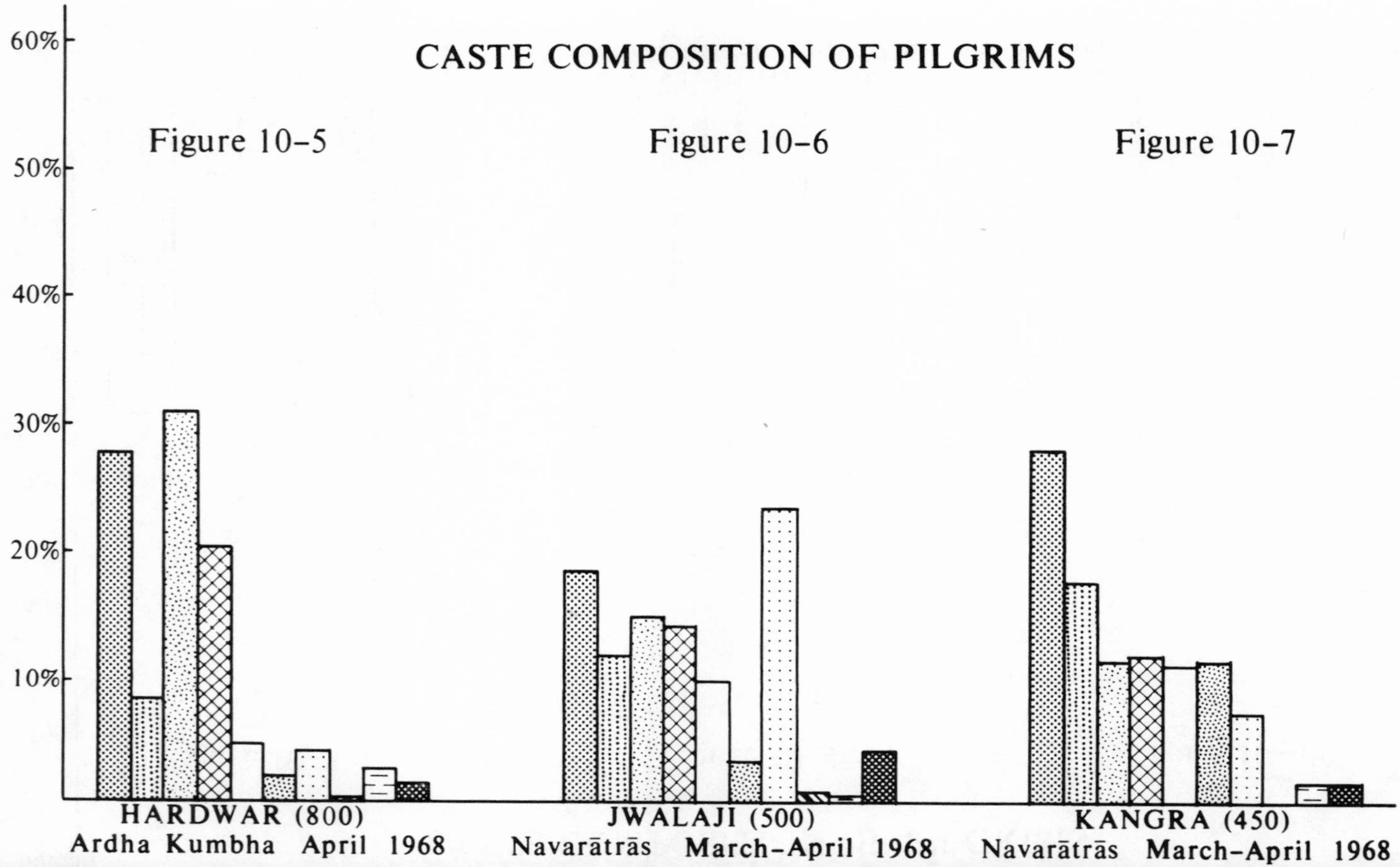

CASTE COMPOSITION OF PILGRIMS

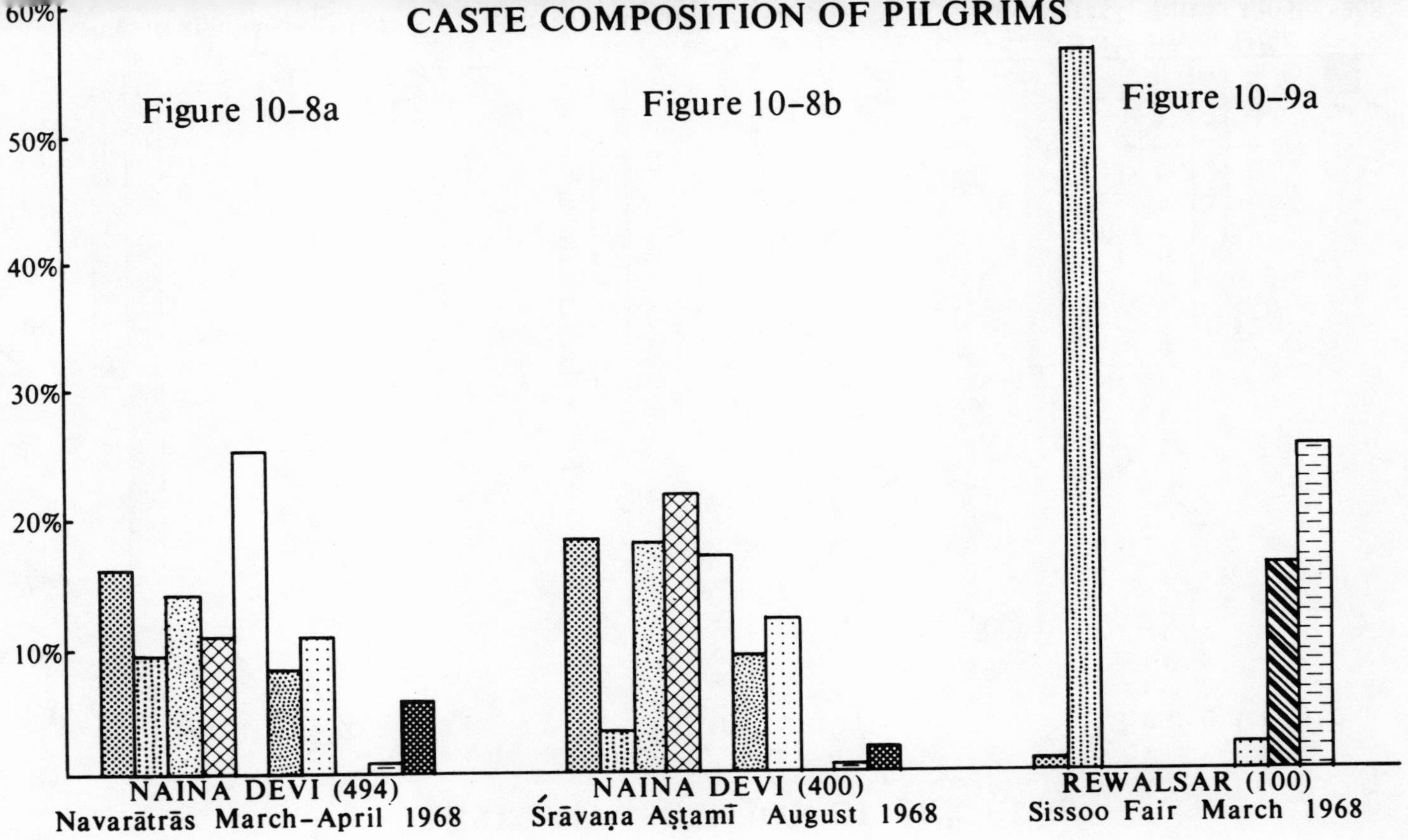

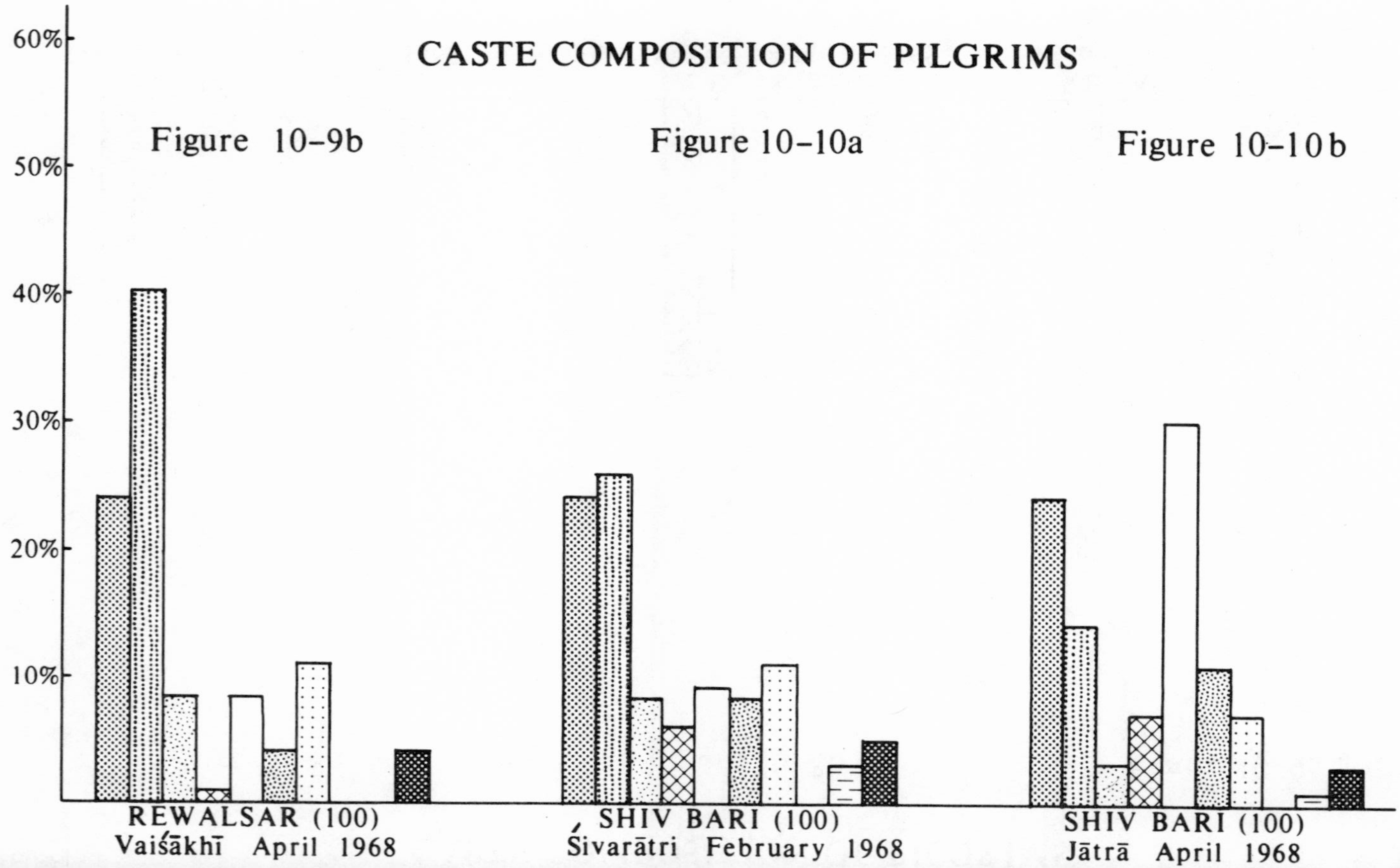
CASTE COMPOSITION OF PILGRIMS
Figure 10–9b
Figure 10–10a
Figure 10–10b
60%
50%
40%
30%
20%
10%
REWALSAR (100)
Vaiśākhī April 1968
SHIV BARI (100)
Śivarātri February 1968
SHIV BARI (100)
Jātrā April 1968

CASTE COMPOSITION OF PILGRIMS

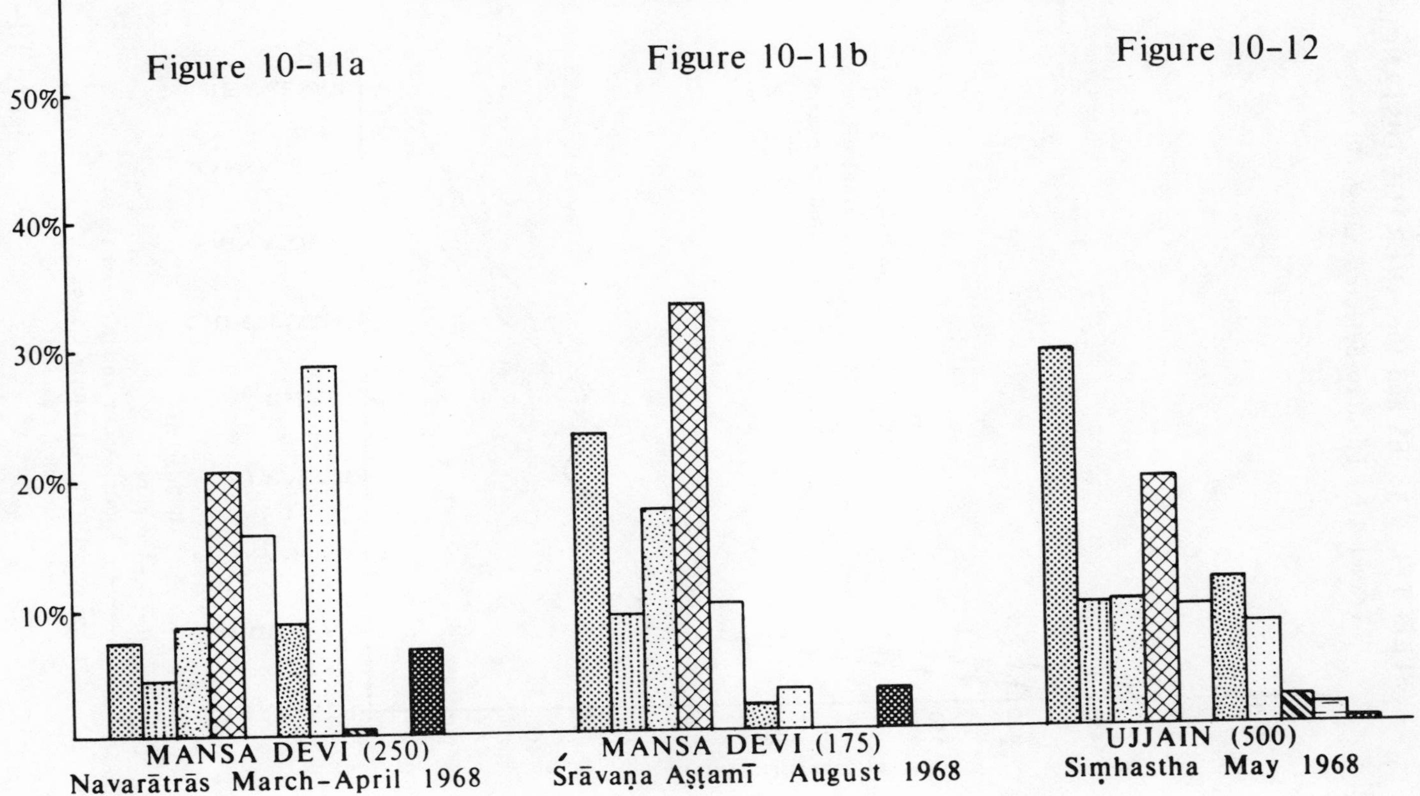

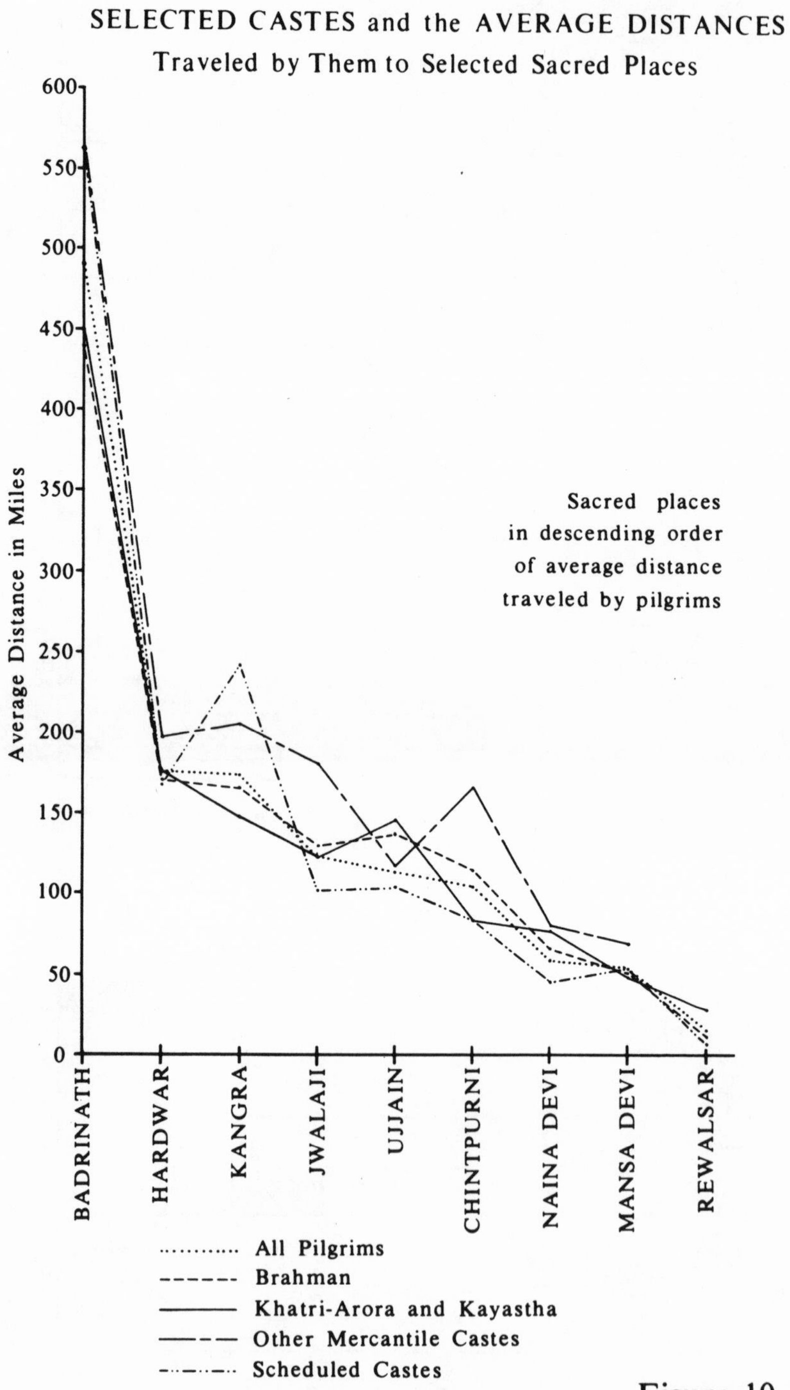
SELECTED CASTES and the AVERAGE DISTANCES
Traveled by Them to Selected Sacred Places
Average Distance in Miles
600
550
500
450
400
350
300
250
200
150
100
50
0
Sacred places
in descending order
of average distance
traveled by pilgrims
BADRINATH
HARDWAR
KANGRA
JWALAJI
UJJAIN
CHINTPURNI
NAINA DEVI
MANSA DEVI
REWALSAR
All Pilgrims
Brahman
Khatri-Arora and Kayastha
Other Mercantile Castes
Scheduled Castes

Figure 10-13

Chapter XI

Sacred Places and the Diffusion of Religious Beliefs

THE DIFFUSION MECHANISM IN GENERAL

Outwardly, the holy shrines may seem to be the end points of a religious purpose, whether a specific one or one that is complex and general. This concept of the significance of sacred places is obviously very narrow. The sacred places are repositories of the religious tradition, as well as active nodes from which certain aspects of religious tradition circulate among the mass of Hindu population. Deleury has aptly noted "the faithful transmission of a literary tradition" through the singing of hymns by illiterate pilgrims of Pandharpur.[1] Many sacred places are not centers for the "propagation" of religious ideas per se, because they are purely sacred foci without being organizational centers.[2] But even such places play their role in the religious consciousness of the vast and varied Hindu population of a large country. When a new sacred place emerges, it does require some mechanism whereby the belief about its sanctity can spread. Theoretically, it may be possible to study the spatial propagation of knowledge about sacred places as "waves of innovation," but in practice it is very difficult.[3] Most of the now enormous literature on spatial diffusion has had the advantage of the availability of requisite data regarding elements that can be measured in one form or another. In the realm of diffusion of information about holy places, particularly in the Indian context, the problem of obtaining required data is yet to be tackled.[4] Nevertheless, it may be useful to study how

[1] G. A. Deleury, *The Cult of Viṭhobā,* p. 88.

[2] Cf. David E. Sopher, *Geography of Religions,* p. 51. Places of this type may include Gangotri, the source of Ganga, in the remote Himalayas, Mount Kailas in Tibet, Amarnath in Kashmir, etc.

[3] A theoretical analogue may be in Torsten Hägerstrand, *The Propagation of Innovation Waves.*

[4] For recent studies that may provide promising guidelines, see Everett M. Rogers, *Bibliography on the Diffusion of Innovations.* Also: Association of American Geographers, *Spatial Diffusion.*

some new sacred places are trying to emerge while the old established religious centers are continuing their role in the circulation of religious ideas.

Let us take an incipient place of pilgrimage where an individual comes to seek the benevolence and help of the deity for some personal problem. Let us further suppose that the problem is "solved" to the satisfaction of the individual, who then gives credit to the deity. The faith thus generated or reaffirmed most likely will make the individual a devotee. He probably will communicate this "fact" to his family and to his acquaintances within his caste. Other members of the caste or his social group may, in their time of need, seek similar aid. If they too receive satisfaction which they attribute to the power of the deity, their experience can set up a chain reaction of pilgrims. If a devotee fails to achieve the desired result, it can be ascribed to lack of faith, improper ritual, or one's *karma*.[5] However, success is characteristically attributed to the power of the deity. A mechanism thus begins to operate by word of mouth to propagate the idea that the deity of a given holy place has power and potency. How far and fast this idea will spread depends upon many factors. A few of these factors may be listed.

(1) The frequency of contacts between the pilgrim and the potential pilgrims within a social stratum or the "contact field" of the pilgrim; (2) the range and mobility of the pilgrim; (3) existence of social barriers between castes which prevent communication; (4) personal receptivity and biases of the potential pilgrims; (5) the existence of requisite preconditions that impel an individual to undertake a pilgrimage; (6) the presence, among a body of potential devotees, of a priest or an organized body of priests who promote the ideas of sanctity of a holy place, or who have vested interests there; (7) the specific methods employed by the priestly castes to promote the sanctity of a given holy place; (8) the existence of another holy place that serves the same purpose; (9) presence or absence of renowned *sādhus* at the sacred place.

In the last chapter we noted that the sacred places visited largely for specific purposes are likely to have a large element of spatially less mobile and socially "lower" caste groups. Such a pilgrim composition is not conducive to the rapid spatial extension of the

[5]As popularly understood, *karma* means the effect of former deeds, performed either in this life or in a previous one, on one's present and future condition.

sanctity of a sacred place. Their networks of social relationships are likely to be limited to relatively small areas. Since social networks may be crucial in the spread of information, the field of such a place is likely to be limited in extent.[6]

One may ask why certain sacred places of local importance (e.g., Shiv Bari) continue to be so despite the fact that the pilgrims include a large proportion of influential higher castes. There is no simple answer. However, the following reasoning may offer some explanation.

To a large extent, and for practical purposes, the prestige of a sacred place depends on whether it is clearly recognized in the traditional religious literature. Thus, the holy places eulogized in the epics or Puranic literature have long become common knowledge, whether through actual reading or through oral tradition. Religious literati throughout India do not question their high sanctity. If a place of pilgrimage today remains local, this means that the Sanskritic religious tradition has not accorded it any prestige by associating it with religious events of import. Without this association, the chances that any local place will be accepted as a high-order place are indeed slim. Unless this happens, Hindus from diverse regions will not likely come as pilgrims.

It is possible, however, that an enterprising priest, for his personal, spiritual, or economic gain, may propagate the belief that a given local place is an ancient, forgotten one of greater sanctity than was hitherto believed. He will then need to establish a link between the given local place and the appropriate part of Sanskritic tradition. He may, indeed, write what is commonly called a *sthala purāṇa*—a local "ancient account" of the specific place. If his effort succeeds, and the grafted aura of antiquity grows, the place may assume a higher stature and enter the "great tradition" of Hinduism.

The fusion of local myths and traditions with the ancient religious literature of the *Purāṇas* is a commonplace fact giving rise to many inconsistencies and even absurdities. Nevertheless,

[6]Anthropologists have shown considerable interest in the study of the intervillage connections of Indian villages. See, for example, Morris E. Opler, "The Extensions of an Indian Village," and William L. Rowe, "The Marriage Network and Structural Change in a North Indian Community." The nature of information flowing through these networks needs more attention from geographers. See, however, a related sociological approach: K. Ishwaran, "Kinship and Distance in Rural India," in Ralph Piddington, ed., *Kinship and Geographical Mobility,* pp. 81–94.

it serves the important function of "knitting together into one religious society the numerous heterogeneous groups in India."[7]

SPECIFIC EXAMPLES OF INCIPIENT STAGE OF DIFFUSION

Our field work has provided us with excellent examples of the efforts that enterprising individuals are making to propagate the sanctity of their incipient shrines. We shall describe briefly two examples.

In Chandigarh, capital of the Punjab and Haryana states (as of 1968), there is a lowly hut *inside* the premises of the local modern Government College. It belongs to a Jogi (a Jogi by caste, not to be confused with *yogi*). Beside his little dwelling is a five-foot-high lump of mud that the Jogi has built. He claims it to be the *smādh* (grave) of his ancestral *guru*. He also insists that this is the original site of the *smādh* within a village that was situated here until evacuated several years ago when Chandigarh city was built.

Government College, allegedly, has made several efforts to evict the Jogi, to level his land for extending the playgrounds. However, he refuses to leave. The *smādh* is sacred, he says, and cannot be smothered by bulldozers. In fact, he told the writer that the blades of the bulldozers break down each time authorities try to level the place. The operator of the machine, it is claimed, no longer agrees to work on the holy site. The Jogi showed the writer a *mūrti* (image) he claims to have found there. Though the image is too disfigured to establish the deity's identity, its appearance has fortified the Jogi's faith that the place is indeed sacred.

When the writer showed interest in the incipient shrine, the Jogi claimed that his ancestor told him in a dream that someone from "abroad" would come and help him to establish this sacred place as a shrine. If the Jogi can find a wealthy devotee (and, of course, if he is not evicted legally), it is entirely possible that there may one day be a shrine of allegedly ancient origin in the modern city of Chandigarh. Some rickshaw pullers in Chandigarh have started to come to this sacred place to pray. They are already a source of the admittedly meager income of this Jogi. He was willing to approach the head of the Department of Ancient Indian History (Dr. Chhabra) in the Punjab University to establish the identity of the image that he claims to have dug up at this spot.

[7]M. N. Srinivas, *Caste in Modern India,* p. 106.

The second example also comes from near Chandigarh. About seven miles away, on the Chandigarh-Simla road, is a small old fortress village named Mani Majra. About a mile from here is the temple of the goddess, Mansa Devi, venerated by pilgrims from adjoining districts, particularly Patiala, Sangrur, and Ambala. This temple, to which pilgrims are chiefly directed, is considered by most to be the real one. Mansa Devi Temple was built in its present form by a Sikh prince of the former princely state of Nabha, named Maharaja Gopal Singh, between the years 1868 V.S. and 1872 V.S. (corresponding to 1811–1815 A.D.).[8]

Nearby is another temple, also called Mansa Devi, built by a former Maharaja of Patiala. Though an imposing structure, this is, according to the priests of the Patiala Temple, one of the several *"sukhnā"* temples.[9] About two hundred yards from the main Mansa Devi Temple, but hidden from it by a low ridge of the Siwaliks, is a small shrine locally known as the Kholiwala Temple. Few pilgrims visit it because all ceremonies are performed at the Mansa Devi Temple. The attendant of the small temple is outwardly a Sikh, but wears the sacred thread. This man—we shall call him Devi Singh—came here from his nearby village a few years ago. He claims that the goddess Mansa expressly "sent him" to attend this temple. A virgin girl in his village fell into a trance one day and the goddess Mansa spoke through her and commanded Devi Singh to serve in the Kholiwala because it is *the real* ancient temple. He obeyed at once and now makes his living from one acre of land that is endowed to the temple, and from the small offerings some pilgrims bring to the goddess during the fairs.

Devi Singh is now making efforts to inform large numbers of pilgrims that the "real" ancient temple has wrongfully been neglected. He claims to have found some coins of the 1870s and 1890s while digging near the temple, thus showing that pilgrims used to patronize it. Also he uncovered some rude carvings of *nāgas* (serpents) and some pumpkin-shaped stones, but more important, an "ancient" image of the goddess. Announcing his finds in the local Hindi newspaper, he attracted the attention of some wealthy pilgrims. By so doing he collected enough money

[8]The date V.S., or the *Vikrama Samvat,* is according to the inscription on the archway of the temple gate. It does not mention the kingdom or principality of the prince.

[9]A *sukhnā* temple is locally any structure a pilgrim builds as a mark of reverence to the goddess, after the wish of the pilgrim has been fulfilled through her grace.

to purchase a phonograph, a number of records with songs of devotion to the goddess, and a pair of loudspeakers. During the few days of pilgrimage he plays these records loudly to catch the notice of visitors to the main temple. With relatively "modern" techniques, Devi Singh apparently is succeeding to some extent in resurrecting the temple, which he now calls the "Adi-Mansa" temple (ancient temple of Goddess Mansa). The larger the number of pilgrims attracted to the temple, the greater the offerings and the better off Devi Singh will be.

Through his devotion to the goddess, he has already discovered an enterprise—the sale of sanctity. By claiming this temple as the ancient one, Devi Singh has now begun to arouse the anger of the priests of the main temple. There is, moreover, a good deal of tension between the priests of the main temple and the priests of the Patiala Temple.[10] Obviously these three temples, apart from being places of worship, are competing economic enterprises—a cut-throat competition indeed!

Neither of the above two shrines has, as yet, become part of the "great tradition"; but it is clear that efforts are afoot to make them so. The two examples give us some insight into the mechanism employed by the interested priests to spread ideas about the sanctity of the shrine. A detailed study of incipient shrines would greatly increase our understanding of the intricate nature of the process of diffusion of beliefs and emergence of sacred places.

DIFFUSION FROM HIGH-LEVEL SACRED PLACES

In the above examples the knowledge about the existence of a sacred place and some ideas about the power and potency of the deity are propagated, largely through the agency of a priest and a body of pilgrims. We shall now turn our attention to a more elaborate mechanism of some better-known sacred places, basing the discussion on our study of Hardwar and some other high-level places.

The high-level sacred places usually comprise several shrines, although there usually is a single most holy spot or area.[11] The

[10] In fact, inside the Patiala temple there is a photograph of a young priest who, we were told, was murdered because of this tension between the two priest groups.

[11] A formulation of the definition of sacred spot and sacred complex has been given by L. P. Vidyarthi, *The Sacred Complex in Hindu Gaya.*

pilgrim body at high-level shrines, as was noted earlier, consists largely of the religious elite, who are usually literate and mobile. In the case of Hardwar, we can additionally distinguish the following main components of the diffusion mechanism.

(1) An organized, but internally highly segmented, community of religious functionaries consisting of the *purohit*s or *paṇḍā*s and their agents; (2) *āśramas* (hermitages), *maṭhs* and *ākhāḍās* (organized headquarters or subcenters of sects or subsects) of sectarian *mahants* (a *mahant* is a kind of pontif) or other respected *sādhus* and sages; (3) institutions of religious education, as well as secular institutions, with an orientation toward the teaching of Sanskrit literature, ancient Hindu medicine, and Hindu philosophy. Publishing houses oriented to printing sacred texts, books, and pamphlets of devotional songs.

The above components propagate or at least keep alive the traditional concepts of religion and religiously oriented education. Although sacred centers are not the only places where religious ideas develop or from which they are propagated, they are, nevertheless, places where religious ideas do assume prominence.

The Role of the Religious Functionaries

The role of religious functionaries is of great importance, especially at the high-level sacred places such as Gaya, Hardwar, Puri, and Pushkar. Although their overall importance is on the decline, they nevertheless provide a fascinating example of an indigenous interlinking mechanism in a religious circulation manifold.

The households of the *purohits* of Hardwar, according to the estimate of Pandit Pradyuman Kumar,[12] number about fifteen hundred. The *purohits* live in the nearby town of Jwalapur, but commute to Hardwar every day for meeting their *jajmāns* (pilgrim clients).[13] Each *purohit* has certain villages or castes in a specific area as the source of his traditional clients. At some sacred places where the limited number of pilgrims of a given small area does not warrant segmentation of priests on the basis of castes or

[12]A *purohit* at Hardwar.

[13]The reason for their living in a locality different from the actual sacred places is that the sanctity of the holy place forbids the *purohits* to carry on their household activities, particularly conjugal relations, at the holy place.

villages, a single priest may claim an entire region.[14]

When a pilgrim visits Hardwar, the agents of a *purohit* usually meet him at the bus or railway station. The first question they ask the pilgrim is "What is your native place of residence?" The moment the place is named, the next question is "What *jāti*?"

Answers to these two questions are usually sufficient to establish whose *jajmān* a given pilgrim is. The agent then conveys him to the proper *purohit*. Through their phenomenal memory and constant actual practice in the identification technique these agents almost always are able to establish the association between the pilgrim and his *purohit*. The *purohits* at Hardwar maintain an elaborate system of record keeping on long ledgers called *bahīs*. These *bahīs* have been kept for generations and are handed down from father to son or even sold to other *purohits*, given in dowry to a son-in-law, or otherwise exchanged as property.[15] The *purohit* records the date and purpose of visit of the pilgrim as well as the names of as many relatives in the father's line as the pilgrim remembers. The purpose is twofold. First, this record serves to establish the identity of the *purohit* as well as of the pilgrim. And second, the *purohit* learns the names of large numbers of relatives of the pilgrim, who may be potential pilgrims. Hence, these records are of genealogical as well as of economic value. The *purohit* helps the pilgrim in the performance of any ritual or ceremony for which the pilgrim may have come. The *purohits* also, if called upon to do so, help the pilgrim in finding a lodging and in some instances even extend loans to pilgrims who run short of money.[16] The pilgrim when leaving gives *dakṣiṇā* to the *purohit* according to the former's desire.[17] In some cases the *purohits* of former princes and rich men have been given large sums of money or even land as *dakṣiṇā*. Through this process, operating over

[14]At Gaya, for example, the Gayawāl *purohit*, popularly known by the appellation "Ḍaṛhīwāl," claims to be the *purohit* of the entire Punjab. He zealously defends his claim through a network of his agents, who meet the pilgrims at the local railway station and convey them to this *purohit*.

[15]For an excellent discussion of the value of the records at sacred places, see B. N. Goswamy, "The Records Kept by Priests at Centers of Pilgrimage as a Source of Social and Economic History."

[16]Many *purohits* provide residence to their *jajmāns* in their own buildings. However, many pilgrims these days prefer to stay in hotels. I know of several instances of the *purohits* lending money to their *jajmāns* purely on faith, without any written record of the payment.

[17]*Dakṣiṇā* is the fee given to the priest for the performance of rituals.

centuries, an elaborate network of *jajmān-purohit* relationships has been built up.

Sometimes the *purohit* visits his rich *jajmān* for financial help or to use the prestige of influential *jajmāns* to induce other people to make pilgrimages. Our interviews with several *purohits* suggest that their practice of making visits to recruit pilgrims has declined, but has by no means disappeared. The decline seems to have come about at least in part due to the spread of information about sacred places through nontraditional media such as newspapers, and through the ease of transportation. Before the railroad era, we were told, bands of pilgrims were escorted by the *purohits* or their agents from their villages or towns to the sacred place. Personal check of the *bahīs* of *purohits* shows that some *purohits* do go on a tour to meet their *jajmāns* and collect considerable money, or grain if they have been given land by the *jajmāns*.

Sometimes a *purohit* may gather a band of pilgrims and serve as their guide on a journey to various shrines in India. The *purohit*, of course, having visited many sacred places himself several times over in this fashion, can be depended upon by the illiterate or semiliterate pilgrims, many of whom may never have gone to distant places before.[18]

The priest-pilgrim network of relationships based on reciprocity (i.e., offerings received for rituals performed) must have been a potent factor in the propagation and continued circulation of the ideas about the sanctity of holy places. It is obvious that for the *purohits* the institution of pilgrimage is of immense economic value. The larger the number of pilgrims who come to them for performance of ceremonies and rituals, the better their business. No wonder then that the *purohits* are always keen to eulogize the sanctity of their holy places.

Although we have pointed up the significance of the priest-pilgrim mechanism of interlinkage, an important question remains unanswered. How could the information about the sanctity of a holy place spread beyond the field of interlinkage between priests and pilgrims? Before the advent of railroads and automobiles the range of *purohits'* as well as pilgrims' travel must have been

[18]Vidyarthi gives a detailed account of the activities of the priests of Gaya. Vidyarthi, *Sacred Complex*, pp. 76 ff. At Hardwar we met a party of about thirty pilgrims who had come from Kashmir with their own *purohit*. The party was to proceed to many holy places in different parts of India.

relatively limited. How then were long-range interconnections established despite linguistic barriers? In other words, we are asking the question Did the potential pilgrims know about the sanctity of a given place first or did the *purohits* acquaint them with it? We are assuming here that the sacred place is situated beyond the field of social networks of the pilgrims at a given time. The answer to the above question cannot be given easily. However, we can suggest a probable process.

In order that a pilgrim may visit a high-order place without having been contacted by a priest or agent of that priest and without having been informed of the merit of the sacred place through a kinship network, we have to assume the pilgrim's knowledge about the place through some other mechanism.

Trade or business may take a person from one region to another and thus afford a chance for him to visit the sacred places of an area not otherwise known to him. Our field study supports this idea. For example, at Jwalaji a family of businessmen pilgrims from Assam was interviewed. The ancestors of this family belonged to Rajasthan (Marwar). Having migrated to Assam, this family is well acquainted with the sacred places of the eastern part of India. Through continued social network in Rajasthan and periodic visits, this family also knows about the holy places of western India. Similarly, a number of pilgrims who come from Calcutta to visit Badrinath are migrant merchants from Rajasthan, Gujarat, and Maharashtra, and belong to the Marwari trading castes. They would, because of their long-range trade connections, have opportunity to travel in different parts of India, and they may be important in carrying the ideas about sacred places from one part of India to the other.

The diffusion of religious literature throughout India at a very early period in history must also be considered an important force in acquainting people of diverse regions with a large number of sacred places. Thus, even without the initial contact with a *purohit* of a sacred place, and even without any trading or commercial visits, a pilgrim may visit a place that he knows about solely from the religious literature. When a potential pilgrim does become an actual pilgrim, he may start his first contact with a *purohit* at a sacred place. Thereafter, the *purohit* and his progeny may assert a "right" on this pilgrim and his descendants. Also, the pilgrim who has made the first visit may become a source of inducement for other pilgrims even though others may not have had acquaintance with religious literature. These pilgrims in turn may develop a network of relationships with the *purohits,* and thus there may result an elaborate mechanism of pilgrimage.

The Role of Āśramas, Maṭhs, *and* Ākhāḍās

At Hardwar and at many other important sacred places there exist a number of institutions like the *āśramas, maṭhs,* and *ākhāḍās.* Through their manifold religious and secular activities they not only help the stature of the sacred places but also may be a source of diffusion of the new interpretations of Hinduism and may even give rise to new sects and subsects.[19]

Āśrama means an abode or residence. In common parlance it connotes the abode of a saint, *sādhu,* or ascetic who is usually engaged in some form of religious instruction. At Hardwar and even more so in the neighboring sacred place Rishikesh, the number, the variety, and the complexity of *āśramas* is evident, Svargāśrama being perhaps the most complex of these. Its activities include religious education, maintenance of an elaborate chain of pilgrim rest houses, free medical aid to pilgrims, plying of motorized boats for crossing the Ganga, and a host of charitable works. The activities are financed entirely through *dāna* (donations) from individuals, particularly from rich business communities in various parts of the country. The Divine Life Society, founded by Swami Sivananda, not only provides various kinds of religious instruction, but also publishes a number of books and pamphlets on subjects such as religion and health, imparts instruction on *yoga,* manufactures and markets several indigenous medicines, and sponsors scores of other beneficial activities. More recently, the Academy of Meditation, the headquarters of the International Spiritual Regeneration Movement, founded by Maharishi Mahesh Yogi, has been carrying on the most publicized campaigns to popularize new interpretations of the ancient concepts of Hinduism

[19]At Ujjain we noticed considerable propaganda of the sect of Mehr Baba. Similarly, at Hardwar the Anand Marg Sect of Bengal has been actively propagating its views. At present there are adherents of Anand Marg in Punjab. Anand Marg literally means the "way of joy" or the "blissful path." This sect has its appeal largely to the upper middle-class people such as lawyers, professors, doctors. The preachers themselves are well-read individuals.

in several countries of the world.[20] These are but a few examples of the nature of *āśramas*. These are potent nodes for the diffusion of religious ideas and interpretations.

The term *maṭh* or *muṭṭ* in ordinary language is now understood to mean the abode of an ascetic, and in legal parlance it connotes a monastic institution established for the use and benefit of ascetics, who generally are the disciples of the head of the institution (generally an acknowledged scholar and religious preceptor).[21] According to the Government of India Report of the Hindu Religious Endowments Commission,[22] the establishment of *maṭhs,* as we know them today, is attributed to Ādi Sankarācārya, in the eighth century A.D. These were presumably established after the model of Buddhist *vihāras,* or monastaries. The *maṭhs* have been used particularly as centers for the dissemination of religious philosophy.[23]

Ākhāḍa literally means a kind of gymnasium. These were originally militaristic ascetic organizations, and their adherents still don their arms at the time of *Kumbha Melas* at Hardwar, Allahabad, Ujjain, and Nasik.[24] The writer had the opportunity to visit several *ākhāḍās* at the *Siṃhastha* fair at Ujjain as well as at Hardwar during 1968. The principal *ākhāḍās* are few in number, but they have numerous branches at a large number of sacred places in northern India. The members of the *ākhāḍās* make regular pilgrimages, particularly to the four places where the *Kumbha* or *Siṃbhastha* fair is held. At these fairs, where millions of pilgrims gather, these ascetics perform various religious activities. The writer has observed the performance of recitations from the holy books, such as the *Rāmāyaṇa,* dramas based upon religious themes and ancient episodes, severe mortificatory yogic practices, like self-torture by fire, and numerous other practices.

All these activities are designed to arouse the religious consciousness of the pilgrims, but they also serve to support the organization

[20]Maharishi Mahesh Yogi has published, among other works, *Bhagavad-Gita : A New Translation and Commentary,* which professes to be "a rediscovery to fulfill the needs of our time."

[21]*Report of the Hindu Religious Endowments Commission* (Delhi : Government of India, Ministry of Law), p. 14.

[22]*Ibid.,* p. 15.

[23]*Ibid.,* pp. 15–22.

[24]For a detailed account of the organization of *ākhāḍās* of the ascetics see G. S. Ghurye, *Indian Sadhus,* chaps. 6 through 11.

of ascetics. Without doubt the institutions of *āśramas*, the *maṭhs*, and the *ākhāḍās* serve as important components of the mechanism of circulation and diffusion of religious beliefs in India.

The role of *muṭṭs* and *āśramas* cannot be fully appreciated without realizing the importance of asceticism and the ascetic (*sādhu*), which lie at the root of the monastic organizations and command high respect in Hinduism. Asceticism as an ideal has been a consistent theme in the Indian culture. As Ghurye has rightly observed, "With this course of life alone can a Hindu secure his release from mundane life."[25] This "release" or *mukti* is undoubtedly the ultimate goal of ideal Hindu life. Thus, the ideal personality type "who is devoting full time to the achievement of *mukti*" is regarded with the highest esteem.[26] It is not without reason, then, that the pilgrims, particularly at the high-level sacred places, flock to the *āśramas* and *muṭṭs*, where the renowned *sādhus* explain the fundamental Hindu concepts. Singer has cogently argued that the ascetic exerts an immediate, continuing, unifying influence in India because of his extraordinary norm, charismatic appeal.[27] Since the ascetic is not bound by any specific caste norm, his appeal penetrates all social strata—from the Brahman to the untouchable—and his message becomes universal. The role of the ascetic in the context of pilgrimage certainly deserves more attention from scholars.

Institutions of Religious Education

Many sacred places have served as centers of religious education and thus have been partly instrumental in keeping the religious beliefs alive. There are several examples, both early and modern, of this role of holy places.[28]

It may be imagined that the role of places of pilgrimage for the preservation and diffusion of education has declined because of the growth of the scientific attitude. The writer believes that the role of the sacred places as centers of learning has in fact increased through

[25]Ghurye, *Indian Sadhus*, p. 2.

[26]Philip Singer, "Hindu Holy Men : A Study in Charisma," p. 32.

[27]*Ibid.*, pp. 127–128.

[28]See, for example, B. C. Law, *India as Described in Early Texts of Buddhism and Jainism* (London : Luzac, 1941); Radha Kumud Mookerji, "Education," in R. C. Majumdar ed., *The History and Culture of the Indian People*, Vol. II, *The Age of Imperial Unity*; K. K. Pillay, *The Sucindram Temple*.

a process of adaptation and reassertion. The establishment of Banaras Hindu University at Varanasi, and Kurukshetra Sanskrit University at Kurukshetra, are but two of the many possible examples of the adaptive and reassertive process. The sanctity of these places is in effect reinforced and the process of diffusion of knowledge, both sacred and secular, made more scientific and rapid through the establishment of seats of higher learning at the renowned sacred places.

Hardwar offers an excellent example of the reassertion of traditional Indian education. The Gurukula Kangri University (near Hardwar) basically stresses the ancient Indian (Vedic) method of instruction, with a great emphasis on Sanskrit, but sciences are also taught. In medicine this university has done remarkable work on the study, revival, and diffusion of *Āyurveda* (ancient Indian medicine). The drugs manufactured by the institute's pharmacy are known and used throughout India, particularly in the North.[29] Other institutes of traditional education have emerged in and near Hardwar, for example, Rishikul Medical School, which combines traditional Indian medicine and modern surgery. Anybody passing through the main bazaar of Hardwar can notice a large number of medical stores selling Indian indigenous medicines. Hardwar thus not only helps to maintain the Hindu religious tradition, but also has adapted itself on more modern lines to become an important center for the diffusion of the reinterpreted ideas, whether they concern liberal education or medicine. The rejuvenation of Indian medicine, its spread, and its role vis-à-vis Western medicine could be a fascinating study in itself.[30]

Other Diffusion Mechanisms

From the above sketch it should be evident that the sacred places form important nodes, both as repositories of traditional Hinduism and as propagators of reinterpreted values and beliefs. The basic reason for this role is that Hindus from diverse regions visit these places and thus provide opportunity and convenience for the growth of such institutions.

[29]For a short account of this institute, see G. S. Ghurye, *Indian Sadhus*, pp. 230–231.

[30]The author is currently engaged in studying the process of diffusion of modernized Ayurvedic medicine and the Indianization of homeopathy—a Western system of medicine.

During the major religious fairs, lectures and discourses by the learned *sādhus* and *sannyāsīs* attract large crowds of pilgrims. The schedules of lectures are widely advertised through handbills and newspapers. Thus, the sacred places during the major fairs become visible centers for the diffusion of new ideas about religion and the spread of information about new cults. Through a combination of several elements an elaborate mechanism of diffusion and circulation is developed whereby the contacts between the sacred place and its pilgrim field are renewed and extended.

The national government and the various state governments are beginning to realize that vast numbers of people gathered at the sacred places can be a useful field for the diffusion of new ideas bearing on the social, economic, and political development of India. At Hardwar on the *Ardha Kumbha,* for example, the Health Department had set up a large (temporary) family-planning exhibition and a clinic, which acquainted thousands of pilgrims with family-planning devices and even extended individual advice to numerous people. Similarly, the ministeries of Agriculture and Industries had their exhibitions. The large number of pilgrims who assemble at sacred places with no cost to the government can provide an inexpensive method for the dissemination of new ideas even to the remoter corners of the country.

CONCLUSIONS

Sacred places seem to have played a significant role in the continued circulation of traditional as well as reinterpreted religious beliefs. The mechanisms for the diffusion and circulation of religious ideas vary, from the complex traditional systems of high-level sacred centers to the relatively simple ones of the incipient shrines. The traditional systems have been based largely on the social relationships between the priest and the pilgrim. These relationships are undergoing changes due to the emergence of new media of communication and transportation.

Chapter XII

Pilgrim Interaction At Sacred Places : The Case of Hardwar

INTRODUCTION

In the last chapter interaction between the pilgrims and the established institutions at the sacred places were the main concern. This chapter explores the nature of interaction within the pilgrim body. Since pilgrims from culturally diverse areas assemble at high-level sacred places, there appears to exist the potential for interpersonal communication and, by extension, for regional intercommunication, leading perhaps to a sharing of values and beliefs as well as to the diffusion of cultural traits. That there is a potential cannot be denied; but there are scholars who have, it seems, overstressed the role of pilgrimages in the process of nation-building, possibly conveying the impression that the potential has already been developed.[1]

The fact that pilgrims at a shrine of a certain level come to participate in a religious experience presupposes the existence of a shared belief in the area from which they come or in the segment of Hindu population that they represent. Therefore, there is no specific compelling reason for the pilgrims to communicate or exchange religious ideas; they already hold certain elements of religious beliefs in common; that is why they come to a specific shrine. Furthermore, the usual object of pilgrimage is to partake individually of the sanctity of a place or to supplicate a deity for specific ends. Thus, the institution of pilgrimage in its elemental form expresses itself as a "relationship" between the devotee and the object of worship or sanctity. It does not, by itself, depend on a relationship among the pilgrims. The interrelationship of the pilgrims is established usually in an indirect manner, through an intermediary, whether it is a holy man from one region interpreting

[1]See, for example, Radha Kumud Mookerji, *The Fundamental Unity of India.* Also Haridas Bhattacharyya, ed., *The Cultural Heritage of India,* chap. 35, pp. 499–500.

religious beliefs in another region, or an organization or sect propagating "new" beliefs in a body of pilgrims who have not heard of them before. Religious intercommunication between pilgrims from different regions is not articulately structured.

A pilgrim, at high-level shrines, is no doubt exposed to the visible variety within the pilgrim body, and is likely to carry the impression that despite apparent diversity there are, nevertheless, certain common religious symbols and goals of Hinduism. The idea of regional diversity in India as well as the idea of a common binding thread is thus impressed on pilgrims' minds. I have already observed in a previous chapter that pilgrimage is *not* a once-in-a-lifetime event and that many pilgrims repeat their visits to a given shrine. These facts, combined with the impressive continuity of the institution of pilgrimage since ancient times must result in a cumulative consciousness about the simultaneous regional diversity as well as broad religious identity within Hinduism. Discussing the wider ties of Indian village, Professor Mandelbaum points out that pilgrimage helps to continually confirm the sense of identification of people with entire India.[2] Similarly, Professor Srinivas asserted that "the concept of the unity of India is essentially a religious one."[3]

The process whereby a pilgrim acquires the sense of identity with the entire Hindu sacred space lies essentially in the realm of psychological perception. The effects of this process are extremely difficult to isolate. Yet, the cumulative effect cannot be ignored unless one chooses to be oblivious of the long historical continuity of the institution of pilgrimage.

In spite of what I have said above, there are, I believe, certain conditions that hinder the full realization of potential pilgrim interaction at the sacred places. Some of these conditions are related to the agro-economic cycle, which is partially dependent on the climatic regime. Other, perhaps more important, factors are directly related to the nature of Hindu society itself. I shall try to illustrate these ideas briefly in relation to Hardwar.

REGIONAL SEASONALITY OF PILGRIMAGE

It has been pointed out earlier that pilgrims from different parts of India show a marked seasonal concentration at Hardwar.

[2]David G. Mandelbaum, *Society in India,* Vol. II, *Change and Continuity,* p. 401.
[3]M. N. Srinivas, *Caste in Modern India,* p. 105.

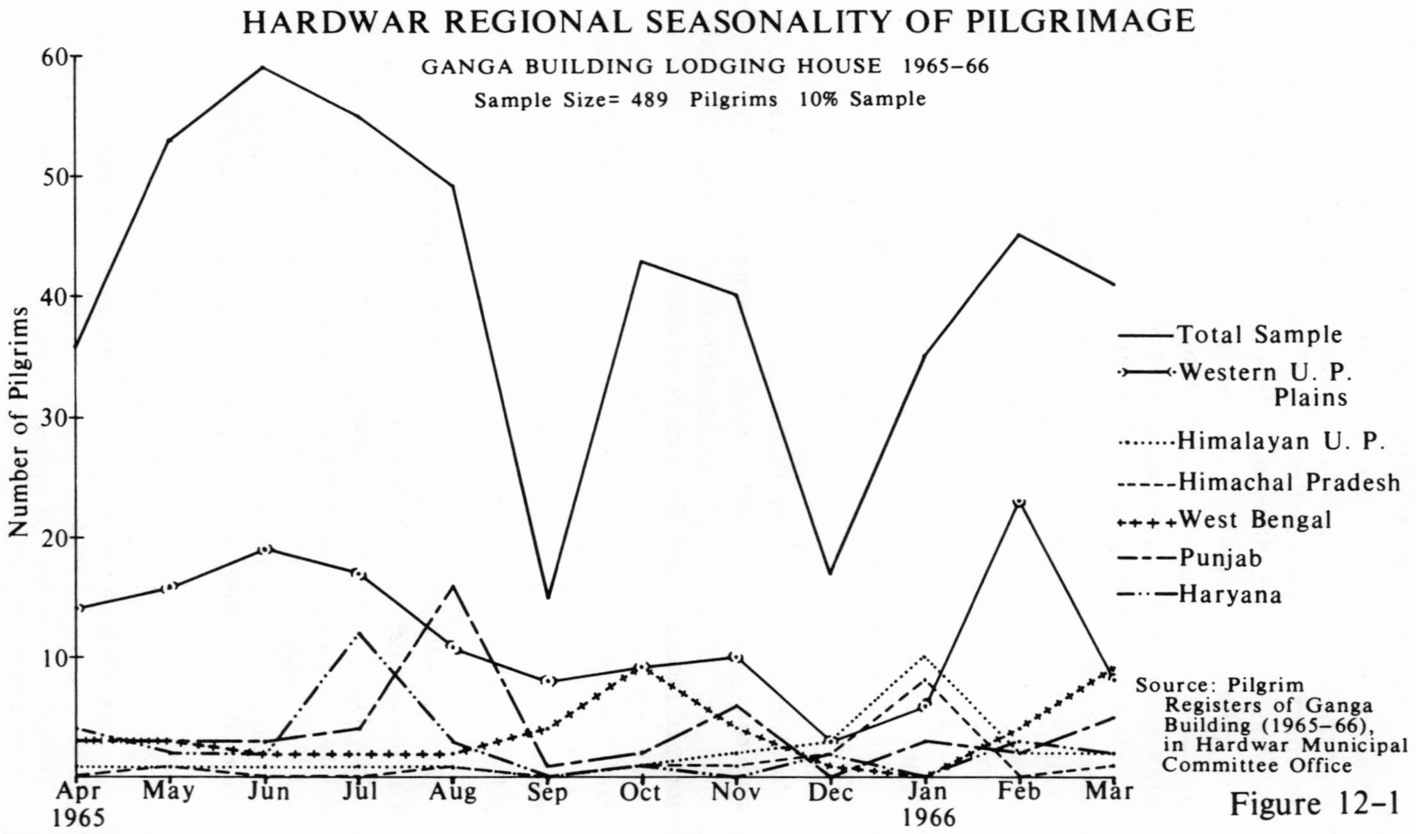
HARDWAR REGIONAL SEASONALITY OF PILGRIMAGE
GANGA BUILDING LODGING HOUSE 1965–66
Sample Size= 489 Pilgrims 10% Sample
Number of Pilgrims
60
50
40
30
20
10
Apr 1965
May
Jun
Jul
Aug
Sep
Oct
Nov
Dec
Jan 1966
Feb
Mar
Total Sample
Western U. P. Plains
Himalayan U. P.
Himachal Pradesh
West Bengal
Punjab
Haryana
Source: Pilgrim Registers of Ganga Building (1965–66), in Hardwar Municipal Committee Office

Figure 12-1

The priestly caste at Hardwar is keenly aware of this through their experience over successive generations. The livelihood of the *purohits* is intimately bound up with the visiting pilgrims who perform prescribed rites and pay appropriate *dakṣiṇā* (ritualistic fee). During my several visits to Hardwar it was brought home to me that to carry on detailed interviews with the priests one must select the slack season of pilgrimage. Careful sampling of the pilgrim registers shows that the peak periods of pilgrim arrivals from different regions are in different parts of the year (fig. 12-1).[4] Thus, pilgrims from western Uttar Pradesh, Haryana, Punjab, West Bengal, and Himachal Pradesh, have their respective peak periods in February, July, August, October, and January. Our observations on the basis of samples from the pilgrim registers are generally in accord with the views of the priests of Hardwar. The existence of regional seasonality tends to reduce interaction between pilgrims of different regions. Of course, during periods of overlap there may be some interaction when the pilgrims from different regions attend the discourses of holy men at Hardwar and even more so at nearby Rishikesh.

The occurrence of regional pilgrim maxima at different times in the year may be related both to the regional agricultural cycle and to the religious occasions especially favored for a holy bath at Hardwar.[5] There may also be the influence of different periods of vacation in schools, colleges, offices, and certain government departments. It is not possible for us to illustrate all these relationships. However, some examples may be cited to demonstrate that such relationships exist. Further inquiry in this field is needed.

The main pilgrimage season for Himachal Pradesh and the Himalayan districts of Uttar Pradesh is January (fig. 12-1).[6]

[4]Each *dharmaśālā* (pilgrim rest house that charges no rent or only token rent), "lodging house," and hotel at Hardwar and other places maintains a register of arrival and departure of pilgrims. However, some of the local managers of these places indulge in unlimited corruption and during peak periods charge illegal rent. Furthermore, records are kept in the most haphazard manner and many pilgrim entries are not made, to avoid detection of overcrowding by the Health Department and the Municipal Committee. Many lodging houses are operated by the *paṇḍās (purohits)* who formerly lodged pilgrims free in their own buildings. The pilgrims now pay rent as they would in a regular hotel. However, because of traditional ties between the *paṇḍās* and their client-pilgrims, the latter tend to reside in their lodging houses. This gives rise to a regional or caste bias in the samples of lodging houses.

[5]Cf. Iravati Karve, "On the Road : A Maharashtrian Pilgrimage," p. 22.

[6]This graph shows the sample from one lodging house only. This particular one

Winter is the slack agricultural season in both of these regions; therefore, pilgrimage during this season does not interfere with the agricultural activity. Many Pahāṛīs (people from the Himalayan region) come to the adjoining plains during the winter months for finding temporary jobs as well as for selling their special products, such as blankets, caps, and woolen garments. The location of Hardwar at the contact zone of mountains and plains makes it convenient for the seasonal migrants of the adjoining hill region to have a holy bath before dispersing themselves in the neighboring plains.

For the pilgrims of western Uttar Pradesh there are two distinct peaks, one in June and the other in February (fig. 12-1). There may be a complex relationship between the agricultural-commercial cycle of activities and pilgrimage. The first peak comes soon after the *kharif* (wet season crop) has been sown. The second comes about a month before the *rabi* (dry season crop) harvest.

The pilgrimage maxima for Haryana and Punjab occur successively after that of Uttar Pradesh. These peaks are paralleled by the correspondingly later sowing of the *kharif* crops in Haryana and Punjab. Thus, a relationship between agricultural calendar and pilgrimage is suggested. A detailed study of the agricultural cycle of different regions in the field of Hardwar is necessary before more specific observations on regional seasonality of pilgrimage can be made. Nevertheless, the overall pilgrimage cycle at Hardwar shows that in the agriculturally busy months of September and December Hardwar has relatively few pilgrims.[7]

The pilgrims from West Bengal usually come during the festival holidays of *Durgā Pūjā* (worship of the goddess Durgā) in the month of October. It seems as though the spatial separation between West Bengal and Punjab is emphasized by their temporal separation at Hardwar.

---

has been selected for illustration because local inquiry at Hardwar suggested that there was no regional bias on the part of the management of this lodging house. It is very difficult to find lodging houses in Hardwar which do not have biases in favor of certain regions.

[7]August and more particularly September are busy months because of tillage for *rabi*; December and January are occupied with irrigation and weeding. The regional seasonality may possibly be affected by the introduction of new seeds of wheat which require a somewhat different agricultural routine.

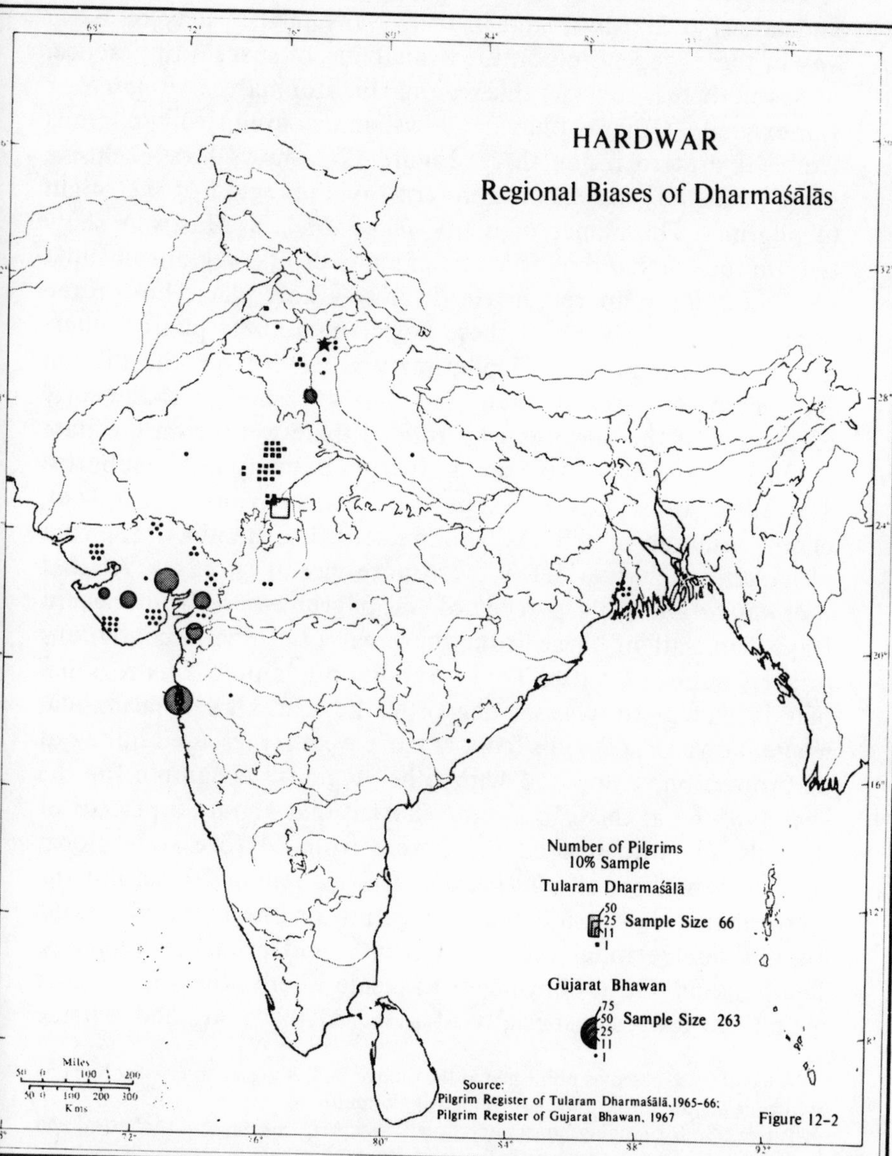
HARDWAR
Regional Biases of Dharmaśālās
Number of Pilgrims
10% Sample
Tularam Dharmaśālā
50
25
11
1
Sample Size 66
Gujarat Bhawan
75
50
25
11
1
Sample Size 263
Miles
50 0 100 200
50 0 100 200 300
Kms
Source:
Pilgrim Register of Tularam Dharmaśālā, 1965–66;
Pilgrim Register of Gujarat Bhawan, 1967
Figure 12-2

REGIONAL BIASES IN THE RESIDENTIAL PATTERN OF PILGRIMS

There are a very large number of *dharmaśālās*, lodging houses, and hotels at Hardwar and in theory any pilgrim may reside in any of these, depending on the availability of space.[8] In practice, however, there is considerable regional bias for many *dharmaśālās*.[9] For example, Gujarat Bhavan allows, almost exclusively, pilgrims from Gujarat to reside there. Figure 12-2 shows how exclusive some of the *dharmaśālās* are in terms of the region of the origin of pilgrims. The names of many *dharmaśālās* at Hardwar show that on the one hand pilgrims from many diverse regions of India have an abiding interest in Hardwar as a holy place, but on the other the exclusiveness of these hostels minimizes pilgrim interaction.[10] A sample of 263 pilgrims was taken from the Pilgrim Register of Gujarat Bhavan (for 1967). It showed that nearly 62 percent of the pilgrims who resided there were from the state of Gujarat, and over 24 percent were from Bombay and its suburbs. The latter apparently were, as their castes strongly suggested, mainly Gujarati merchants who are settled in Bombay. The case of Tularam Dharmaśālā is even more clear (fig. 12-2). At that *dharmaśālā* about 94 percent of the pilgrims were from eastern Rajasthan—all of these from the areas of formerly contiguous princely states of Kota, Tonk, Bundi, and Jaipur. This regional bias is evident to a lesser degree in the Karnatak Dharmaśālā, where, however, pilgrims from Mysore were represented quite out of proportion, compared with other regions. A sample for the year 1965–66 at this *dharmaśālā* showed that about 30 percent of the pilgrims who resided there were from Mysore state alone. It is true that not all *dharmaśālās* show a regional bias, but the fact remains that residential segregation on the basis of regions inhibits interregional mixing of people and exchange of ideas. The pilgrims find it convenient to reside where others from their region are lodged, especially at a sacred place situated outside

[8]A list of these places is published at the time of each *Kumbha* and *Ardha Kumbha* by the *melā* Committee and the Municipal Committee.

[9]It is less so for lodging houses and hotels, where, of course, rent is charged and there is less discrimination on the basis of regional origin.

[10]Some of the names of *dharmaśālās* that show their regional nature are Punjab-Sindh Kshetra, Karnatak Dharmaśālā, Gujarat Bhavan, Andhra Dharmaśālā (in Rishikesh). Some have nonregional names, but strong regional exclusiveness of pilgrims, e. g., Bhola Giri Ashram allows mostly Bengali pilgrims.

their language area. The residential pattern of pilgrims at Hardwar thus appears to be a microcosmic replica of the regional cultural variety of India at large. Just as the interregional communication is limited in India as a whole, so is the interaction between pilgrims of different regions at Hardwar.

CASTE BIASES IN THE RESIDENTIAL PATTERN OF PILGRIMS

Intimately related to the partial regional segregation in the residential pattern of pilgrims at Hardwar is the caste bias, which, in some cases, fortifies the regional bias because many castes tend to be region-specific. Since few pilgrims from the former untouchable castes make pilgrimages to high-level shrines, there should be, theoretically, little basis for caste separation in the residential pattern. At Hardwar, however, pilgrims of the scheduled castes are, it seems, increasing in number. An indication of this is that a new pilgrim rest house by the name of Gandhi Harijan Dharmshala has come into existence. While the visits of a perceptible number of Harijan pilgrims to Hardwar is a tangible evidence of the process of "Sanskritization," yet even at the sacred place they remain, in practice, the same untouchable group.[11]

Chandi Ram Sindhi Dharmshala provides us with an example of the residential pattern of a caste group which also happens to be region-specific. A sample (375 pilgrims) for the year 1965–66 from the pilgrim registers of this *dharmaśālā* showed that over 51 percent of the pilgrims who resided in this building registered themselves as of "Sindhi" caste.[12] A further inquiry into the castes of other pilgrims in the sample revealed that the castes of most other pilgrims in this *dharmaśālā* could be subsumed under the wider "Sindhi" caste.

CONCLUSIONS

The above description shows quite clearly that the seasonal separation and existing residential patterns of pilgrims, based on regional or caste bias, do not constitute a favorable mechanism

[11]"Harijan" (Man of God) is the term coined by Mahatma Gandhi to be used in place of "untouchable" and synonymous pejoratives.

[12]Strictly speaking, Sindhi is not a caste. In practice, however, Hindus with that appellation have many attributes of a caste. Most Hindu Sindhis are of the Lohāṇā trading caste; other trading groups make up most of the remainder.

for interregional pilgrim interaction. Hardwar is perhaps not a unique example. Future studies of other sacred places may provide a better understanding of the nature of pilgrim interaction. Hardwar clearly reflects the broader aspects of Hinduism in India at large. The diversity of pilgrims at Hardwar is a replica of the regional diversity of India. The seasonal separation and a considerable degree of residential segregation of pilgrims based on regional and caste differentiation reflect regional and social diversity within Hinduism. Nevertheless, Hardwar remains a major focus for the expression of shared belief in the sanctity of this sacred place. Thus, a commonality of religious beliefs exists side by side with the variegated social and spatial patterns of Hinduism.

Chapter XIII

Summary of Conclusions

In the preceding pages we have studied only one aspect of the religious circulation in India—the pilgrimages of the Hindus to their sacred places. Since the character of places and spatial organization lie at the core of geography, the nature of circulation generated by sacred places has been treated as a problem in geography.

The antiquity and the continuity of the institution of pilgrimage in Hinduism has been demonstrated by mapping sacred places described in the epic *Mahābhārata,* the *Purāṇas,* and later sources. It seems clear that the broad outline of the sacred realm of Hinduism was established some centuries before the beginning of the Christian Era. Since then it has undergone relatively minor changes, taking into consideration the immense span of time involved.

The route pattern of ancient pilgrimage suggests at least two favorable zones or corridors of contact between the North and the South. These corridors seem to have been favored for the southward expansion of plow agriculture. The areas less suited for this mode of cultivation remained outside the domain of Hinduism and in part continue to be occupied by tribal peoples. Thus, the Hindu sacred realm of the past was also broadly coincident with the extent of the material culture of Hinduism, as distinct from the cultures of the forest-dwelling tribes practicing hunting and gathering and slash-and-burn agriculture. No wonder the process of Hinduization in these latter areas has been slow.

Among the many deities associated with sacred places on an all-India scale, Śiva—originally a Dravidian deity—occupies the dominant position, followed by Viṣṇu and the pre-Aryan Mother Goddess. Thus, despite Aryanization, the pre-Aryan deities (whatever their present form in the context of Hinduism) continue to command allegiance. On the other hand, most of the purely Aryan deities have been relegated to a minor position. I believe, therefore, that the significance of the pre-Aryan deities in the present context of Hinduism needs a reappraisal.

Association of Hindu sacred places with flowing water seems to be a spatial expression of the pervasive concept of ritual purification by bathing. Since this concept itself might have been of proto-Dravidian origin, a deeper understanding of the site association of Hindu holy places may be achieved by directing more attention to the study of the religious belief pattern of the ancient Dravidians.

Our study shows that the pilgrims' perception of the ranks of holy places reflects the absence of a unified system of ranking within Hinduism itself. This, in turn, is the result of the existence of a variety of cults in Hinduism, and the syncretistic character of the Hindu belief pattern. However, for analytical purposes at least, five levels of sacred places can be objectively derived. These are pan-Hindu, supraregional, regional, subregional, and local.

The five levels of sacred places cannot be considered to constitute a formal hierarchy because they do not represent steps in a single system, and each successively lower level is not necessarily subordinate to the level above it. Nevertheless, an objective ordering allows us to observe the sociological and cultural characteristics within their corresponding pilgrim fields.

The highest-level sacred places can be regarded as nodes in a religious circulation manifold, in which the ritually high castes and the economically high classes from different cultural regions of India participate. Pilgrimage at this level is an expression of some of the highest common beliefs of Hinduism carried by a thin stratum of religious elite—mostly literate. Spiritual aspects of the Hindu religion and the ideal of purification of the soul are the chief motivating factors at the highest levels. Religious circulation at this level continuously reaffirms the extent of the Hindu sacred realm. India as a spatial entity has had little meaning to the Hindus outside of the framework of religion until the modern era. Certainly, without such a sense of "India" there never would have been a "freedom movement" and the nationalist activities even of the nineteenth century, and the Indian national renaissance, leading ultimately to independence.

The regional and subregional-level shrines reflect the great variety in the belief patterns of Hinduism and are intimately related to the material and mundane aspects of life. The deities at such shrines tend to become highly personalized and are propitiated for specific material gains and for the resolution of anxiety arising out of the problems of everyday life. Pilgrimages at these levels are often undertaken for the performance of several obligatory life-cycle rites. At these levels religion tends to become a problem-solving social mechanism in which the sociological, rather than the spiritual, aspects dominate. The pilgrim congregation includes a perceptible, and in certain cases a major, proportion of scheduled castes and large elements of semiliterate and illiterate population. The pilgrim fields of these shrines tend to remain restricted because beyond the regional cultural milieu the pilgrims cannot establish a personalized "relationship" with the deities. Moreover, the social and economic networks of the pilgrims of such shrines are usually restricted to a single linguistic, dialectic, or other cultural region or subregion. On the whole (excepting local shrines), it can be maintained that the higher the level of a holy place, the higher the proportion of ritually high caste pilgrims, and the more general the purpose of the visit.

The scheduled-caste pilgrims distinctly favor the Mother Goddess shrines, especially where animal sacrifice can be performed. The practice of blood sacrifice has disappeared at several of the Mother Goddess shrines and is likely to decline where it is still prevalent. Such places can be of great value for the study of the process of Sanskritization, both in reference to pilgrims of the scheduled castes and to the ritual complex of the shrines.

The relationship between castes of pilgrims and the distances they travel to reach a sacred place is very complex. It is clear, however, that up to the regional-level shrines, different castes do not show much divergence in the distances traveled for pilgrimage. At the supraregional and the pan-Hindu level certain differences become obvious. The mercantile castes as a whole travel the longest distances, followed by the ritually higher Brahmans. This may be, in part, due to the relatively higher economic level of the former caste groups. At the lower-level shrines commitment or vow is an important reason for travel; therefore, distance to the sacred place becomes less significant. At the higher levels the purposes of travel are general; therefore, religiously motivated individuals undertake the pilgrimage. Moreover, when distance becomes a critical factor the more affluent castes have a greater ability to go on a pilgrimage. These relationships need further inquiry through a sampling of individuals of different castes and economic groups in the fields of various shrines.

Some of the salient components of the diffusion mechanism of sacred places have been illustrated, especially with reference to Hardwar. Diffusion of religious literature in India, particularly the *Purāṇas,* has provided the basic corpus for recognition of sacred places. The priest-pilgrim relationships have concurrently tended to fix the fields of the places of pilgrimage. In recent decades faster means of travel and nontraditional media of communication have widened the pilgrim fields. Thus, the traditional diffusion mechanism seems to have been in part supplanted by the modern one, which is less dependent on the traditional social relationships. High-level places continue to diversify their role in spreading the traditional and reinterpreted patterns of beliefs.

The Hindu places of pilgrimage are the symbols of the religious beliefs of Hinduism; they reflect its vitality, resilience, and syncretism. They broadly define and continually reemphasize the Hindu sacred space. They have knitted the linguistically diverse Hindu population socially, culturally, and spatially at different integrative levels. Their significance is to be measured in their capacity to generate and maintain a massive system of religious circulation.

Appendix

Pilgrim Samples and Caste Groupings

PILGRIM SAMPLES

A total of 5,454 pilgrims were interviewed at twelve sacred places, as is shown in the Introduction, in table 1-1, and an effort was made to achieve a representative sample, since under the conditions of the fairs a strict random sample was out of the question. The samples were taken at such spots at the sacred places where the greatest mixing of pilgrims could be expected. In the case of sacred places where one temple was the main focus of pilgrimage, samples were taken either inside the sacred precincts or close to the main entrance or exit. At the places where bathing was the chief object of pilgrimage, interviews were carried out at the bathing *ghāṭs,* as in the case of Hardwar and Ujjain. At Hardwar about two hundred pilgrims were also interviewed inside the *dharmaśālās,* which, local inquiry suggested, had no regional or caste biases for pilgrims' residence. In the case of Badrinath a special adjustment had to be made, because it is located very close to the Indo-Tibetan border and some difficulty was experienced in carrying on interviewing of pilgrims for more than two days. Therefore, one hundred interviews were carried out in the Badrinath temple precincts, while the rest were done at Rishikesh. This shifting, however, did not cause any serious problem, because Rishikesh is the point of departure for the buses going to Badrinath. Interviews at Rishikesh were carried out at the place where passenger tickets for Badrinath are issued, and where the Health Department checks the immunization certificates of the passengers before tickets for the buses can be issued.

THE QUESTIONNAIRE

The questionnaire was printed in English and Hindī. However, the questions were asked in Hindī or Panjābī except at Rewalsar, where the help of an interpreter was necessary because many pilgrims spoke dialects of Tibetan. When a pilgrim was in a hurry, only four basic questions were asked: the district of origin, caste, profession, and the purpose of his pilgrimage. At the places where samples were taken twice, save for

Rewalsar, only these four questions were asked on the second occasion.[1] At Rewalsar all questions were asked on both occasions because the first one was primarily a Buddhist festival, and the second was dominated by Hindus and Sikhs. At Ujjain only the four basic questions were asked because necessary help could not be arranged. But a sample of 500 pilgrims was nevertheless obtained in view of the immense gathering of the *Siṃhastha* fair.

The date and the names of the sacred place, the occasion, and the interviewer were recorded.

Each pilgrim was asked for information about these seven items: (1) male or female; residence: (2) town or village, (3) tehsil, (4) district; (5) profession; (6) caste; (7) purpose of visit (e.g., *sukhnā, darśaṇa, muṇḍana, snāna,* etc.).

The following eleven questions were then asked.

(8) How many times have you visited this place?

(9) Which sacred places did you visit while coming to this place (in order of visit)?

(10) Which sacred places do you intend to visit before reaching home (in order of intended visit)?

(11) Which sacred places have you ever visited in your lifetime?

(12) Any place of pilgrimage nearer to your home than this place?

(13) Which in your opinion are the three most sacred *tīrthas* in the whole of India?

(14) For how many days are you going to be away from home while on this *yātrā*?

(15) Who is attending to your work at home while you are on this *yātrā*?

(16) To which place do people from your area usually go for *yātrā*?

(17) Are you alone or with a group or family?

(18) Which languages can you speak?

CATEGORIES OF CASTES OR COMPARABLE GROUPS

In our questionnaire the *jāti* (caste) of pilgrims was recorded. The numerous *jātis* of the pilgrims were later grouped into ten categories for the purpose of analysis.[2]

[1]These places are Baijnath, Chintpurni, Jwalaji, Kangra, Mansa Devi, Naina Devi, Rewalsar, Shiv Bari.

[2]The following works proved helpful for arriving at the caste categories: *Census of India,* 1931, Vol. I, part 2, table XVII, "Race, Caste or Tribe"; *Census of India,* Paper No. 2, 1960, *Scheduled Castes and Scheduled Tribes Arranged in Alphabetical Order*; J. H. Hutton, *Caste in India,* 4th ed. (Bombay: Oxford University Press, 1963); Sir Denzil Ibbetson, *Panjab Castes* (Lahore, 1916); R. V. Russell, *The Tribes*

(1) *Brahman.* This includes all Brahmans, whatever their present occupation or regional origin.[3]

(2) *Rajput.* All Rajputs, whether professing Hinduism or Buddhism (as in the case of pilgrims from the districts bordering Tibet), are included in this category. This category is also likely to include some pilgrims who claim to be Rajputs although they may actually belong to artisan castes.

(3) *Khatri-Arora and Kayastha.* Khatri and Arora castes are essentially Punjabi mercantile castes, while Kayasthas, a caste traditionally considered scribes, belong to north central and eastern parts of India, particularly Bengal. Ideally the Kayasthas should be in a separate category, but they were so few in number in my sample and somewhat equivalent to the Khatris of Punjab in their respective hierarchical position that it seemed reasonable to combine them in this category. At Badrinath and Ujjain only were the Kayasthas significant in number. In the text this whole caste group (Khatri-Arora and Kayastha) has been referred to simply as Khatri-Arora.

(4) *Other Mercantile Castes.* Mercantile castes other than Khatri-Arora are grouped together. This category also includes Jains, because our samples indicate that most of them are merchants by profession. In the text this group has been referred to as "mercantile castes" only.

(5) *Cultivating Castes.* This group combines all Hindu and Sikh Jats as well as other cultivating castes according to the 1931 Census. However, it does not include the cultivating Brahmans and Rajputs.

(6) *Artisan Castes and "Clean" (non-scheduled) Service Castes.* Both Hindu and Sikh artisan castes and service castes are combined in this group. In the text they are termed simply as "artisan castes." This group is the equivalent of "industrial" and "transport" castes of the 1931 Census.

(7) *Scheduled Castes.* This group is based on the 1961 Census. Both Hindu and Sikh scheduled castes have been combined. In some instances a particular caste may be in the scheduled caste category in one state and not in the other. In such cases, the Census definition has been accepted.

(8) *Scheduled Tribes.* The 1961 Census has been the chief guide in grouping the tribes except where the respondents declare themselves as Rajputs (as in the case of pilgrims to Rewalsar and Ujjain). The Gaddī tribe of Himachal Pradesh has castes almost equivalent to the Hindus

---

and Castes of the Central Provinces of India (London, 1916); Joseph E. Schwartzberg, "The Distribution of Selected Castes in the North Indian Plain," and "Caste Regions of the North Indian Plain."

[3]David E. Sopher, "Pilgrim Circulation in Gujarat," p. 396, follows the 1931 Census classification and includes the cultivator Brahmans with what he terms the "agrarian castes." However, the Brahmans who are not primarily cultivators are grouped by him with merchant castes as "high-status service castes."

of the plains; therefore, even though the Census considers them a scheduled tribe, it is more logical for our purpose to put them in the caste they consider themselves to belong to. For example, a Gaddī tribal who considers himself Brahman has been included in the Brahman category rather than as a member of the "scheduled tribe."

(9) *Unclassified.* Some Hindus did not wish to return their caste, while a few simply mentioned "Hindu" as their caste. Similarly a number of Gorkhas (at Bhagsunag) did not return their specific caste. These individuals have been combined in this category.

(10) *Sikh.* While most Sikh pilgrims returned their specific caste, some only mentioned "Sikh." Those who did state their caste have been grouped with the appropriate caste. Only the ones who did not give their caste name have been put in this category.

The first seven caste groupings (excluding "other mercantile castes") closely approximate Schwartzberg's scheme with respect to castes, arranged by functional categories on a roughly hierarchical basis, in his sample of villages in Hoshiarpur district of Punjab.[4] Although the caste hierarchy of one region may not be strictly comparable to that of the other, the broad groupings are applicable to most of the pilgrims in our study area. They combine the concept of hierarchy as well as the traditional functions of the castes. Moreover, a finer classification would have made interpretations difficult by reducing the number in the several categories. This is particularly to be avoided in cases where only one hundred pilgrims were interviewed on a given occasion. The last three categories are necessitated in our study because of the presence of tribal and Buddhist pilgrims at Rewalsar, of Gorkhas at Bhagsunag, and of several Hindu and Sikh pilgrims who did not name their caste.

[4]Schwartzberg, "Caste Regions," p. 96. The presence of large numbers of mercantile castes (other than Khatri-Arora) requires a separate category in our analysis. The Khatri-Arora caste group is important mostly in Punjab, Haryana, and Delhi, while the other merchant castes have a much wider distribution although their proportion in any given region may be small.

Bibliography

PUBLISHED WORKS

Abul-Fazl-i-'Allami. *'Ain-i-Akbari of Abul-Fazl-i-'Allami.* Translated into English by H. S. Jarrett, revised and further annotated by Sir Jadu-Nath Sarkar. Calcutta : Royal Asiatic Society of Bengal, Vol. 3, 1948.

Agni Purāṇa : A Collection of Hindu Mythology and Traditions (Sanskrit). Edited by Rājendralāla Mitra. 3 vols. Calcutta : Bibliotheca Indica, The Asiatic Society of Bengal, 1879.

Agrawala, Vasudeva S. *Devī-Māhātmyam : The Glorification of the Great Goddess.* Varanasi : All-India Kashiraj Trust, 1963.

———. *Matsya Purāṇa—A Study : An Exposition of the Ancient Purāṇa-Vidyā.* Varanasi : All-India Kashiraj Trust, 1965.

Āitareya Brāhmaṇa (Rigveda Brahmanas). Translated from the original Sanskrit by A. B. Keith, Cambridge : Harvard University Press, 1920.

Aiyangar, K. V. Rangaswami, ed. *Kṛtyakalpataru of Bhaṭṭa Lakṣmīdhara, Tīrthavivecana Kāṇḍam.* Gaekwad's Oriental Series No. 98. Baroda : Oriental Institute, 1942.

Aiyangar, S. Krishnasvami. *Some Contributions of South India to Indian Culture.* Calcutta : University of Calcutta, 1942.

Ali, S. M. *The Geography of the Purāṇas.* New Delhi : People's Publishing House, 1966.

Allchin, Bridget and Raymond. *The Birth of Indian Civilization.* Penguin Paperback, 1968.

Anonymous. "Viṭhobā of Pandharpur." *Indian Antiquary* 2 (September 1873) : 272–273.

Anonymous. *Madura—A Tourist Guide.* Madras : Higginbotham and Co., 1913.

Association for Asian Studies. "The Proto-Dravidian Inscriptions of the Indus Civilization Being Deciphered." *Newsletter* 15 (December 1969) : 86–87.

Association of American Geographers. *Spatial Diffusion.* Commission on College Geography Resource Paper No. 4. Washington, D. C. : Association of American Geographers, 1969.

Ayyar, P. V. Jagadisa. *South Indian Shrines.* Madras : Madras Times Printing & Publishing Co., 1920.

Bacon, Thomas. *The Orientalist* (Vol. 1). Manchester : Ainsworth, 1842.

Balaratnam, L. K. "South-Indian Fasts and Festivities." In Mythic Society, *Quarterly Journal* (Bangalore) 34 (1943) : 68–73.

Banerjee, N. R. *The Iron Age in India*. Delhi : Munshiram Manoharlal, 1965.

Banton, Michael, ed. *Anthropological Approaches to the Study of Religion*. New York : Frederick A. Praeger, 1966.

Barth, A. *The Religions of India*. Translated by Rev. J. Wood. 3rd ed. London : Kegan Paul, 1891.

Bartholomew, J. G. *A Literary and Historical Atlas of Asia*. London : J. M. Dent & Sons, 1912.

Barua, Hem, and J. D. Baveja. *The Fairs and Festivals of Assam*. Gauhati (Assam) : D. N. Dutt Barua, 1956.

Basham, A. L. *The Wonder That Was India : A Survey of the Culture of the Indian Sub-continent before the Coming of the Muslims*. New York : Grove Press, 1959.

Beals, Alan R. "Conflict and Interlocal Festivals in South Indian Region." *Journal of Asian Studies* 23 (June 1964) : 99–113.

Berreman, Gerald D. *Hindus of the Himalayas*. Berkeley and Los Angeles : University of California Press, 1963.

Bharati, (Swami) Agehananda. *The Ochre Robe*. Seattle : University of Washington Press, 1962.

———. "Pilgrimage in the Indian Tradition." *History of Religions* 3, no. 1 (1963) : 135–167.

———. *The Tantric Tradition*. London : Rider and Company, 1965.

———. "Pilgrimage Sites and Indian Civilization." In *Chapters in Indian Civilization*, edited by J. W. Elder, Vol. I, pp. 85–126. Dubuque (Iowa) : Kendall/Hunt Publishing Company, 1970.

Bhattacharya, Batuknath. "Festivals and Sacred Days." In *The Cultural Heritage of India*. Vol. IV, *The Religions*, edited by Haridas Bhattacharya. Calcutta : Ramakrishna Mission, 1956.

Bhattacharyya, Haridas, ed. *The Cultural Heritage of India*. Vol. IV, *The Religions*. Calcutta : Ramakrishna Mission, 1956.

Bhowmick, Prabodh Kumar. "Four Temples in Midnapur, West Bengal." *Man in India* 40 (1960) : 81–108.

Bishop, Carl Whiting. "The Origin and Early Diffusion of Traction Plough." *Antiquity* 10 (1936) : 261–281.

Bose, Nirmal Kumar. "Culture Zones of India. *Geographical Review of India* 18, no. 4 (1956).

Briggs, George Weston. *The Chamars*. London : Oxford University Press, 1920.

Broek, J. O. M. *The Santa Clara Valley, California : A Study in Landscape Changes*. Utrecht : University of Utrecht, 1932.

———. "The Relations between History and Geography." *The Pacific Historical Review* 10, no. 5 (1941) : 321–325.

Brush, John E. "The Distribution of Religious Communities in India." *Annals, Association of American Geographers* 39 (1949): 81–98.

Buck, Cecil Henry. *Faiths, Fairs, and Festivals of India.* Calcutta: Thacker, Spink and Co., 1917.

Bühler, G., trans. *The Laws of Manu.* Oxford University Press: 1886. Reprinted, Delhi: Motilal Banarsidass, 1964.

Burgess, James. "The Ritual of the Temple of Rameshvaram." *Indian Antiquary* 12 (Bombay, 1883): 315–326.

Census of India, 1931. Vol. I, *India,* part 1, *Report by J. H. Hutton.* Delhi: Manager of Publications, 1933; and Volume I, part 2, table XVII, pp. 525–533.

Census of India. Paper No. 2, 1960. *Scheduled Castes and Scheduled Tribes Arranged in Alphabetical Order.* New Delhi: Manager of Publications, 1960.

Census of India, 1961. Vol. V: *Gujarat,* Part VII-B: *Fairs and Festivals.* Delhi: Manager of Publications, Government of India, 1961.

Census of India. Paper No. 1, 1962. 1961 *Census—Final Population Totals.* Delhi: Manager of Publications, Government of India, 1962.

Census of India, 1961. Vol. II: *Andhra Pradesh,* Part VII-B (11): *Fairs and Festivals, Kurnool District.* Delhi: Manager of Publications, Government of India, 1963.

Census of India, 1961. Vol. II: Part II-A (ii): *Union Primary Census Abstracts.* Delhi: Manager of Publications, Government of India, 1963.

Census of India, 1961. Vol. II: *Andhra Pradesh,* Part VII-B (9), B (12), B (18), B (19), B (20): *Fairs and Festivals.* New Delhi: Manager of Publications, 1965.

Census of India, 1961. Vol. XIII: Punjab, Part VII-B: *Fairs and Festivals.* New Delhi: Manager of Publications, Government of India, 1965.

Chakravarty, Chintaharan. *The Tantras.* Calcutta: Punthi Pustak, 1963.

Chanda, Anil K. *Report of the Commissioner for Scheduled Castes and Scheduled Tribes for the year* 1961–62 (eleventh report), parts 1 and 2. Delhi: Manager of Publications, 1963.

Chatterjee, S. P., ed. *The National Atlas of India.* Preliminary edition. Calcutta: Ministry of Education and Scientific Research, 1957.

Chattopadhyaya, Debiprasad. *Lokāyata: A Study in Ancient Indian Materialism.* New Delhi: People's Publishing House, 1959.

Chattopadhyaya, Ksetreschandra. "Religious Suicide at Prayag." *Journal of the U. P. Historical Society* 10 (1937): 65–79.

Chunder, Bholanauth. *The Travels of a Hindu.* 2 vols. London: N. Trübner, 1869.

Cohn, Bernard S. "Structural Change in Rural Society." In *Land Control and Social Structure in Indian History,* edited by Robert Eric Frykenberg, pp. 53–121. Madison, Milwaukee, and London : University of Wisconsin Press, 1969.

Cohn, Bernard S., and McKim Marriott. "Networks and Centers in the Integration of Indian Civilization." *Journal of Social Research* 1, no. 1 (1958) : 1–9.

Crooke, William. "Tanjore." In *Encyclopaedia of Religion and Ethics,* Vol. 12, p. 192. New York : Charles Scribner's Sons, 1908–1927.

———. "Tirupati." In *Encyclopaedia of Religion and Ethics,* Vol. 12, pp. 345–346. New York : Charles Scribner's Sons, 1908–1927.

———. "Indian Pilgrimage." In *Encyclopaedia of Religion and Ethics,* Vol. 10. Edited by James Hastings. New York : Charles Scribner's Sons, 1956.

Cunningham, Alexander. *The Ancient Geography of India.* London : Trübner, 1871.

Das, Dyal. "Tax on Pilgrims." *Indian Historical Records Commission, Proceedings,* Vol. 31, part 2, pp. 102–105. Mysore, January 1955.

Das, R. K. *Temples of Tamilnad.* Bombay : Bharatiya Vidya Bhavan, 1964.

Datar, Balwant N. *Himalayan Pilgrimage.* Delhi : Publication Division, Government of India, 1961.

Datta, Jatindra Mohan. "Influence of Religious Belief on the Geographical Distribution of Brahmins in Bengal." *Man in India* 42 (1962) : 89–103.

Dave, H. J. *Immortal India.* 4 vols. Bombay : Bharatiya Vidya Bhavan, 1959–1961.

Deffontaines, Pierre. *Géographie et Religions.* Paris : Gallimard, 1948.

———. "The Religious Factor in Human Geography; Its Force and Its Limits." *Diogenes,* No. 2 (Spring 1953) : 24–37.

De La Saussaye, P. D. Chantepie. *Manual of the Science of Religion.* Translated by Beatrice S. Colyer-Fergusson. London : Longmans, Green and Co., 1891.

Deleury, G. A. *The Cult of Viṭhobā.* Poona : Deccan College Post-Graduate and Research Institute, 1960.

Del Vasto, Lanza. *Le Pèlerinage aux Sources.* Paris : Société des Editions Denoël, 1943.

De Planhol, Xavier. *The World of Islam (Le Monde Islamique : Essai de Géographie).* New York : Cornell University Press, 1959. English translation, Cornell University.

Devi-Dayal, Pandit. *Mufid-i-Alam Jantri* (Urdu). Jullundur (Punjab) : Pandit Chunilal. Annual Publication.

Dey, Nando Lal. *The Geographical Dictionary of Ancient and Medieval India.* Calcutta Oriental Series, No. 21, E-13. London : Luzac and Co., 1927.

Diehl, Carl Gustav. *Instrument and Purpose : Studies on Rites and Rituals in South India.* Lund (Sweden) : C. W. K. Gleerup, 1956.

Dikshitar, V. R. R. *The Matsya Purāṇa, a Study*. Bulletin of the Department of Indian History and Archaeology, No. 5. Madras : University of Madras, 1935.

Director General of Observatories. *Rashtriya Panchang* (English). Delhi : Manager of Publications, 1967 (Annual).

Dubois, Abbe, J. A. *A Description of the Character, Manners and Customs of the Hindus of India. . . .* Translated from the French manuscript. 2d ed. Madras : J. Higginbotham, 1862.

Dutt, Nripendra Kumar. *The Aryanization of India*. Calcutta : N. K. Dutt, 1925.

Ehrenfels, Baron Omar R. *Mother-Right in India*. Hyderabad Deccan : Oxford University Press, 1941.

Eliade, Mircea. *Images and Symbols : Studies in Religious Symbolism*. New York : Sheed and Ward, 1961. Originally published in French (1952) under the title *Images et Symboles*.

———. *The Sacred and the Profane* : *The Nature of Religion*. New York : Harper and Row, 1961.

———. *The Two and the One*. New York and Evanston : Harper and Row, Torchbooks, 1965.

Elliott, H. M. *Early Arab Geographers*. Calcutta : Susil Gupta, 1956.

Encyclopaedia of Religion and Ethics. New York : Charles Scribner's Sons, 1908–1927. Vol. 12.

Farquhar, J. N. *An Outline of the Religious Literature of India*. London : Oxford University Press, 1920. First Indian reprint, Delhi : Motilal Banarsidass, 1967.

Fickler, Paul. "Fundamental Questions in the Geography of Religions." (translated from "Grundfragen der Religionsgeographie," *Erdkunde* : *Archiv für wissenschaftliche Geographie*, Vol. 1, 1947, pp. 121–44, in *Readings in Cultural Geography*, edited by Philip L. Wagner and Marvin W. Mikesell, pp. 94–117. Chicago : University of Chicago Press, 1962.

Fischer, Eric. "Some Comments on a Geography of Religion." *Annals, Association of American Geographers* 46 (1956) : 246–247.

Fleure, H. J. "Sacred Cities; Chiefly in the European Quadrant of the World." *Geographical Teacher* 12 (1923–24) : 434–440.

Garuḍa Purāṇa. Edited by Ramasankara Bhattacharyya. Varanasi : Chowkhamba Sanskrit Series Office, 1964.

Ghurye, G. S. *Gods and Men*. Bombay : Popular Book Depot, 1962.

Ghurye, G. S. *Indian Sadhus*. Bombay, Popular Prakashan, 1964.

Ghurye, G. S. *Religious Consciousness*. Bombay : Popular Prakashan, 1965.

Glasenapp, Helmuth Von. *Heilige Stätten Indiens*. Munich : Georg Müller Verlag, 1928.

Goetz, Hermann. *The Early Wooden Temples of Chamba.* Leiden: E. J. Brill, 1955.

Goswamy, B. N. "The Records Kept by Priests at Centers of Pilgrimage as a Source of Social and Economic History." *Indian Economic and Social History Review* 3, no. 2 (June 1966): 174–184.

———. "Pahari Painting: The Family as the Basis of Style." *Marg* 21, no. 4 (September 1968): 17–62.

Goswamy, B. N., and J. S. Grewal. *The Mughals and the Jogis of Jakhbar.* Simla: Indian Institute of Advanced Study, 1967.

Gumperz, John J. "Religion and Social Communication in Village North India." *Journal of Asian Studies* 23 (June 1964): 89–97.

Gupte, Rai Bahadur, B. A. *Hindu Holidays and Ceremonials, with Dissertations on Origin, Folklore and Symbols.* Calcutta and Simla: Thacker, Spink and Co., 1919.

Gyani, S. D. *Agni Purāṇa: A Study.* Varanasi: Chowkhamba Sanskrit Series Office, 1964.

Hägerstrand, Torsten. *The Propagation of Innovation Waves.* Lund Studies in Geography, Ser. B. Human Geography No. 4. The Royal University of Lund, Sweden, Department of Geography, 1952.

———. *Innovation Diffusion as a Spatial Process.* Translated by Allan Pred. Chicago: The University of Chicago Press, 1967.

Hamilton, Walter. *A Geographical, Statistical and Historical Description of Hindostan.* 2 vols. London: John Murray, 1820.

Harper, Edward B., ed. *Religion in South Asia.* Seattle: University of Washington Press, 1964.

Havell, E. B. *Benares (The Sacred City).* London: Blackie and Son, 1905.

Himachal Pradesh District Gazetteers, Chamba. Simla: Government of Himachal Pradesh, 1963.

Himachal Pradesh. *Census,* 1961. *District Handbook, Bilaspur.* Simla: Superintendent of Census Operations, 1965.

Hindu Religious Endowments Commission. *Report of the Hindu Religious Endowments Commission* (1960–1962). Government of India, Ministry of Law. Delhi: The Manager of Publications, 1962.

Hirt, Howard F. "The Dravidian Temple Complex: A South Indian Cultural Dominant." *Bombay Geographical Magazine* 8–9 (1961): 95–103.

Hopkins, Edward Washburn. *The Religions of India.* Boston: Ginn and Co., 1895.

Hopkins, Washburn. "Economics of Primitive Religion." *Journal of the American Oriental Society* 20 (1899): 303–308.

Hsu, Shin-Yi. "The Cultural Ecology of the Locust Cult in Traditional China." *Annals, Association of American Geographers* 59 (1969): 731–752.

Hurst, John F. *Indika: The Country and the People of India and Ceylon.* New York: Harper, 1891.

Hutchison, J., and J. Ph. Vogel. *History of the Panjab Hill States.* 2 vols. Lahore: Superintendent Government Printing, 1933.

Hutton, J. H., *Census of India,* 1931. Vol. I, India. Part 1, *Report.* Delhi: Manager of Publications, 1933.

Ibbetson, Sir Denzil. *Panjab Castes, Being a Reprint of the Chapter on "The Races, Castes and Tribes of the People" in the Report on the Census of the Panjab, Published in* 1883, *by the late Sir Denzil Ibbetson.* Lahore, 1916.

Imperial Gazetteer of India. 26 vols. New ed. Oxford: Clarendon Press, 1907–09.

India (Republic). Ministry of Information and Broadcasting. *Festivals of India.* Delhi: Ministry of Information and Broadcasting, Publications Division, 1956.

———. *Temples of North India.* Delhi: Ministry of Information and Broadcasting, Publications Division, 1959.

Indian Historical Records Commission. *Proceedings of Meetings.* Delhi: Government of India Press, December 1937 and January 1955.

Issac, Erich. "Influence of Religion on the Spread of Citrus." *Science* 129 (1959): 179–186.

———. "Religion, Landscape and Space." *Landscape* 9 (1959–60): 14–18.

———. "The Act and the Covenant; the Impact of Religion on the Landscape." *Landscape* 11 (1961–2): 24–37.

———. "Myths, Cults and Livestock Breeding." *Diogenes,* No. 41 (1963): 70–93.

———. *Religious Geography and Geography of Religion.* University of Colorado Studies, Series in Earth Sciences, No. 3, *Man and the Earth.* Boulder: University of Colorado Press, 1965.

Jacques, Claude. "Les Pèlerinages en Inde." In Sources Orientales, *Les Pèlerinages,* pp. 157–197. Paris: Editions du Seuil, 1960.

James, O. E. *Cult of the Mother-Goddess.* New York: Frederick A. Praeger, 1959.

Kalhaṇa. *Kalhaṇa's Rājataraṅgiṇī, A Chronicle of the Kings of Kaśmīr.* 2 vols. Translated, with an Introduction and Commentary, by M. A. Stein. Westminster: Archibald Constable and Co., 1900.

Kalyāṇa, Tīrthāṅka. Vol. 31, no. 1. Gorakhpur: The Gita Press, 1957.

Kane, P. V. "The Two Epics." *Annals of the Bhandarkar Oriental Research Institute,* Vol. XLVII (1966), pp. 11–58.

Kantawala, S. G. *Cultural History from the Matsya Purāṇa.* Baroda: M. S. University, 1964.

Karve, I. "On The Road: A Maharashtrian Pilgrimage." *Journal of Asian Studies* 22 (November 1962): 13–30.

Keay, F. E. *Ancient Indian Education; An Inquiry into its Origin, Development and Ideals.* Oxford University Press, 1918.

Kosambi, D. D. "The Basis of Ancient Indian History." *Journal of the American Oriental Society* 75 (1955): 35–45 and 226–237.

———. *The Culture and Civilization of Ancient India in Historical Outline.* London: Routledge and Kegan Paul, 1965.

———. "Living Prehistory in India." *Scientific American,* February 1967, pp. 105–114.

Kristensen, W. Brede. *The Meaning of Religion: Lectures in the Phenomenology of Religion.* Translated by John B. Carman. The Hague: Martinus Nijhoff, 1960.

Kunhan Raja, C. "The Hindu Temples and Their Role in the Future Life of the Country." In *Brahmavidya,* Vol. 11, no. 1, 1947.

Kuriyan, George. "Geography and Religion." *Indian Geographical Journal* 36 (1961): 46–51.

Lal, Kanwar. *Holy Cities of India.* Delhi: Asia Press, 1961.

Law, Bimala Churn. *Geographical Essays.* 2 vols. London: Luzac and Co., 1937.

———. "Sacred Places of Vaishnavas." In *United Provinces Historical Society: Journal.* Vol. 10 (1937), p. 80.

———. *Holy Places of India.* Calcutta: Calcutta Geographical Society, 1940.

———. *Tribes in Ancient India.* Bhandarkar Oriental Series No. 4. Poona, 1943.

———. *Historical Geography of Ancient India.* Paris: Société Asiatique de Paris, 1954.

Leach, Edmund R. "Magical Hair." *The Journal of the Royal Anthropological Institute* 88 (1958): 147–164. Reprinted in *Myth and Cosmos,* edited by John Middleton, pp. 77–108. Garden City (N.Y.): Natural History Press, 1967.

Lewis, C. A. "The Geographical Texts of the *Purāṇas*: A Further Critical Study." *Purāṇa* 4 (January 1962): 112 ff.

Lewis, Oscar. *Village Life in Northern India: Studies in a Delhi Village.* Urbana: University of Illinois Press, 1958. Also Random House, Vintage Books, September 1965.

Library of Congress. *List of References on the Origin and Early Migration of the Hindus.* New York: Library of Congress, Division of Bibliography, May 4, 1921.

Maclean, Rev. J. H. "Kanchipuram." In *Encyclopaedia of Religion and Ethics.* Vol. 7, pp. 644–648. New York: Charles Scribner's Sons, 1908–1927.

Madras, Government of. *Administration Report of The Hindu Religions and Charitable Endowments (Administration) Department.* Madras: Government of Madras, 1962.

The Mahābhārata, Translated into English Prose from the Original Sanskrit Text by Pratap Chandra Roy. Vol. 2, *Vana Parva*. Calcutta : Datta Bose and Co., n.d.

The Mahābhārata, Āraṇyakaparvan. For the first time critically edited by Vishnu S. Sukthankar. Poona : Bhandarkar Oriental Research Institute, 1941–2.

Mahajan, V. D., et al. *Political and Cultural History of Ancient India*. Delhi : S. Chand, 1962.

Mahamahopadhyaya, Harprasad. "Dakshini Pandits at Benares." *The Indian Antiquary* 41 (January 1912) : 7–13.

Mahesh Yogi, Maharishi. *Bhagavad-Gita* : *A New Translation and Commentary*. London, Los Angeles, Rishikesh : International S. R. M. Publications, 1967.

Maity, Pradyot Kumar. *Historical Studies in the Cult of the Goddess Mansa* : *A Socio-Cultural Study*. Calcutta : Punthi Pustak, 1966.

Majumdar, R. C., general editor. *The History and Culture of the Indian People* : *The Classical Age*. Bombay : Bharatiya Vidya Bhavan, 1962.

Mandelbaum, David G. "Introduction : Process and Structure in South Asian Religion." *Journal of Asian Studies* 23 (June 1964) : 5–20.

———. *Society in India*. 2 vols. Berkeley and Los Angeles : University of California Press, 1970.

Marriott, McKim. "Little Communities in an Indigenous Civilization." In *Village India* : *Studies in the Little Community*, edited by McKim Marriott. Chicago : University of Chicago Press, 1955.

———. "Changing Channels of Cultural Transmission in Indian Civilization." *Journal of Social Research* 4, nos. 1-2 (1961) : 13–25.

Mate, M. S. *Temples and Legends of Maharashtra*. Bombay : Bharatiya Vidya Bhavan, 1962.

Matsya Purāṇa. Cultural History from the Matsya Purāṇa, by Kantawala, S. G. Baroda : M. S. University, 1964.

Mazumdar, B. P. *The Socio-Economic History of Northern India*. Calcutta : Firma K. L. Mukhopadhyay, 1960.

Mecking, Ludwig. "Benares, ein Kulturgeographisches Charakterbild." *Geographische Zeitschrift* 19 (1913) : 20–35 and 77–96.

Mitra, A. *Fairs and Festivals in West Bengal*. Alipore (West Bengal) : Government Press, 1953.

Mookerji, Radha Kumud. *Ancient Indian Education (Brahmanical and Buddhist)*. London : Macmillan, 1947.

———. *The Fundamental Unity of India*. Bombay : Bharatiya Vidya Bhavan, 1960.

Nilakanta Sastri, K. A. *A History of South India*. Madras : Oxford University Press, 1958.

———. *Development of Religion in South India*. Bombay : Orient Longmans, 1963.

Niyogi, Puspa. *Contributions to the Economic History of Northern India (From the Tenth to the Twelfth Century A.D.)*. Calcutta : Progressive Publishers, 1962.

O'Malley, L. S. S. *Popular Hinduism*. Cambridge : University Press, 1935.

Opler, Morris E. "The Extensions of an Indian Village." *Journal of Asian Studies* 16 (1956) : 5–10.

———. "The Place of Religion in a North Indian Village." *Southwestern Journal of Anthropology* 15 (1959) : 219–226.

Otto, Rudolph. *The Idea of the Holy*. New York : Oxford University Press, 1958. (First published 1923.)

Pargiter, F. E. *The Purāṇa Text of the Dynasties of the Kali Age*. London : Oxford University Press, 1913.

———. *Ancient Indian Historical Tradition*. London : Oxford University Press, 1922.

Patnaik, Nityananda. "Administration of Jagannath Temple in the 18th Century." *Man in India* 43 (1963) : 214–217.

Pavitrananda, Swami. "Pilgrimages and Fairs : Their Bearing on Indian Life." In *The Cultural Heritage of India*. Vol. IV, *The Religions*, edited by Haridas Bhattacharyya. Calcutta : Ramakrishna Mission, 1956.

Payne, Earnest A. *The Śāktas*. Calcutta : Y.M.C.A. Publishing House, 1933.

Piddington, Ralph, ed. *Kinship and Geographical Mobility*. Leiden : E. J. Brill, 1965.

Pillay, K. K. *The Sucindram Temple*. Adyar, Madras : Kalakshetra Publications, 1953.

———. "The Temple as a Cultural Centre." *Journal of Oriental Research* 29 (1959–60) : 83–94.

Punjab, *Punjab District Gazetteers*. Vol. VII-A, *Ambala District*, 1923–24. Lahore, 1925.

———. Vol. VII-A, *Kangra District*, 1924–25. Lahore, 1926.

———. Vol. VIII-A, *Simla District*. Lahore, 1908.

Punjab. *Punjab* [*Panjab*] *States Gazetteers*. Vol. VIII, *Bilaspur State*. Lahore, 1904.

———. Vol. XII-A, *Mandi State*. Lahore, 1904.

———. Vol. XXII-A, *Chamba State*. Lahore, 1904.

Pusalker, A. D. *Studies in the Epics and Purāṇas*. Bombay : Bharatiya Vidya Bhavan, 1963.

Quanungo, K. R. "Some Side-lights on the History of Benares, Political and Social, Thrown by Selections from the Peshwas' Daftar, Poona." Indian Historical Records Commission, *Proceedings of Meetings*, Vol. XIV (Dec. 1937), pp. 65–68. Delhi : Manager of Publications, 1938.

Radhakrishnan, S. *The Hindu View of Life*. London : George Allen and Unwin, 1927.

Ragam, V. R. *Pilgrim's Travel Guide*. 2 vols. Guntur : Sri Sita Rama Nama Sankirtana Sangham, 1957 and 1963.

Ramaswami Ayyar, C. P. "Temples as Centers of Indian Artistic Life." *Adyar Library Bulletin* (Madras), Vol. 15 (1951), pp. 59–61.

Ramesan, N. *Temples and Legends of Andhra Pradesh*. Bombay : Bharatiya Vidya Bhavan, 1962.

Redfield, Margaret Park, ed. *Human Nature and the Study of Society : The Papers of Robert Redfield*. Vol. 1. Chicago : University of Chicago Press, 1962.

Redfield, Robert. "The Social Organization of Tradition." *Journal of Asian Studies* 15 (1955) : 13–21.

———. "Societies and Cultures as Natural Systems." *Journal of the Royal Anthropological Institute of Great Britain and Ireland,* Part I & II (1955), pp. 19–32.

Redfield, Robert, and Milton B. Singer. "The Cultural Role of Cities." *Economic Development and Cultural Change* 3 (October 1954) : 53–73.

Renou, Louis. *The Nature of Hinduism*. Translated by Patrick Evans. New York : Walker and Company, 1962.

Rogers, Everett M. *Bibliography on the Diffusion of Innovations*. Diffusion of Innovations Research Report No. 4. Michigan State University, Department of Communication, July 1966.

Roussel, Romain. *Les Pèlerinages à Travers les Siècles*. Paris : Payot, 1954.

Rowe, William L. "The Marriage Network and Structural Change in a North Indian Community." *Southwestern Journal of Anthropology* 16 (1960) : 299–311.

Roy, Dilip Kumar, and Indra Devi. *Khumbha, India's Ageless Festival*. Bombay : Bharatiya Vidya Bhavan, 1955.

Roy Chaudhury, Pranab Chandra. *Temples and Legends of Bihar*. Bombay : Bharatiya Vidya Bhavan, 1965.

Russell, R. V. *The Tribes and Castes of the Central Provinces of India*. London : Macmillan and Co., 1916.

Rutter, Eldon. "The Muslim Pilgrimage." *Geographical Journal* 74 (1929) : 271–273.

Sachau, Edward C. trans. *Alberuni's India*. 2 vols. London : Trübner, 1910. (Book originally written between 1007 and 1033 A.D.).

Saraswati, Baidyanath. "The Holy Circuit of Nimsar." *Journal of Social Research* 8, no. 2 (1965) : 35–49.

Sarkar, B. K. *The Folk Element in Hindu Culture*. London : Longmans, Green and Co., 1917.

Sauer, Carl O. "Foreword to Historical Geography." *Annals, Association of American Geographers* 31, no. 1 (1941) : 1–24.

Schwartzberg, Joseph E. "The Distribution of Selected Castes in the North Indian Plain." *Geographical Review* 55 (1965) : 477–495.

———. "Caste Regions of the North Indian Plain." In *Structure and Change in Indian Society,* edited by Milton Singer and Bernard S. Cohn, pp. 81–113. Chicago : Aldine Publishing Co., 1968.

Shafer, Robert. *Ethnography of Ancient India.* Wiesbaden : Otto Harrassowitz, 1954.

Shejwalkar, T. S. "The *Mahābhārata* Data of Aryan Expansion in India." *Bulletin of the Deccan College Research Institute* 5 (21 January 1944) : 201–219.

Shukla, J. D. (Officer In-Charge, Ardh Kumbh). *Report on the Arrangements for Hardwar Ardh Kumbh Mela held on 13th April,* 1945. Publisher not known. Available in the Hardwar Municipal Committee Office.

Singer, Milton. "The Cultural Pattern of Indian Civilization : A Preliminary Report of Methodological Field Study." *Far Eastern Quarterly* 15 (1955) : 23–36.

———. "The Great Tradition in a Metropolitan Center : Madras." *Journal of American Folklore* 71 (1958) : 347–388.

Singer, Milton, ed. *Traditional India : Structure and Change.* Philadelphia : American Folklore Society, 1959.

———. *Krishna : Myths, Rites, and Attitudes.* Honolulu : East-West Center Press, 1966.

Singh, R. L. *Banaras : A Study in Urban Geography.* Banaras : Nand Kishore and Bros., 1955.

Singh, Sher. "Buffalo Sacrifice in Kamaksha Temple at Kao, Himachal Pradesh." *Folklore* 7, no. 11 (November 1966) : 418–421.

Singh, Ujagir. "Evolution of Allahabad." *National Geographical Journal of India* 4 (September 1958) : 109–129.

Sircar, D. C. "The Śākta Pīṭhas." *Journal of the Royal Asiatic Society of Bengal* 14, no. 1 (1948) : 1–108.

———. "The Dravidian Problem." *Man in India* 35 (1955) : 31–37.

———. *Studies in the Geography of Ancient and Medieval India.* Delhi, Patna, Varanasi : Motilal Banarsidass, 1960.

Slater, Gilbert. *The Dravidian Element in Indian Culture.* London : Earnest Benn, 1924.

Smith, Vincent A. *The Oxford History of India.* 3d rev. ed. Oxford, 1961.

Sopher, David, "Language and Religion." In *India : A Compendium,* edited by Raye R. Platt. New York : American Geographical Society, 1962.

———. "Landscape and Seasons : Man and Nature in India." *Landscape* 13 (1964) : 14–19.

Sopher, David E. *Geography of Religions.* Englewood Cliffs, N. J. : Prentice Hall, 1967.

———. "Pilgrim Circulation in Gujarat." *Geographical Review* 58, no. 3 (1968) : 392–425.

Soundara Rajan, K. V. "The Kaleidoscopic Activities of Medieval Temples in the Tamil Nad." Mythic Society, *Quarterly Journal* (Bangalore) 42 (1952) : 87–101.

Sources Orientales. *Les Pèlerinages.* Paris : Éditions du Seuil, 1960.

Spate, O. H. K., and E. Ahmad. "Five Cities of the Gangetic Plain." *Geographical Review* 11 (1950) : 260–278.

Spate, O. H. K., and A. T. A. Learmonth. *India and Pakistan : A General and Regional Geography.* 3d ed. London : Methuen and Co., 1967.

Spencer, George W. "Religious Networks and Royal Influence in Eleventh Century South India." *Journal of the Economic and Social History of the Orient* 12 (1969) : 42–56.

Sprockhoff, Joachim-Friedrich. "Zur Problematik einer Religionsgeographie." *Mitteilungen der Geographischen Gesellschaft in München* 48 (1963) : 107–121.

Srinivas, M. N. *Religion and Society among the Coorgs of South India.* Bombay : Asia Publishing House, 1952.

———. *Caste in Modern India.* Bombay : Asia Publishing House, 1962.

———. *Social Change in Modern India.* Bombay : Allied Publishers, 1966. First published by the University of California Press, Berkeley and Los Angeles, 1966.

Stein, Burton. "The State, the Temple and Agricultural Development : A Study in Medieval South India." *Economic Weekly,* 4 February 1961, pp. 179–187.

———. "Social Mobility and Medieval South Indian Hindu Sects." In *Social Mobility in the Caste System in India,* edited by James Silverberg, pp. 78–94. The Hague : Mouton Publishers, 1968.

Steiner, R. *Festivals and Their Meaning.* Translated from German by G. Adams. London : Anthroposophical Publishing Co., 1958.

Thirunaranan, B. M., and N. Ananta Padmanabhan. "Tiruttani—Study of a Temple Town." *Indian Geographical Journal* 32 (1957) : 1–24.

Thomas, P. *Hindu Religion, Customs and Manners.* 3rd. ed. Bombay : D. B. Taraporevala Sons and Co., Ltd., 1956.

Thurston, Edgar. *Castes and Tribes of Southern India.* Vol. 5. Madras : Government Press, 1909.

Underhill, Muriel M. *The Hindu Religious Year.* Calcutta : Association Press, 1921.

United Provinces. *District Gazetteers of the United Provinces of Agra and Oudh.* Vol. XXXV, *Almora District,* 1911.

———. Vol. XXXVI, *Garhwal,* 1910.

———. Vol. XXXIV, *Nainital District,* 1904.

———. Vol. II, *Saharanpur District,* 1909.

Valisinha, Devapriya. *Buddhist Shrines in India*. Colombo : Mahabodhi Society of Ceylon, 1948.

Van der Leeuw, G. *Religion in Essence and Manifestation : A Study in Phenomenology*. 2 vols. New York : Harper and Row, Torchbook, 1963 (translation of 1933 German edition).

Vasishtha, Mehta. "The Ancient Geography of North-West India." *National Geographical Journal of India* 8, parts 3–4 (1962) : 197–214.

Vāyu Purāṇa, A System of Hindu Mythology and Tradition. Edited by Rājendralāla Mitra. 2 vols. Calcutta : Bibliotheca Indica, Asiatic Society of Bengal. Vol. 1, 1880; vol. 2, 1888.

Venkatesvara, S. V. *Indian Culture through the Ages*. Vol. 1, *Education and the Propagation of Culture*. London : Longmans, Green and Co., 1928.

Vidyarthi, L. P. *The Sacred Complex in Hindu Gaya*. Bombay : Asia Publishing House, 1961.

Ward, W. *A View of the History, Literature, and Religion of the Hindus*. 2 vols. Vol. 2, *Religion*. Mission Serampore Press, 1815.

Watson, Francis. "Pilgrims to Badrinath." *Geographical Magazine* 34 (1961) : 421–428.

Watters, Thomas, ed. *On Yuan Chwang's Travels in India* (629–645 A.D.). London : Royal Asiatic Society. Vol. 1, 1904, vol. 2, 1905.

Wayman, Alex. "Climactic Times in Indian Mythology and Religion." *History of Religion* 4, no. 2 (Winter 1965) : 295–318.

Weber, Max. *The Religion of India : The Sociology of Hinduism and Buddhism*. Glencoe, Ill. : The Free Press, 1958.

Wheeler, J. Talboy. *Ancient and Hindu India (The Brahmanic Period)*. Calcutta : Punthi Pustak, 1961.

Wheeler, Sir Mortimer. *Early India and Pakistan : to Ashoka*. New York : Frederick A. Praeger, 1959.

Wilkins, W. J. *Modern Hinduism, Being an Account of Religion and Life of the Hindus in Northern India*. London : T. Fisher Unwin, 1887. Chapter 4, "Pilgrimages," pp. 240–298.

William, Monier. *Religious Thought and Life in India*. London : John Murray, 1883 (especially chapter 17, "Temples, Shrines and Sacred Places").

Wilson, H. H., trans. *The Vishnu Purana*. Calcutta : Punthi Pustak, 1961 (reprint). Originally published in London in 1840.

Winternitz, M. *A History of Indian Literature*. Calcutta : University of Calcutta, 1927.

Wright, Caleb. *Lectures on India*. Boston : Caleb Wright, 1851.

———. *India and Its Inhabitants*. St. Louis, Mo. : J. A. Brainerd, 1860.

———. *Historic Incidents and Life in India*. St. Louis, Mo. : J. A. Brainerd, 1861.

UNPUBLISHED SOURCES

Elmore, Wilber Theodore. "Dravidian Gods in Modern Hinduism: A Study of Local and Village Deities of Southern India." Ph.D. Dissertation, Lincoln, Nebraska, 1915.

India. Home Department, Land Revenue Branch. Document No. 29-37 f, dated November 25, 1839. National Archives, New Delhi.

India. Imperial Record Department. "Government of Bombay to submit statement of income derived from and expenses incurred on Hindu and Muhammadan places of worship." Document No. 19-19, of August 17, 1835. National Archives, New Delhi.

———. "Pilgrim tax and registration of barbers during annual fair at Allahabad." Document No. 26, of August 29, 1836. National Archives, New Delhi.

———. "Rawal's succession to Badrinath temple in Garhwal District." Document No. 10, of May 22, 1847. National Archives, New Delhi.

Pilgrim Register of Chandi Ram Sindhi Dharmaśālā (1965–6), kept in the Office of Hardwar Municipal Committee.

Pilgrim Register of Gandhi Harijan Dharmaśālā (1965–6), kept in Gandhi Harijan Dharmaśālā, Hardwar.

Pilgrim Register of Ganga Building (1965–6), kept in the office of Hardwar Municipal Committee.

Pilgrim Register of Gujarat Bhawan (1967), kept in Gujarat Bhawan, Hardwar.

Pilgrim Register of Karnatak Dharmaśālā (1965–6), kept in Karnatak Dharmaśālā, Hardwar.

Pilgrim Register of Tula Ram Dharmaśālā (1965–6), kept in the office of Hardwar Municipal Committee.

Singer, Philip. "Hindu Holy Men : A Study in Charisma." Ph.D. dissertation, Syracuse University, Department of Anthropology, 1961.

Stein, Burton. "The Tirupati Temple : An Economic Study of a Medieval South Indian Temple." Ph.D. dissertation, University of Chicago, Department of History, 1958.

Stoddard, Robert H. "Hindu Holy Sites in India." Ph.D. dissertation, State University of Iowa, Department of Geography, 1966.

Index

level of sacredness of, 125, 146; map showing origins of pilgrims to, 126; purposes of pilgrimage to, 155, 158; frequency of visits to, 160, 161; and religious travels of pilgrims, 164–170, 173; as a *dhām,* 170n; ceremonies at, 173; distances traveled to, by pilgrims of various castes, 189, 200
Bahīs (records), 28, 208, 209
Bahtis, 177
Baijnath, 12, 101, 103, 104, 107, 145; perception of degree of sacredness of, 101, 106; pilgrim field of, 117–120, 124, 144; level of sacredness of, 125, 146; purposes of pilgrimages to, 156; frequency of visits to, 161; and religious travels of pilgrims, 164, 166, 168; caste composition of pilgrims to, 176, 194
Banaras Hindu University, 214
Bania, 183
Baranasi (Varanasi), 77. *See also* Vārāṇasī
Barvaha, 46
Basham, A. L., 59, 93
Bathing, ritual, 3, 76–77, 86, 88, 90n, 149, 150, 158, 170, 226. *See also* Rivers, sanctity of
Beas River, 48
Beasa, 113
Bengal, 35, 36–37, 53, 68, 74, 79. *See also* West Bengal
Bhadratunga, 47
Bhadravata, 46
Bhagirathi, 51; River, 52
Bhagsunag, 12, 103, 104, 232; perceived degree of sacredness of, 101; pilgrim field of, 117–119, 124, 144–145; level of sacredness of, 125, 146; purposes of pilgrimages to, 156; frequency of visits to, 161; and religious travels of pilgrims, 164–166, 168; caste composition of pilgrims to, 177, 195
Bhagvān (knowledge of the Cosmic Reality), 148–149
Bhajans (religious songs), 149
Bhakti-yoga (path of unmixed devotion), 3
Bharati, Agehananda, 2, 4, 5, 24
Bhaviṣyat Purāṇa, 59
Bhetā (songs), 160
Bhojki Brahman caste, priests of, 186
Bhrigutunga, 50
Bhutan, pilgrims from, 122, 144
Bhuvanakośa (geographical lists of tribes), 59
Bihar, 35
Blood sacrifice. *See* Animal sacrifice
Bombay, pilgrims from, 127, 222
Brahmā, 41, 90–93, 97–98; map of sacred places of, 89
Brahman pilgrims: places considered most sacred by, 106–112; and caste composition of pilgrims to sacred places, 176–177, 179–184, 193–199; and level of sacred places visited, 186–188; distances traveled by, 188–191, 200, 227; category of, 231
Brāhmaṇas, 3n
Brahmani, 50
Brahmaputra, valley of, 36
Brahmasara, 51
Brahmasthana, 51, 53
Brahmavarta, 49, 50
Brindaban, 113
Buddha-Gaya, 101
Buddhism, and Hinduism, 76, 212
Buddhist pilgrims, 103n, 122, 141, 144, 155, 230. See also *Sissoo* fair
Burhanpur Gap, 39

Calcutta, pilgrims from, 127, 210
Carmaṇvatī, 30, 66, 69, 72. *See also* Chambal River
Caste *(jāti)*: and pilgrim activity, 26, 105–115, 151–152, 175–200, 202–203, 208, 223, 227; categories, 230–232
Census of India, 11, 27
Chambal River, 46. *See also* Carmaṇvatī
Champa, 51, 52
Chamunda, 101
Chandigarh district, 138, 171, 204
Charmanwati, 46. *See also* Carmaṇvatī
Chaudharies, 177
China: Locust Cult in, 151n; Buddhist pilgrim from (*See* Hsüan-tsang)
Chintpurni: pilgrims at, 12, 103, 104, 107; perceived degree of sacredness of, 101–102, 106, 107, 109, 111, 113–114; pilgrim field of, 118–122, 124, 132; level of sacredness of, 125, 146; maps of origins of pilgrims to, 134, 135; diversity of pilgrims to, 138; purposes of pilgrimage to, 155; frequency of visits to, 161; and religious travels of pilgrims, 164, 166, 168; goddess at, 174; caste com-

Gangotri, 50n, 86, 170
Garuḍa Purāṇa, sacred places mentioned in, 61–65 (map, 62), 67. See also *Purāṇas*
Gaṭh-joṛ ceremony, 183
Gaurisikhara, 51, 52. *See also* Gaurīśikhara
Gaurīśikhara, 66. *See also* Gaurisikhara
Gaya, 98, 150n, 207; ancient, 50, 51
Gayā, 30, 62, 65, 66, 68, 70, 71, 72, 73, 74, 79
Gazetteers, 11, 21, 27–28
Geographical, Statistical and Historical Description of Hindostan, A, 21
Geography, historical-cultural, 14
Ghurye, G. S., 152, 213
Girivraja, 72
Glasenapp, Helmuth von, 22
Godavari River, 53, 54, 55
Gods. *See* Deities
Gokarṇa, 53, 70, 75
Gomatī, 62, 66, 69, 72
Gomati, confluence of, 51
Goparatra, 50
Gorkhas, 144–145, 177, 232
Goswamy, B. N., 28
Gṛhasthas (householders). 18
Grierson, G. A., 141
Gujarat, 37, 40; pilgrims from, 210, 222
Gurgaon, 130
Guru, the tenth, 141n
Gurukula Kangri University, 214

Hardwar, 6, 12, 19, 50n, 65, 90, 103, 104, 117, 211n, 212, 229; perception of degree of sacredness of, 101, 102, 106–115; distance traveled by pilgrims to, 118, 119; pilgrim field of, 123, 124, 127, 130; level of, as a sacred place, 125, 146; map of origins of pilgrims to, 128; ceremonies at, 149, 150, 154, 161; purposes of pilgrimages to, 155, 158, 171; frequency of visits to, 161; and religious travels of pilgrims, 164–168, 170; caste composition of pilgrims to, 178, 185, 187, 196; distances traveled to, by pilgrims of various castes, 189, 191, 200; diffusion of beliefs and ideas at, 206–207, 211, 212, 215, 228; religious functionaries at, 207–208; institutions of higher education at, 214; seasonal and residential separation of pilgrims at, 216–224
"Harijan," the term, 223n
Haryana, 12, 232n; pilgrims from, 121, 127, 180, 218, 219, 220
Hastinapur, 40
Health Department, 215, 219n, 229
Heilige Stätten Indiens, 22
Hemakūṭa, 66
Hermitages. See *Āśramas*
Hilltops, sanctity of, 86–87
Himachal Pradesh, 11–13; pilgrims from, 102, 121, 127, 138, 144, 145, 191, 218, 219; pilgrims to, 102, 138n; goddess shrines of, 154, 160, 174, 186; Gaddī tribe of, 231–232. *See also* Gaddīs
Himālaya, 72
Himalaya, sanctity of, 86
Hindī-speaking area, pilgrims from, 130, 132, 138, 144. *See also* Delhi
Holy men, 3, 6, 98, 149
Holy Places of India, 22
Hopkins, Edward Washburn, 58
Horse sacrifices, 41. *See also* Animal sacrifice
Hoshiarpur, 138, 180
Hsu, Shin-Yi, 151n
Hsüan-tsang, 75–76
Hurst, John F., 21

Ibn Haukal, 77
Immortal India, 22
Imperial Gazetteer of India, The, 11, 27
Indika: The Country and the People of India and Ceylon, 21
Indra, 93
Indus River, 47, 65, 93. *See also* Sindhu
Institutions, religious, and diffusion of ideas, 207–215
Instrument and Purpose, 152–153
International Spiritual Regeneration Movement, 211
Investiture of sacred thread, 150, 154
Isaac, Erich, 25

Jacques, Claude, 23
Jagannath Puri, 113, 170n
Jains, 183, 231
Jajmāns (pilgrim clients), 207–209
Jambukesvara, 82
Jammu-Kashmir, 127
Jamvu Marga, 45–46
Jāti. See Caste *(jāti)*
Jatismara, 51